Keeping Faith in Practice

Keeping Faith in Practice

Aspects of Catholic Pastoral Theology

Edited by
James Sweeney
with Gemma Simmonds and
David Lonsdale

scm press

© The editors and contributors 2010

Published in 2010 by SCM Press
Editorial office
13–17 Long Lane,
London, EC1A 9PN, UK

SCM Press is an imprint of Hymns Ancient and Modern Ltd
(a registered charity)
St Mary's Works, St Mary's Plain,
Norwich, NR3 3BH, UK
www.scm-canterburypress.co.uk

British Library Cataloguing in Publication data

A catalogue record for this book is available
from the British Library

978-0-334-04323-2

Typeset by Regent Typesetting, London
Printed and bound by
Lightning Source Inc

Contents

Foreword

STEPHEN PATTISON

All Western pastoral and practical theology has been fundamentally shaped and influenced by Catholicism. From St Augustine of Hippo and Gregory the Great, through to Karl Rahner and the liberation theologians in more recent times, the Catholic Church has been a major contributor to evaluating and offering paradigms for Christian faith in practice. Unfortunately, in the modern British context, Catholicism has not featured very prominently in the development of practical theology. When James Woodward and I were putting together *The Blackwell Reader in Pastoral and Practical Theology* a decade ago, it was not at all clear who the British Catholic practical theologians might be. While we knew of some individuals and courses engaged in moral and pastoral theology, it seemed that practical theology, a term that comes directly from the Reformed tradition, was not a label with which Catholics then identified. We published the *Reader* knowing that Catholic authors and Catholic thought were severely under represented. Despite our best efforts, however, we were unable to identify and obtain the sorts of authors and contributions that we wanted from this tradition. It seemed to me, both then and now, that in many ways Catholicism was the sleeping giant of pastoral and practical theology in our midst, with so much to offer by way of tradition, experience and insight to the wider ecumenical and theological communities.

Keeping Faith in Practice, then, represents part of the first, very welcome contemporary stirrings of that huge and rich tradition; I am personally delighted that Catholics are now so very much more interested in making common cause with practical theologians of other hues. There is a treasure trove of fascinating material here that does much creatively to break the unfortunate silence of the past. While the book has a clear focus on Britain and British writers, it is enriched by material and authors from other parts of the Western world such as France and the USA. (Why is it that British practical theologians know almost nothing of the important tradition of Catholic practical theology that flourishes in very sophisticated forms just across the channel?) This in itself reminds us of one of the great strengths of Catholicism: its internationalism and polylingualism. Another strength is the theological and philosophical depth and profundity of much Catholic thought that can bring illuminative insight to bear in ways that are underexplored in Protestantism.

This book does much to explain where Catholic pastoral and practical theology has come from in Britain, and what it has to offer to thinkers and practitioners both within and outside the Catholic church. It exemplifies some of the creative ways in which an old and complex tradition can be brought into dialogue with contemporary experience, sometimes in surprising ways. So it is a pleasure to welcome it unequivocally as an earnest of greater and deeper contributions to come.

Readers will recognize that Catholic practical theology in Britain in the new, overt form expounded and exemplified herein, is a somewhat tender plant. While there are shoots of real interest and methodological innovation, it would not take much for these to perish, as they have in the past, if a handful of institutions and people were to de-commit from the quest to make Catholic thinking and working part of mainstream practical theology. My hope for the authors and readers of this book is that this will be the beginning of an important dialogue and learning experience for Catholics and non-Catholics alike. Non-Catholics need to learn from this venerable, fertile tradition, while Catholics themselves will also need the support and interest of their non-Catholic peers to grow and develop in a sustainable way. This book would seem to be the ideal place for this mutual learning and critique to begin. I know I will be speaking for many colleagues in the hitherto Protestant-dominated British and Irish Association for Practical Theology when I welcome it here publicly as an extremely important step in the development of British practical theology, not just Catholic practical theology. And the editors and authors are to be congratulated for bringing this much-needed resource into the public domain.

Stephen Pattison
Former Chair, British and Irish Association for Practical Theology
University of Birmingham

Acknowledgements

The suggestion about the need for a text on Catholic approaches to pastoral and practical theology was first floated about six years ago. The encouragement it met from all quarters was very pleasing. Teachers and students and writers and researchers agreed that something was missing from the published literature. Not that there was a dearth of Catholic publications in the pastoral field, but these did not address their subjects in the precise terms of practical theology as it is practised in, mainly, non-Catholic circles. 'Catholicism', said Stephen Pattison, 'is the sleeping giant in practical theology.'

Our thanks go to all who have contributed to realizing the dream of this volume: the participants in the colloquium and international conference at Heythrop College, University of London, in 2007 which led directly to the publication, and in a special way those who authored chapters; the staff of the Pastoral and Social Studies Department at Heythrop and other colleagues in the College for their support; and Birute Briliute for help in preparing the text. We are grateful too for the encouragement of colleagues in the community of scholars in practical theology, and especially Stephen Pattison for his enthusiasm for the project and his Foreword. Thanks also to: Henri-J. Gagey of the Institut Catholique in Paris, who has given wise advice throughout; Natalie Watson of SCM Press who has been most helpful and encouraging – and patient too with the delays in bringing the work to completion; the two anonymous referees whose helpful comments on the proposal were much appreciated.

Our aim has been to meet the expectations of this diverse constituency of interest. In the future, there is much more that will need to be done to advance the mutual enrichment of the various traditions of pastoral and practical theology. We offer this book as a first contribution.

James Sweeney, Gemma Simmonds, David Lonsdale
August 2009

Contributors

Kathleen A. Cahalan is Associate Professor of Theology, Saint John's University, School of Theology-Seminary, Collegeville, MN, and formerly Convenor of the Practical Theology Group, Catholic Theological Society of America.

Andrew Cameron-Mowat SJ is Lecturer in Pastoral Liturgy at Heythrop College, University of London.

Louis-Marie Chauvet is Professor Emeritus of Theology at the Institut Catholique, Paris.

Lilian Dube is Assistant Professor of Theology and Religious Studies at the University of San Francisco.

Henri-Jérôme Gagey is Professor of Fundamental Theology and former Dean of the Faculty of Theology at the Institut Catholique, Paris.

Nicholas M. Healy is Professor of Theology at St John's University, New York.

Bernard Hoose is Senior Lecturer in Christian Ethics at Heythrop College, University of London.

Brendan Killeen is Visiting Lecturer in Canon Law at Heythrop College, University of London.

Michael Kirwan SJ is Lecturer in Theology and Head of Department of Theology at Heythrop College, University of London.

David Lonsdale is Senior Lecturer in Christian Spirituality and Dean of Postgraduate Studies at Heythrop College, University of London.

David McLoughlin is Senior Lecturer in Theology at Newman University College, Birmingham.

Martin Poulsom SDB is Lecturer in Theology at Heythrop College, University of London.

Robert Schreiter CPPS is Bernardin Center Vatican II Professor of Theology at the Catholic Theological Union, Chicago.

Gemma Simmonds CJ is Lecturer in Christian Spirituality at Heythrop College, University of London.

James Sweeney CP is Senior Lecturer in Pastoral Theology and Head of Department of Pastoral and Social Studies at Heythrop College, University of London, and Secretary of the Catholic Theological Association of Great Britain.

Peter Tyler is Senior Lecturer in Pastoral Theology at St Mary's University College, Twickenham.

Clare Watkins is a theologian and former Vice-Principal of the Margaret Beaufort Institute of Theology in the Cambridge Theological Federation.

Introduction

JAMES SWEENEY CP
WITH GEMMA SIMMONDS CJ AND
DAVID LONSDALE

The enterprise of pastoral and practical theology has a long and complicated history, much of which is referred to in the chapters of this book, and it has taken several routes. Writing on the topic of 'practical theology' in the English-speaking world has come mainly from the Protestant tradition, with the result that specific Catholic resources for teaching and research are hard to come by. A pragmatic concern to fill a gap in available resources lies at the origins of this volume. A colloquium was held at Heythrop College, University of London, in January 2007 to explore the nature of pastoral theology and whether there is, in fact, a specifically Catholic approach. This was followed by an international conference of scholars in November 2007 to examine the topic in greater depth, and the papers presented at that meeting form the basis of this volume.

Our purpose is to engage with the ongoing discussions about the place of, and the procedures for, this kind of theological enterprise, and to contribute a Catholic voice to what has become a rather well-delimited and ecumenical field. The aim is to clarify some fundamental points of the Catholic approach and to explore issues that need further discussion and would benefit from greater mutual exchange between these two traditions. The terms 'pastoral' and 'practical', and the question of which is the more appropriate, have been much debated in the literature, but without reaching consensus. They are not exact synonyms, but may be said to denote the same broad field of human-faith practice under different aspects. While we have stuck with 'pastoral' in the sub-title, both terms are in evidence throughout the text.

JAMES SWEENEY, GEMMA SIMMONDS, DAVID LONSDALE

The Status of Pastoral and Practical Theology

The practice of theology as disciplined enquiry into the divine takes its place today among the various disciplines of the sciences and the humanities and the many cultural currents that characterize contemporary society. Not only is theology situated within the diversity of forms of knowledge and of social and personal values, with their proper autonomy, but it is deeply marked by this context. It must account for its validity as intellectual enquiry and earn its credibility in a pluralist culture. It has not always done so well in these respects. There has been a certain dissociation of theology, or some forms of it, from the world of the human and the everyday business of living and coping with immediate needs; a gap has opened up between theological sources of wisdom and social and public issues; there is a rift between faith and life, between the gospel and culture. Consequently, theology has lost traction in both the academic world and the world at large. It has something of an image problem; the very word is suspected of authoritarian overtones, and it is bracketed with 'theocracy' as a throwback to medieval times. To brand a discussion point 'theological' is to accuse it of obscurity, delving into trivia, and avoiding the real matter in hand.

Practical and pastoral theology, however, is self-conscious in confronting precisely this context directly. Its focus is the sustained exploration of the links between, on the one hand, the realities of human, personal and social experience and, on the other hand, the Christian theological tradition, with its varied resources of wisdom and insight and the message of the gospel and the saving truth it proclaims.

This, however, is a project that has to be validated. The risk for pastoral/practical theology is to become merely a paraphrase of human-spiritual experience, enclosed in itself and unable to express the fundamental truth claims of Christian faith. The difference, put starkly, is between a practical theology that by making theology more practical renders it more *theological*, and a practical theology that is merely expressive and gives up on any binding claim of the truth of faith.

There is an expectation that practical theology should come up with practical 'answers' to whatever are the troubling questions of the day. The various practical disciplines (moral theology, canon law, liturgy, catechesis, evangelization, spirituality, justice advocacy, faith-based social action, etc.) are all sites where there is an alliance between theological principle and experiential wisdom. However, care should be taken not to require more of theology than it can deliver; it is suited more to diagnosis and interpretation than to direct prescription. As Karl

Rahner observed with reference to ecclesial decision-making (although it applies more widely):

> the decisions of the Church are not really made in practical theology, for that is a matter for the whole Church (and within this totality it is a matter for official authority), even if the theory of practical theology, as actually carried on, is itself one factor in the Church's practice . . . Consequently, it [practical theology] is 'critical' towards the Church while it cannot annexe the latter's decisions.[1]

Practical forms of theology do not 'hand down' practical answers in the manner of an 'applied' theology. Rather, practical theology engages with practice and practitioners in the joint task of determining action. It is inexorably, therefore, an engaged and an ecclesial exercise; and Catholic pastoral/practical theology is inevitably marked by the Catholic ecclesial structure.

Catholic Pastoral Theology

It is not the case that a Catholic contribution to the discipline of practical theology has been missing – far from it – but the way in which the practical dimensions of theology are conceptualized tends to be different in Catholicism. There is a long Catholic tradition of *pastoral* theology, linked to biblical and systematic theology on the one hand and moral and ascetical theology on the other, and dealing with ministry, mission and Christian living. More recently, since the Second Vatican Council (1962–65), this has broadened into a praxis-oriented theology that takes greater account of culture and society (and more recently gender and ecology) and the place of the Church in the world. These developments have given a new impetus to Catholic social teaching as well as influencing the emergence of liberation and other forms of contextual theology.

On one view, all theology is ultimately practical, in service of the life and practice of faith; and if there is a problem, it is that theological work has too often cut itself off from practical and pastoral concerns. Another view is that traditional pastoral theology has been underdeveloped theoretically and reduced to 'hints and tips' for ministry and mission. The terminology of practical/pastoral has signalled two ways of handling this matter, with 'practical' referring to praxis-oriented and 'pastoral' to ministry-oriented approaches; but this is not really so satisfactory and does not take us very far. Behind the terminological question the issue is not so much about the nature of pastoral/practical theology, but about the theological enterprise itself.

This was the fundamental issue that arose at the initial colloquium: not so much about specific Catholic approaches and resources in pastoral theology – a Catholic *how* question – but whether and how it might be defined – *what* it is, and indeed whether a *specific* form of theology called 'pastoral' really exists in Catholicism. The issue is more than definitional semantics, for the approach taken in relation to 'what' determines the 'how'. This has given shape to this volume. After two scene-setting chapters, the first main section (Part Two) focuses on fundamental questions, while the typical Catholic make-up and approach is addressed in Part Three.

Contents

The book's title captures what we see as the aim across this whole enterprise: we must both keep faith practical and have faith in the significance of practice.

The essays are grouped in three parts. The introductory Part One sketches the broad landscape of today's pastoral theology, in two moves: James Sweeney's survey of the main orientations of contemporary Catholic theology and David McLoughlin's and Gemma Simmonds's account of the emergence of a local pastoral theology in Britain and Ireland. Part Two sets out the fundamental perspectives. First, Michael Kirwan reflects on the task of reading the signs of the times, arguably the foundation of the whole enterprise; then Robert Schreiter, from the USA, supplies the range of contextual factors to be taken into account; Henri-Jérôme Gagey, writing from the French experience, both traces the genealogy of pastoral theology from deep within Catholic systematic theology and considers its status as a theological discipline; Kathleen A. Cahalan too probes the disciplinary question, from a United States point of view; Nicholas M. Healy focuses on ecclesiology, an essential feature in any Catholic approach; and Martin Poulsom underscores the way a change in Catholic theology has come about with a case study of a prominent Catholic theologian, Edward Schillebeeckx. Part Three develops particular aspects of Catholic pastoral theology as it is worked out in practice. The first two chapters discuss what is involved in setting about the task. It has to be an interdisciplinary exercise, and Louis-Marie Chauvet examines some of the challenges and pitfalls for theologians adopting sociological or anthropological frameworks. It is an exercise in which the elements of historical experience and religious tradition are in play, and Clare Watkins, developing an ecclesiological approach, argues these should be seen as unified rather than (as is often the case, she maintains) disparate. Four pastoral disciplinary fields (among the many possible) are then explored – Andrew Cameron-Mowat on liturgy, Peter Tyler on mysticism and pastoral care, Bernard Hoose on moral theology and Brendan Killeen on canon law. Two chapters draw us further afield: Lilian Dube, as an African woman theologian, provides a glimpse of the pressing practical issues that arise in the global South, beyond the Western context; and David Lonsdale moves beyond the confines of theology itself with an exploration of the place where literature and pastoral theology meet. Finally, a practical theology research methodology developed by Heythrop's ARCS project team is described as a possible model for this kind of theological enterprise by way of a case study.

Catholic Pastoral Theology – Characteristic Notes

The specific characteristics of Catholicism are necessarily influential in shaping its theology. In particular, its international character is reflected in these essays in that, although primarily written in the context of Britain and Ireland, they include significant contributions from the United States and France as well as from Africa. There is a vast international literature – from other European and other English-speaking countries and the Southern hemisphere – to be drawn on in developing Catholic pastoral and practical theology. The theology now emerging from Africa, Asia and Latin America is deeply practical in orientation; one immediately thinks of liberation theology, as well as other contextual theologies.

It is abundantly clear in the essays that a foundational role is played by Vatican II's *Gaudium et spes* (the Pastoral Constitution on the Church in the Modern World). While there continues to be a lively critical debate about the merits of this key document, one of its successes has been to put in place an overarching framework for practical theological enquiry, one that is both ecclesiological and societal. This also highlights another characteristic of Catholicism: the close (and properly critical) attention its theologians must pay to magisterial declarations. The Council documents and subsequent papal encyclicals, as well as some strong episcopal teaching texts (for example, by the CELAM conferences of the Latin American bishops at Medellín, Puebla, Santo Domingo and Aparecida, and the United States bishops' pastoral letters on war and peace and the economy, and *The Common Good* document of the bishops of England and Wales), have authoritative status; they are markers in the developing Catholic tradition, to be absorbed within theological reflection.

One of the most striking features of Catholicism in recent times has been the sea change in its theological approaches. The tight constraints of Neo-Scholasticism have given way to a greater theological pluralism; the Bible is no longer seen as little more than a useful source of proof texts and is given its proper status as the fountain-head of all theology; the full scope of the Christian tradition, and especially the patristic resources, have been recovered; an inductive approach, working from human experience and history, has emerged, displacing the previously dominant deductive approach; and theology is practised as vital engagement with the business of Christian living rather than what has often been perceived as an arid exercise in intellectual speculation. This transformation of the practice of Catholic theology is arguably the most significant fruit of the Second Vatican Council. It is in this context that the issues of Catholic pastoral theology can be revisited.

Note

1 Karl Rahner, 1972, 'Practical Theology within the Totality of Theological Discipline', in *Theological Investigations*, vol. IX, London: Darton, Longman & Todd, pp. 101–14, here pp. 103–4.

PART ONE

Theology – The Catholic Scene

Introduction to Part One

There is no definitively established form of pastoral theology. Its history, across different contexts and traditions, largely determines its character. Because it is practical and relates to practice, pastoral theology is always in need of finding its bearings anew. There is a historical immediacy to this form of theology that gives it a different tone from the 'timelessness' sometimes associated with classical theological themes such as Trinity or Christology (which is not to say that systematic theology does not also develop). This historical immediacy is particularly obvious in Catholic pastoral theology. The perspectives reflected in this volume arise from a history that is a major theological story in its own right, one dominated by the Second Vatican Council (1962–65).

The impulses that were emerging in the pre-conciliar era and what has transpired in the Council's aftermath (in both theology and the life of the Church) are fundamental contextual factors shaping contemporary Catholic pastoral theology; and Robert Schreiter, who has written extensively on 'context' from the United States, will develop this theme in Part Two, while Henri-Jérôme Gagey, with specific reference to the French scene, will explain the evolutions within systematic theology that have delivered a specific approach to Catholic pastoral theology.

But in a first move and to set the scene, Chapters 1 and 2 in Part One survey the landscape and tease out some of the issues for Catholic pastoral theology, both in today's theological context and in the specific ecclesial context of Britain and Ireland. James Sweeney sketches the contours of, and tensions within, Catholic theology as pastoral theology's larger setting. It becomes clear that practical questions and issues, in particular the great overarching issues of social and cultural change, play a determinative role; and not only for pastoral theology as such, but even for the exploration of the central doctrines of Christianity. David McLoughlin and Gemma Simmonds (with additional input from the editors) then trace the emergence of a local – British and Irish –

9

Catholic pastoral theology, relying on their close personal involvement over the years. This is a history that still has to be fully researched; however, what becomes clear is that the first steps of practice and reflection on practice have borne fruit in a pastorally engaged theology, but the second step of more considered reflection and research requires more adequate resources of personnel, time and funding. Until now such resources have been very limited.

I

Catholic Theology and Practice Today

JAMES SWEENEY CP

In Historical Perspective – Vatican II

The Second Vatican Council (1962–65) was an event that left an indelible mark on Catholic life and theology. It was summoned to be a 'pastoral council'. Pope John XXIII surprised the Church by announcing the Council in January 1959 within months of his election, and caused some alarm within the Vatican Curia, whose high officials were hardly consulted. What need was there, some asked, for a Council? The question was all the more pressing as the Pope made it plain that this Council, unlike others, should not be about condemning errors or rectifying abuses, or even about resolving doctrinal matters. Its concerns were to be 'pastoral'. What did it mean?

The underlying reasons for summoning the Council remain something of a mystery. Pope John famously attributed it to a sudden inspiration of the Holy Spirit, but as an accomplished historian he knew that it would be epoch-making, and this certainly was his intention. He was an optimist, and believed that the Catholic Church, having come through the convulsions of the modern period intact, was well poised to make a new contribution to the progress of humanity and undertake a new historical mission of supplying moral and spiritual foundations for the striking technological advances that were transforming society (*Humanae salutis*, the Apostolic Constitution convoking the Council, 1961). Another significant factor was the mounting tensions within Catholic theology. Research in the biblical, patristic and liturgical fields by outstanding Catholic scholars such as Yves Congar and Henri de Lubac was still held in check by the dominance of scholastic theology in the Roman institutions.

The eventual achievements of Vatican II were profoundly pastoral, but they also embodied doctrinally significant shifts. The everyday changes in the life of the Church – in the liturgy, the active role of the laity, ecumenical relations – were far-reaching; and underlying them was a new emphasis in the doctrine on the Church correcting an excessively institutional model and reinstating a more biblical ecclesiology that appealed to patristic sources. This opened the way for a new understanding of ecclesial authority. The Council's doctrine of episcopal collegiality set the primacy and infallibility of the Pope as defined by the First Vatican Council in 1870 in the wider context of the worldwide college of bishops and the Church as a whole.

Vatican II was above all a council about the relationships that are constitutive of the Church: the relationships of union with God and of communion with each other, of which the Church is 'sacrament, sign and instrument' (*Lumen gentium*, 1); the relationship with the modern world (*Gaudium et spes*), with other churches and ecclesial communions (*Unitatis redintegratio*), with other faiths (*Nostra aetate*), and of religious freedom (*Dignitatis humanae*). The breadth of the conciliar programme in these and its other documents suggests that the Catholicism that had consolidated itself institutionally over the previous century had somehow become exhausted and a fresh approach was required.

This notion of some mid-twentieth-century exhaustion of Catholicism was not how things seemed at the time. On the contrary, according to Adrian Hastings, what was apparent was 'the sheer vitality and range of committed ability, lay and clerical, present in the Church at that time and just waiting for a new lead' (Hastings 1991, p. 4).[1] But intractable problems began to emerge at the time of the Council around institutionalization, and they have troubled the Church ever since. Institution-building had been the very hallmark of Catholicism's nineteenth-century restoration, and it was strikingly successful, to a large degree because it was in tune with the social forces of the time that were reshaping society itself on a new institutional and bureaucratic model. By the 1960s, however, new forces – an educated laity, lay apostolic movements, a reinvigorated theology, the biblical and liturgical renewal – put established structures, and therefore the ecclesial authorities, under pressure, just as was happening in the secular sphere. The centralized power within the Church, which had grown significantly after the declaration of papal infallibility at Vatican I, collided with the hopes and aspirations springing up at the grass roots.

The Catholic Church that emerged from the Vatican II era, while allowing for some developments, was structurally and doctrinally continuous with its historic reality, but pastorally – and, one might say, spiritually and culturally – it was much changed.[2] This was not the result of the Council alone. Vatican II was a breakthrough moment, but, as with all such moments, it met strong internal opposition. And as the Church belatedly embraced the world and modernity the force of the modern project was already faltering. In the 1960s, the 'expressive revolution', ushering in the era of postmodernity, made the post-conciliar pastoral approach immensely complicated.

Much has been written about the causes of the negative trends that swept across Catholicism in the wake of the Council.[3] For some the Council itself was to blame; the Church was the author of its own misfortunes. What the result of an adamant 'no change' policy, favoured by the Council 'conservatives', would have been for late twentieth-century Catholicism is an unanswerable 'what if?' question. What is clear is that society and culture were changing in some deep way. The patterns of change varied from country to country and continent to continent, but a common feature everywhere was a transformation in how the individual related to the social order. Society and culture became less determining (or less obviously determining) of individuals' lives, and the space for personal expression expanded; a new kind of personal autonomy was emerging. This was evident in the West in its burgeoning consumerism, but it was also what the new independence in the post-colonial countries betokened. It was held in check in the Communist countries of Eastern Europe, but with the result that the social system became ever more hollowed out, as its collapse in 1989 was to make clear. The poverty in the countries of the South gave rise to a mounting sense of injustice, a protest against the cruelty of an economic order that could simply crush individual persons and communities.

Stability and social order came under severe pressure, dramatized in the student uprisings of 1968, the anti-Vietnam War protests and the Prague Spring; and the shock was felt in the Church as well. Although the demise of 1960s utopianism was inevitable, to be replaced by the more sober 1970s and the economic shock of the first oil crisis, the underlying shift in the individual's relationship to society and culture was set to continue.

Theology

Vatican II shifted Catholic theology definitively into a new gear.[4] The 'progressive' forces at the Council[5] set out to overcome the rigid scholasticism of the Roman schools and its inadequate form of Thomism and replace it with a theological approach attuned to history, one that

was biblically based and which retrieved lost – and particularly the
patristic – features of the tradition. They succeeded, and the Council
documents are testimony to this renewed theological approach. However, there were major differences within the progressive camp; these
were masked while the main battle was being fought, but they emerged
very quickly once the Council was over.[6]

What follows is a sketch of the new landscape of Catholic theology
and some of its neuralgic points. These themes are covered in greater
depth in subsequent chapters. My concern is to explore how Catholic pastoral-practical theology is located within the current practice of
theology as a whole, and specifically in relation to the issue of faith and
human experience.

The polarization of post-conciliar Catholic theology could hardly be
more dramatic. On the one side, Karl Rahner, Yves Congar, Edward
Schillebeeckx and Hans Küng, and on the other, Henri de Lubac, Jean
Daniélou, Hans Urs von Balthasar and Joseph Ratzinger, gathered
around two competing journals – *Concilium* and *Communio* – founded
after the Council to propagate its teaching (as the editors variously
interpreted it). Many ways of explaining the divide have been suggested:
Thomist versus Augustinian; progressive versus conservative; mission
versus identity; secular versus sacred; even embrace of the world versus fear of the world. One of the significant points of difference that
is crucial in relation to a pastoral theology is around the theological
approach to history.[7]

The fundamental pastoral text of the Council is *Gaudium et spes*
(*GSp*) (1965), the 'Pastoral Constitution on the Church in the Modern
World' (or, in the official Latin version, *in mundo huius temporis* – 'in
the world of this time'). This is the only constitution (the most solemn
form of conciliar text) named as 'pastoral',[8] and it is around its interpretation that some of the most fundamental controversy has raged.
This is hardly surprising, given the outright rejection of modernity by
Pope Pius IX in the nineteenth century that had long been determinative of Catholicism.[9]

Gaudium et spes is in the line of church social teaching convention-
ally dated from Pope Leo XIII's encyclical *Rerum novarum* (1891), but
it was a major shift in approach.[10] It adopted an explicitly biblical and
theological perspective and relied less on the natural law approach of
the earlier encyclicals, which had tended to reinforce a two-tier nature–
grace cosmology and to distance Church from World as two distinct
'perfect societies'. The Pastoral Constitution portrayed the Church
as thoroughly integrated within humanity and contemporary history:

'The joy and hope, the grief and anguish of the men of our time, especially those who are poor or afflicted in any way, are the joy and hope, the grief and anguish of the followers of Christ as well' (*GSp*, 1). No longer a Church set apart but a pilgrim Church (*Gaudium et spes*, 45, 57; *Lumen gentium*, 48, 50).

Gaudium et spes signals a shift to historical consciousness. In his opening address to the Council, Pope John made the observation (seen as controversial at the time) that 'the substance of the ancient doctrine of the deposit of faith is one thing, and the way in which it is presented is another' (*Gaudet Mater Ecclesiae*, 1962), thus giving official approval to a freeing-up of Catholic theology from a rigid essentialism and propositionalism. The conciliar decree on revelation, *Dei Verbum* (*DV*) (1965), confirmed this by insisting on the dynamic character of divine revelation itself as 'realized by words and deeds':

The works performed by God in the history of salvation show forth and bear out the doctrine and realities signified by the words; the words, for their part, proclaim the works, and bring to light the mystery they contain. (*DV*, 2)

Jesus Christ, sent as 'a man among men', speaks the words of God (Jn. 3: 34), and accomplishes the saving work which the Father gave him to do . . . He did this by the total fact of his presence and self-manifestation – by words and works, signs and miracles, but above all by his death and glorious resurrection from the dead, and finally by sending the Spirit of truth. (*DV*, 4)

Christ the Lord . . . commanded the apostles to preach the Gospel . . . this was faithfully done: it was done by the apostles who handed on, by the spoken word of their preaching, by the example they gave, by the institutions they established, what they themselves had received. (*DV*, 7)

The implications of this in terms of human history were what the Council attempted to work through with the Pastoral Constitution. History is more than a human and secular reality, it is a *locus theologicus*:

The Church has a visible social structure, which is a sign of its unity in Christ: as such it can be enriched, and it is being enriched, by the evolution of social life – not as if something were missing in the constitution which Christ gave the Church, but in order to understand this constitution more deeply, express it better, and adapt it more successfully to our times ... Whoever contributes to the development of the community of mankind on the level of family, culture, economic and social life, and national and international politics, according to the plan of God, is also contributing in no small way to the community of the Church insofar as it depends on things outside itself. (*GSp*, 44)

Gaudium et spes was the beginning, but in no way the conclusion, of a great theological debate in Catholicism. It became a fundamental reference point, but one that needed clarification and deepening. The lines of its teaching were developed in subsequent papal encyclicals;[11] it was the inspiration of the Medellín and Puebla gatherings of the Latin American Episcopal Conference (CELAM) in 1968 and 1979 and their emphasis on the option for the poor; and it gave impetus to the theology of liberation in Latin America as well as European political theology (Guttiérez 1988; Metz 1980).

The criticism of *GSp*, however, is that it is naive and therefore in some way pastorally deficient. In this assessment – by no means only from conservatives[12] – *GSp* is overly optimistic about social progress, couched in terms of development rather than liberation, reflects a European-American mindset, relaxes the necessary tension between the Church and the world, and underplays the reality of sin and the tragic in human history and the dimension of the cross in Christian life. These may be seen, benignly, as limitations of a text that was the first of its kind and drawn up in the heat of the Council's deliberations.[13] However, it is alleged by some that the limitations are more fundamental and can be traced to the manner of *GSp*'s embrace of history.

The radical critique of *GSp* and of contemporary Catholic theology inspired by it is that its method of reading, and therefore its actual reading, of history buys into the dominant narrative of modernity.[14] What is truly problematic for Christian theology and practice, from this point of view, is modernity itself. Modernity sundered the organic unity, both intellectual and institutional, of the high medieval period, dissolved any reference to transcendent reality as an intrinsic feature of human existence, privatized faith and religion, and transformed the social order on a this-worldly, utilitarian and technological basis (Rowland 2003).[15] It stands in radical opposition to the Christian vision of reality.

This is clearly a historical critique, and not a simple reversion to the deductive approach and scholastic categories of pre-conciliar theology. But it is a radically different reading of history from the predominant view in the Council. Vatican II was self-conscious in 'throwing open the windows of the Church', in John XXIII's phrase, and it accepted – and not exactly uncritically – the significance of modernity and the social developments that came in its wake; this was the predominant orientation in the Council debates. A critique of modernity had long been standard Catholic fare, but in the Council it appeared to be vanquished, even if the emerging *GSp* text was subject to detailed criticism and hostility from conservative quarters.

A critical dividing line in Catholic theology, therefore, can be seen as between those who, while they may be critical of its concrete formulations, adopt the *GSp* starting-point, and those who, while acknowledging the importance of many of *GSp*'s specific social teachings, find it unacceptable, deficient or problematic as a starting point for Catholic theology. The alleged naivety of *GSp* is not the point; what lies in the background are fundamental questions about the significance of human-secular history in relation to divine revelation, about Christian faith and contemporary experience and, ultimately, the relationship of redemption and creation – all crucial foundational issues for any pastoral-practical theology.

Dividing Lines in Catholic Theology

According to John McDade, the 'location' Vatican II proposed for theology, as 'the sphere of "proper speech" about God', is 'in the middle of human history and experience'. This reshaped the agenda of theology so that it 'necessarily involves questions about its engagement with the world and its development, its orientation within particular social situations, and fundamental questions about its methodology and hermeneutics' (McDade 1991, pp. 423–4). In the period immediately after the Council, the transcendental theology of Karl Rahner was influential in articulating this new agenda. In Rahner's theological anthropology – where 'man as subject is the event of God's absolute self-communication' (Rahner 1978, p. 191) – the human is seen as the expression of the divine, the divine as inscribed in the human and, as McDade puts it, 'the mystery of Christ is to be found in the *humanum*, within the complex of human experience and history' (1991, p. 424). The link between faith and experience or revelation and history is ultimately direct rather than extrinsically established. Given this perspective, theology could no longer rest within its own disciplinary domain. Post-conciliar theology's anthropological turn now caused it to rely heavily on the human and social sciences.

Edward Schillebeeckx was a leading exponent, taking great pains to re-educate himself in a wide range of contemporary socio-philosophies, especially hermeneutics and Frankfurt School critical theory. In discussing both the theological tradition and contemporary issues, he pays close attention to experience – the historical context that lies behind the Scriptures and church doctrine and the structured experience of society today. His writings on church ministry exemplify this, going beyond doctrine and investigating the evolution of the forms of ministry in the history of the Church, and his agenda is explicitly set by the modern-day crisis of ministry in the Church and how this should be met (Schillebeeckx 1981 and 1985).

One effect of this orientation to history as *locus theologicus* is that it becomes less possible to construct grand theological syntheses. A theology attentive to the concrete *humanum* will lean to the particular rather than generalizations, and more likely be expressed in 'fragments' (Forrester 2005). Schillebeeckx, for example, has not written any comprehensive account of the Church in the world, the major theme of his later work, to stand alongside his great sacramental and Christological studies; and on the question of how doctrine stands in relation to human experience and dogma to history – about which he fell under Roman suspicion – he has been judged less than fully convincing even by sympathetic commentators (Schreiter 1997).

Deep conflicts over this post-conciliar theological approach were signalled by the attack mounted by Hans Urs von Balthasar on Rahner, with the charge that his theology portrayed Christian revelation as no more than bringing to light what was universally present immanently in human history (von Balthasar 1969).[16] Von Balthasar may be seen as a kind of Catholic Karl Barth. His theology is placed solidly within the revealed Word of God and 'at the centre of the contemplative Church's experience', a theology in the mode of doxology, as John McDade explains, and 'grounded in an experiential sense of God's engagement with us' (McDade 1991, p. 427). While rejecting the 'this worldly' orientation of much of contemporary theology, von Balthasar nevertheless holds, in a rather non-Barthian way, to a vision of human nature as 'the essential language of the *Logos*' (Riches and Quash 1997, p. 135). In his exposition of the analogical relation of similarity/dissimilarity between the creature and the divine he seeks to forge a deep connection with contemporary culture and philosophy, but he portrays these as broken and needing to be 'reset', and so the emphasis is put on dis-similarity over similarity.

High philosophy versus low sociology would be one way of distin-guishing the avenues into theology of the neo-conservative Balthasar and the post-conciliar Schillebeeckx. The polemics throw into sharp relief a very practical issue – the risk of reducing theology to social commentary. Just as pastoral care and spirituality are sometimes criti-cized for succumbing to a kind of psychological 'Babylonian captivity', so too the commanding heights of systematic theology can come under threat.[17] Pastoral theology, so reliant on social science methodologies to carry out its tasks, is especially vulnerable to the loss of its theological character. These challenges do not become any less acute today, and a balanced and *Catholic* theology has to steer a steady course. It is per-haps ironic, then, that what heightens the foundational philosophical issues is a social factor – the postmodern turn.

Contemporary Context

The theological agenda is, in the end, always shaped by practical matters, and today is no exception. Not only has systematic theology become more historically and practically attuned, but a variety of 'practical theologies' have arisen, the most prominent being Latin-American-inspired liberation theology, which saw its task as a refocusing of theology itself, and which then gave rise to the specific liberation theol-ogies – feminist, black, etc. – as well as theologies rooted in other social contexts – African, Asian, and so forth. At the same time, powerful secularizing trends across the Western world destabilizing the social status of religion have generated new political theologies in both radi-cal (Metz) and more conservative (Radical Orthodoxy, communitarian) forms. This turn to practice is a turn to history and an anthropologi-cal turn; it is in tune with modern culture's all-encompassing turn to the subject and the postmodern turn. Within the consequent prolif-eration of 'theologies', pastoral theology or practical theology has to seek its own niche, either as a distinct 'branch' or 'sub-discipline' or 'project'.[18]

Postmodernity, according to Lieven Boeve, sets a new context in which the openness to the world deriving from *Gaudium et spes* has to be fundamentally re-articulated. He puts the matter bluntly: is it the case that '[b]ecause of the loss of plausibility of the modern dialogue partner . . . the modern-theological project of dialogue with modernity becomes implausible, but also that the concept of dialogue itself in theology is disputed' (Boeve 2007, p. 151). In Boeve's analysis, post-modernity overcomes modernity by its radical pluralization of the cultural and religious sphere and suspicion of modernity's totalizing frameworks; the effect is that the hold of tradition in human affairs (taken-for-granted values and customary practices) is finally vanquished.[19] The resulting social 'de-traditionalization' radically disrupts any sense of continuity between Christian faith and the life of humanity. This continuity is what *GSp* seems to envisage. In Boeve's view, however, *GSp*'s real importance lies more in what it does than in what it says, its approach and method as developed in Part 1 rather than the contingent teachings of Part 2. He maintains that 'the Constitution did not favour the modern world of the early 1960s as such, but allied itself with the contemporary, critical consciousness, present in the contemporary philosophy of personalism' (Boeve 2007, p. 158).

When transposed to the postmodern pluralized context, this critical theological consciousness is forced to acknowledge that Christianity can no longer rely on being self-evidently an engagement with the *humanum*.[20] The assumption of continuity between the concerns of faith and the life of humanity no longer holds. This is evident only from within the specificity, and now narrowed reach, of faith. As a result, the Church's dialogue with the world now becomes structurally and explicitly a dialogue with 'the other', with those – individuals and institutions – who do not live within the Christian narrative of salvation. This brings about an 'interruption' in the self-understanding and unfolding of the Christian mission, which over the centuries had come to assume its own historical credibility. However, for Christianity to accept this postmodern 'interruption' – acknowledging now its own specificity, re-assuming the particularity of its salvation narrative, transcending its own totalizing tendencies and its closure to 'the other', engaging in a genuinely open dialogue in service of truth – is simply to be coherent with its origins. For it is by interrupting our closed narratives that God's Word is broken open, the crucifixion of Jesus being the climactic instance. 'Interruption' is a theological category not an unfortunate social fact.[21]

Boeve's postmodern reading is in stark contrast to the anti-modern stance of the radical critics of *Gaudium et spes* – those for whom the only coherent position is the rejection of modernity and what comes in its wake. Their critique is all-encompassing. The modern social order in its totality is suspect: the nation state, born in modernity, has displaced the true basis of human solidarity and is a 'simulacrum of the Body of Christ' (Cavanaugh 2007); secular ethics, codified as human rights, manifests a utilitarian philosophy and lacks foundations in the order of being (Rowland 2003); sociology, the child of modernity, is actually a displaced and illegitimate theology (Milbank 1990). While these critics give a guarded welcome to postmodern trends insofar as they critique modernity, their real theological effort lies less in post-modern dialogue than in the retrieval of the pre-modern.[22]

The two stances, postmodern and anti-modern, find some common ground in holding to the specificity of the Christian narrative and the particularity, in contrast to more universalist conceptions, of the path that flows from it; but they diverge in their valuation of the secular and their way of appropriating the *humanum*. Anti-moderns do not acknowledge the secular as autonomous from the religious. Here, a distinction needs to be made: between, on the one hand, a radical autonomy such that the secular is removed from the sovereignty of God, and, on the other hand, that autonomy which social sectors (politics, law, education, etc.) achieve from religious hegemony as a result of the societal process of institutional differentiation. Accommodation to the latter form of autonomy does not necessarily involve denial of God's dominion. However, once the differentiated social order central to modernity becomes established, it becomes difficult, and perhaps impossible, to retrieve pre-modern philosophical positions, so closely tied are they to pre-modern social structures.[23]

Broadly speaking, these two stances – postmodern and anti-modern – are the poles that delimit the field of Catholic theology today. They imply different evaluations of the *locus theologicus* that is human history and the manner of relating faith and human experience. Which of these underlying theological views is taken, therefore, will determine the role attributed to practical-pastoral theology and its manner of proceeding.

Conclusion

This chapter started by situating contemporary Catholic pastoral theology in the context of Vatican II as a 'pastoral' Council. Given that the axis of theology itself has now shifted so significantly towards the practical, with a proliferation of practical theologies, the description of the Council as *pastoral* is merited. What has been less clear is the Council's pastoral *implementation*, its effects on everyday Catholic practices. As is well known, the pastoral and practical results of the Council – in terms of ecclesial relationships, liturgy, catechesis and the various fields of pastoral care – have been less than satisfactory. However, the practice that the Council did definitively transform is the Catholic practice of theology. It reaffirmed theology as a practical rather than (only – or primarily) a theoretical enterprise. This is borne out even in the case of the anti-modern critics of *Gaudium et spes*, for the root of their objection is that document's perceived *historical* inadequacy for the contemporary reading of the gospel.

What now remain are the many troubling questions of pastoral practice in the contemporary Church, and the role that pastoral-practical theology can play in relation to them. Its precise function is to be attentive to the realities of practice in a sustained way, critically assessing change and facilitating creative evangelical initiative. Whether ecclesial practices in the concrete put the emphasis on the practicalities of *human living* in relation to the gospel (as the champions of *Gaudium et spes* might want) or on the practicalities of *Christian life and witness* to the gospel (the preference of its critics), these practices need to be interpreted, assessed, evaluated and theologically understood in their concreteness. This is a pragmatic task, and one that takes us beyond ideological confrontations. While there is a certain antipathy to this cooler approach among some, since its properly critical procedures do not corroborate the heats of strong religious enthusiasm, this theological approach offers the hope of rendering theology practical and effective in the day-by-day life and action of the ecclesial community.

Notes

1 The view that, nevertheless, there was a certain 'exhaustion' is put by Mathijs Lamberigts, 2007.

2 The issue of continuity versus discontinuity is hotly debated; see James Sweeney, 2009.

3 The well rehearsed litany of woes – falling church attendance, dissent from church teaching, drop in vocations, abandonment of their ministry by priests and religious, etc.

4 We can note here that engagement with official church teaching (an ongoing relationship with the *magisterium*) is a distinctive – and constitutive – feature of Catholic theology, pastoral as well as systematic. The relationship has been a troubled one over recent decades.

5 The terms 'progressive' and 'conservative' came into vogue at the time of the Council to identify opposing tendencies. They are useful for descriptive purposes but less so in terms of the variety and complexity of theological positions. Today,

the two 'camps' are usually identified – and not without polemics – as 'liberal' and 'traditional'.

6 For an account of the process of the Council and how the interests and organizational dynamics of the various groupings of bishops shaped it, see Wilde, 2007.

7 The differences between these two tendencies is mapped by Robert Schreiter in his chapter in this volume.

8 Of the 16 texts promulgated by Vatican II, four have the status of constitutions, including the 'pastoral' constitution *Gaudium et spes*. Its note 1 explains: 'Although it consists of two parts, the Pastoral Constitution "The Church in the World Today" constitutes an organic unity. The constitution is called "pastoral" because, while resting on doctrinal principles, it seeks to set forth the relation of the Church to the world and to the men [*sic*] of today. In Part I, therefore, the pastoral emphasis is not overlooked, nor is the doctrinal emphasis overlooked in Part II' (Flannery 1975, p. 903).

9 *Syllabus of Errors* (1864). It is primarily on *GSp*'s abandonment of these positions and Vatican II's teaching on religious freedom (*Dignitatis humanae*) that the *intégriste* followers of Archbishop Lefebvre reject the Council.

10 The shift in approach had already been signalled by Pope John XXIII's two social encyclicals *Mater et magistra* (1961) and *Pacem in terris* (1963).

11 Paul VI, *Populorum progressio* (1967); *Octagesimo adveniens* (1971); *Evangelii nuntiandi* (1975); John Paul II, *Laborem exercens* (1981); *Sollicitudo rei socialis* (1987); *Centesimus annus* (1991); Benedict XVI, *Caritas in veritate* (2009).

12 See McDonagh 1991.

13 It is the only document that, not having a prior draft, was proposed and formulated during the Council itself. The suggestion of a statement on the Church *ad extra*, to complement the *ad intra* vision of *Lumen gentium*, was made by Cardinal Suenens of Belgium on 4 December 1962.

14 These anti-modern critics, as they are sometimes called, may deflect this criticism from *GSp* itself onto its reception and interpretation by theologians in the post-conciliar period.

15 For an extensive reading of the process of socio-cultural-religious transformation from 1500 to the present day, see Charles Taylor's *A Secular Age* (2007). Taylor, however, does not hold with a wholesale theological or philosophical rejection of modernity.

16 The bitterness of this attack puzzled Rahner (see Marmion 1998, pp. 283–9).

17 In David Tracy's words, '*The* problem of the contemporary systematic theologian . . . is actually *to do* systematic theology' (Tracy 1978, p. 238).

18 See the chapters by Henri Gagey and Kathleen Cahalan in this volume.

19 For Ulrich Beck what this dynamic leads to is not postmodernity but 'new modernity' and its many associated risks (Beck 1992).

20 The term 'humanum' comes from Horkheimer and refers to all that is truly human and worthy of mankind.

21 Boeve acknowledges his indebtedness to Metz for the category of interruption.

22 This is because the genealogy of the flaw in the modern social order

leads back beyond the onset of modernity to the late medieval period, to the univocity of being of Duns Scotus and the nominalism of William of Ockham which undermined the metaphysics of the human as participation in the divine. So Milbank on Scotus: 'finite and infinite being are seen as equally and univocally "in being" – hence *esse* threatens to become greater than God and God to be idolatrously reduced to the status of a partner with his Creation in causal processes'. Milbank 2005 (2nd edn), p. xxiv; also Milbank, Pickstock and Ward 1999. See a discussion of these issues from a Catholic perspective by Fergus Kerr (Kerr 2000).

23 See my discussion of this point with reference to Jose Casanova and William Cavanaugh (Sweeney 2007).

Bibliography

Giuseppe Alberigo (ed.), 1995–2006, *History of Vatican II*, 5 vols (English version edited by Joseph A. Komonchak, translated by Matthew J. O'Connell), Maryknoll, NY: Orbis; and Leuven: Peeters.

Hans U. von Balthasar, 1969, *The Moment of Christian Witness*, San Francisco: Ignatius Press.

Ulrich Beck, 1992, *Risk Society: Towards a New Modernity*, London: SAGE (English translation by Mark Ritter).

Lieven Boeve, 2007, 'Beyond the Modern and Anti-modern Dilemma', in Johann Verstraeten (ed.), *Scrutinizing the Signs of the Times in the Light of the Gospel*, Leuven: Peeters, pp. 151–66.

William Cavanaugh, 2007, 'The Church', in P. Scott and W. Cavanaugh (eds) *Blackwell Companion to Political Theology*, Malden, MA: Blackwell.

Austin Flannery (general ed.), 1975, *Vatican Council II: Vol. I: The Conciliar and Postconciliar Documents*, Northport, NY: Costello; and Dublin: Dominican Publications.

Duncan Forrester, 2005, *Theological Fragments: Explorations in Unsystematic Theology*, London: Continuum/T&T Clark International.

Gustavo Gutiérrez, 1988, *A Theology of Liberation: History, Politics and Salvation*, London: SCM Press.

Adrian Hastings (ed.), 1991, *Modern Catholicism*, London: SPCK.

Fergus Kerr, 2000, 'A Catholic Response to the Programme of Radical Orthodoxy', in Laurence Hemming (ed.), *Radical Orthodoxy? A Catholic Enquiry*, Aldershot: Ashgate, pp. 46–59.

Joseph A. Komonchak (ed.), 1995, *History of Vatican II*, Maryknoll, NY: Orbis; and Leuven: Peeters.

Mathjis Lamberigts, 2007, '*Gaudium et spes*: A Council in Dialogue with the World', in Johann Verstraeten (ed.), *Scrutinizing the Signs of the Times in the Light of the Gospel*, Leuven: Peeters, pp. 17–21.

John McDade, 1991, 'Catholic Theology in the Post-Conciliar Period', in A. Hastings (ed.), *Modern Catholicism*, London: SPCK, pp. 423–4.

Enda McDonagh, 1991, 'The Church in the Modern World (*Gaudium et Spes*)', in A. Hastings (ed.), *Modern Catholicism*, London: SPCK, pp. 96–112.

Declan Marmion, 1998, *A Spirituality of Everyday Faith: A Theological*

Investigation of the Notion of Spirituality in Karl Rahner, Leuven: Peeters.

J. B. Metz, 1980, *Faith in History and Society: Toward a Practical Fundamental Theology*, London: Burns and Oates.

John Milbank, 1990 (2nd edn 2005), *Theology and Social Theory: Beyond Secular Reason*, Oxford: Blackwell.

John Milbank, Catherine Pickstock and Graham Ward (eds), 1999, *Radical Orthodoxy: A New Theology*, London: Routledge.

Karl Rahner, 1978, *Foundations of Christian Faith*, London: Darton, Longman & Todd.

John Riches and Ben Quash, 1997, 'Hans Urs von Balthasar', in David F. Ford (ed.), *The Modern Theologians*, 2nd edn, Oxford: Blackwell, pp. 134–51.

Tracey Rowland, 2003, *Culture and the Thomist Tradition: After Vatican II*, London: Routledge.

Edward Schillebeeckx, 1981, *Ministry*, London: SCM Press.

Edward Schillebeeckx, 1985, *Church with a Human Face*, London: SCM Press.

Robert Schreiter, 1997, 'Edward Schillebeeckx', in David F. Ford (ed.) *The Modern Theologians*, 2nd edn, Oxford: Blackwell, pp. 158–9.

James Sweeney, 2007, 'Catholic Social Thought as Political', in Johann Verstraeten (ed.), *Scrutinizing the Signs of the Times in the Light of the Gospel*, Leuven: Peeters, pp. 207–20.

James Sweeney, 2009, 'How should we Remember Vatican II?', *New Blackfriars* 90, no. 1026, pp. 251–60.

Charles Taylor, 2007, *A Secular Age*, Cambridge, MA: Belknap Press of Harvard University Press.

David Tracy, 1978, *Blessed Rage for Order*, New York: Seabury.

Johan Verstraeten (ed.), 2007, *Scrutinizing the Signs of the Times in the Light of the Gospel*, Leuven: Peeters.

Max Weber, 1947, *The Theory of Social and Economic Organization*, New York: Oxford University Press.

Melissa Wilde, 2007, *Vatican II: A Sociological Analysis of Religious Change*, Princeton, NJ: Princeton University Press.

2

Pastoral and Practical Theology in Britain and Ireland – A Catholic Perspective

DAVID MCLOUGHLIN AND
GEMMA SIMMONDS CJ

The Catholic pastoral theology that has developed in these countries bears witness to a clear tradition with rich resources and much potential, but it also points to certain weaknesses in providing impetus for new developments. Too few people have been deployed, with the result that major events and happenings could so claim the immediate attention of those with authority that long-term initiatives could falter and come to nothing. This leaves behind an amazing plethora of limited and unfinished initiatives in the hands of practitioners with little time or energy for theorizing or critical reappraisal.[1]

When the publishers Herder & Herder and Burns & Oates decided to initiate a series on Pastoral and Practical Theology for the English-speaking world in 1968, they commissioned Karl Rahner to provide the first volume, *Theology of Pastoral Action*, and a young American Dominican theologian, Daniel Morrisey, to work with Rahner to adapt it for an English-speaking readership.[2] The approach, unsurprisingly in the years just after Vatican II, was ecclesiocentric; but unusually for the transcendental theology then in vogue in Catholic circles it recognized the natural pragmatism of the Anglo-Saxon mindset. This initial attempt at collaboration between one of the great systematicians of the modern era with our cooler engagement with the real, the secular and the particular has remained a *leitmotif* of Catholic pastoral engagement in these islands ever since. This has something of a different feel from the new university-based discipline of practical theology which, according to its leading British proponent, Professor Stephen Pattison, is self-confessedly postmodern, and celebrates its necessary fragmentary and periodic quality (Woodward and Pattison 1999, pp. 14, 304).

The Catholic approach, insofar as it is possible to discern commonalities, can be characterized by four of the characteristics of that initial Rahner/Morrisey text. First, the framework of the Church's essential *kerygma*, the fruit of sustained theological reflection across the centuries. Second, and this was what Rahner/Morrisey focused on, the correlation of Christ and society and the possibility of the gospel addressing the contemporary world and humanity through different media, focusing on the ways a divine word can be expressed and the means by which such a word can be heard and received. Third, the exploration of the lived pastoral experience of the Church in its life, sacraments, liturgy, education, religious life and apostolic witness – with reflection tested in creative action. And finally, how this can enable decisions to be reached and action implemented. So: '*Kerygma*, correlation, experimentation, combine to produce action for today's and tomorrow's Church' (Rahner 1968, p. 23). In all of the above the assumption is that the basic model of pastoral theology is ecclesial, and the primary model of church is local. This had already been succinctly anticipated by Herbert McCabe OP, when he said: 'The Church is mankind pausing, as it were, to say where it is going and what it is doing under the power of the Spirit' (McCabe 1966, p. 68).

Influences from the Catholic World

Rahner's incarnational perspective underpinned his pastoral theology. Christ is the sacrament of God and the Church is the sacrament of Christ and so of God's self-gift to humanity, a reality both historical and social. Hence the Church is the sacrament of the divine saving presence and the promise of full reconciled life to come. This is anticipated in one of his earliest texts, *Hearers of the Word* (1969), in which he argues that human beings are the creatures who by nature and grace are open to the divine word wherever that may be expressed. He will return to this later in his concept of the 'supernatural existential', suggesting that human nature itself is qualified by an essential capacity for the divine. What this provided was a formal theological underpinning for a renewed commitment to the human condition expressed in the struggle of Marie-Dominique Chenu, Yves Congar, Henri de Lubac and others for a real theological engagement with the modern world and in particular late industrial society, such as the French worker priest experiment.

The Canadian theologian Bernard Lonergan adapted Rahner's transcendental method to produce a philosophy of how we come to knowledge (Lonergan 1957). He later developed this in his magiste-rial *Method in Theology* (1972), where pastoral and practical theology is subsumed under one of the forms of conversion. Lonergan had enormous influence on a number of British and Irish theologians. His emphasis in *Method* on conversion, and so on the turn to experience, was taken up and commented on by Donal Dorr and Jean-Pierre Jossua in papers at a seminar at St Patrick's College, Maynooth, in 1973.[3] Lonergan's emphasis on the turn away from the subject as isolated knower to a renewed emphasis on engaged and transforming experi-ence was taken up by many thinkers, leading to new forms of engaged theology.

The transcendental theology of Rahner, Lonergan and the early von Balthasar became commonplace in seminary courses in Britain and Ireland in the late 1960s and early 1970s, long before it was attended to in some of the British universities. It inspired a generation of clergy to a renewed social engagement based on a dynamic theological under-standing of creation and incarnation. This underpinning of social engagement by the vision of the great doctrines is a typical element of Catholic pastoral theology at its best.

Another theologian based in Canada, Gregory Baum, pursued a faithful and radical working out of the Church's social teaching within a critical reading of church and society. He was trained as a sociologist and political theorist, and has always been unusually sensitive to the social context of both political and theological theories long before the coining of contextual theology. This approach has been picked up fruit-fully in recent years in Britain by Paul Vallely (1998).

A further external influence was the Pastoral Leadership Program of the Institute of Pastoral Studies at Loyola University in Chicago, which a number of Irish and British priests and religious followed in the 1980s and 1990s. There they encountered the work of the Jesuit Bill Thomp-son on Matthew's Gospel showing how it was possible to be faithful to a critical reading and see its radical implications for their own context. They also benefited from the work of Patricia O'Connell Killen, David Killen and John de Beer on 'everyday theology' (Killen 1983; Killen and Killen 1986, pp. 277–87). This presented a four-source model for theological reflection and developed ways of thinking about sources for theological reflection within different settings. The four sources were: tradition (Scripture, doctrine, history and popular lore); action (actions, thoughts and feeling in one's lived narrative); positions (one's convictions, beliefs and opinions); and culture (ideas and artefacts, social structure and physical environment).

The opening up of the more classical categories to include popular lore, lived narratives, opinions and physical environment was a liberation to those whose experience was of the old late scholastic model of theology with its emphasis on historical 'authorities'. It provoked the mature students attending these courses to develop a working model for ministers and leaders to do theology in a local setting. While this was transformative of individuals' ministries it had little effect on structures of lay or clerical theological formation in the Catholic community on the east side of the Atlantic.

The Catholic Contribution to Practical Theology

Of the 22 contributors to the fine *Blackwell Reader in Pastoral and Practical Theology* only two are Catholic, of whom only one is from the British Isles. The lack of a substantive Catholic input, leaving aside editorial policy, needs to be reflected on. Catholic theology in Britain and Ireland tended to develop, until very recently, with little serious input from the universities. Part of the reason was the tradition of sending gifted students for the priesthood to Rome, Lisbon, Valladolid, Paris, Leuven and Innsbruck. On returning, they had very little in common with those who had studied theology in home seminaries and universities. Nor indeed were many encouraged to sustain a serious intellectual life unless they went on to work in the seminaries. The pastoral and practical theology that does exist has a mixed and messy history. Catholic academic institutes were, until recently, with the exception of Maynooth and its curious history of British governmental support, simply seminaries, religious order houses of formation and teacher training colleges. Those of the latter that have survived are now centres of higher education or new universities in which theology as a discipline, once privileged by their Catholic foundation, has had to fight, as elsewhere, to retain independence or autonomy – and in general they are straining to do so.

The scene has changed markedly, however, over recent decades, and there is now a very significant Catholic presence in most university faculties.[4] This is testimony to a flowering of Catholic theology (and theologians) in these countries. It has highlighted, among other things, the considerable resources available to the Catholic practical and pastoral theologian.

These include: a rich body of church social teaching, both centrally generated (for example the social encyclicals) and home grown (for example *The Common Good*, 1996) and the documents of the first global Church Council, Vatican II; a tradition of engagement at the grass roots, for example in the worker apostolate coming out of the Cardijn Christian Worker movement;[5] access to the great theological retrieval of the early and middle twentieth century (Congar, de Lubac, Chenu); more recently, a radical social and political rereading of the scriptures, influenced by the flow-back to Europe of the see–judge–act method enriched by its practitioners in South America and Africa; the active encouragement of local church leaders and national hierarchies, in documents such as, in England and Wales, the *Easter People* and *The Common Good*, to seek ways for a serious engagement in civil society on the basis of clearly enunciated theological and pastoral principles; the lobbying and charitable organizations – Caritas, the Catholic Agency for Overseas Development (CAFOD), Progressio, the Scottish Catholic International Aid Fund (SCIAF) and Trócaire in Ireland – with their outreach to schools and parishes, and the involvement in their work of creative and engaged theologians; the resources of the religious orders of women and men with their wealth of experience and inter- and intra-congregational global networks.

These resources and influences on Catholic pastoral and practical theology are rich and broad, although it is worth noting that the stimuli often come from outside the British Isles, while finding a new context and resonance here. This becomes clearer as we look at the groups and individuals who have contributed to this inchoate Catholic pastoral theology and the main themes that have emerged over the last fifty years.

An Emerging Pastoral Theology – Practice and Reflection

While the theological foundations for Vatican II's programme of *aggiornamento* or updating were laid by the great continental theologians such as Yves Congar and Henri de Lubac, theological curiosity and pastoral creativity were also ripening in Britain and Ireland prior to the Council, particularly in some lay circles and among the growing number of university-educated Catholics. The liturgical movement was under way and had its enthusiasts. As early as 1920 the University Catholic Societies Federation was founded and affiliated to the international Pax Romana organization. In 1940, under the influence of Cardinal Hinsley, Sword of the Spirit (later to become CIIR and later still Progressio) was launched; and in 1942 the Newman Association was founded, providing a forum for lay intellectual engagement. This resulted in, for example, its Philosophy of Science group, which met from 1954 to 1967, and the very significant empirical research of the Newman Demographic Survey, which produced professional statistical data relating to parishes, education and vocations from 1953 until the disbandment of the unit in 1964.[6]

With the new impetus given by the Council, theologians and practitioners worked to synthesize theological reflection and pastoral experience leading in turn to transformative teaching and practice. The influence of liberation theology and the context from which it arose has been notable here. Returning missionaries, based on their experience among Christians in the developing world, were influential in opening up rich resources and a critical methodology for reflecting on pastoral practice (for example, Dorr 2000 and 2004).

There were ground-breaking pastoral initiatives among the marginalized of the inner cities, which resulted in publications reflecting the influence of a socially engaged praxis on pastoral theology. The movement among women and men religious and their associates to develop a new form of social insertion was influenced by the radical restructuring of religious communities in the Americas from the 1970s onwards.[7]A model of engaged presence was developed that was slowly transformative of the social environment and in which the religious community acted as a nexus for emerging relationships and developments (see Smith 1983; Sweeney 1994).[8] Parishes too have been the site of pastoral theological insight and exploration and secular priests have made, and continue to make, serious contributions to the development of a new pastoral theology.[9]

In the period after the Council, a group of young intellectuals initiated a serious dialogue with radical socialism. Gathering at Spode House, the Dominican Hawksyard Priory, the Slant Group, as it was named after the journal of that name which they founded, became known for its serious engagement with social, economic and political issues in the light of the Catholic tradition in its broadest theological and sacramental forms. This was a collective attempt by a loose alliance of Catholic intellectuals – clerical, religious and lay – to engage critically with the political and social reality of the 1960s and the Church's apparent inability to play the creative and critical counter-cultural role of its foundational documents.[10]

Another influential forum was provided by the Downside Symposia of the 1960s and 1970s; under the aegis of the Benedictines these gatherings engaged in a wide-ranging reflection on topics of Christian life such as work, worship, priesthood, inter-communion and theology in the University. These meetings of some of the most creative theological minds in the British Catholic scene at the time were pastoral, practical and ecumenical. More recently, there has been the project in the West of Ireland to develop local theological resources independent of traditional academic institutions – sometimes referred to as 'Mayo theology'.

Another site for theological engagement has been within the development agencies, including those that are inter-church or independent, and bishops' conferences' bodies (CAFOD, SCIAF, Progressio, Trócaire, Caritas-social action, Christian Aid, Housing Justice, Church Action on Poverty, etc.) and on university or governmental panels dealing with public issues. These have offered a pragmatic framework for the elaboration of Catholic social thought, and theologians from the seminaries and universities have been regularly involved.

The encounter between the mystical tradition and transformative praxis gave rise to new streams in the spiritualities of the religious orders. Following *Perfectae caritatis*, Vatican II's decree on the adaptation and renewal of religious life, religious returned to their historical roots and foundational documents in search of a contemporary interpretation of their charism. For many this became foundational in the rediscovery of their spiritual identity and a renewed opening of those spiritual traditions to a wider lay audience in both the Catholic and wider Christian spheres. The renewal of the Ignatian tradition has also made a major contribution to the spiritual formation and education of clergy, religious and lay people of different Christian traditions, and has given them fresh ways of integrating prayer and daily life, contemplation and action.[11]

A major shift in the Catholic landscape since Vatican II, both in Britain and in Ireland, has been the handing over into lay hands of schools previously run by religious orders. This reflects the ageing profile of religious and the acute fall in vocations, but it also resonates with the Council's call to the laity to holiness and leadership within their personal and professional vocations. This has prompted theological reflection on the pastoral role of education and educators, as well as the process of handing on the charism, or identifying particularities, of the orders to their collaborators so that their historical mission in the Church can be continued (Lydon 2009). Gerald Grace and Ronald Valenti suggest that 'the Church's "best kept secret" may indeed be its heritage of Catholic social teaching, but its second best kept secret is the living culture and practice of contemporary Catholic education in all its forms' (2009). This has been the bedrock for significant educational writing, with a cross-over into practical theology, by scholars such as John Sullivan (2001) and the late Terry McLaughlin (Carr et al. 2008).

In England and Wales the highpoint of serious engagement by the Catholic community with the contemporary realities of social life was the Liverpool Pastoral Congress of 1980 and the document the bishops produced in response to its debates and conclusions, *The Easter People*. This was a rereading of the British scene in the light of the main themes of Vatican II. The preparatory work was done with groups of lay people from across the country representing parishes and with the active apostolic associations and lay movements. Theologians from the seminaries and colleges met with these groups for over a year, helping them come to terms with the theology of Vatican II and to begin to formulate the issues and questions to be addressed. The commitment of so many people was extraordinary and the energy it generated had enormous potential. People returned to their home communities fired up to share a new pastoral theological vision and encourage a renewed engagement with culture and society. The bishops' response in *The Easter People* was a huge success and it was studied in groups in dioceses around the country.

The project, however, failed to fulfil its potential. Some of the Congress's proposals were met with a cold response when they were relayed by Cardinal Basil Hume to the Synod of Bishops on the Family in Rome later that year. Then, when it was announced that the new Pope, John Paul II, was going to make a visit to Britain in 1982, all energy went into preparing for that momentous event. The consequence was that the momentum faded and an opportunity to develop a new pastoral strategy and a new capacity for pastoral reflection and action was lost. In addition, the untimely death of the bishop who was the natural theological leader in the hierarchy, Francis Thomas of Northampton, who had begun applying the process in his own diocese leading to a three-day regional synod that mapped out the next ten years of pastoral development, was another nail in the coffin of a unique moment of opportunity in English and Welsh Catholic history. The twelve months it took to replace him brought the whole process to a halt.[12]

Articulating a Pastoral Theology

Catholic pastoral journals – *The Furrow* and *Doctrine & Life* in Ireland and *The Pastoral Review* in Britain (previously *Clergy Review*, then *Priests & People*) – function as a forum for the dialogue of practitioners and academics, where the hermeneutical circle operates between pastoral experience and different theological disciplines. On a more directly popular level, *Intercom* is a pastoral and liturgical resource magazine, published in Ireland and widely used by priests and pastoral workers in many countries. In the field of spirituality, *The Way* in Britain and *Religious Life Review* and *Spirituality* in Ireland offer a forum for writing and reflection that reaches a worldwide audience.

Some exceptionally good writing emerged from the post-Vatican II agencies and groupings, and this set the standard for serious social and theological engagement, inspiring a new generation of radical clergy and lay activists. Spode House and other centres like it became special places for open discussion and debate, prayer and mysticism, retreats and rallies. In Ireland, Dermot Lane has helped groups reflect on the post-Vatican II turn to experience in Catholic theology. He argues creatively for a way forward between a purely theoretical theology and a simply practical, thoroughgoing Christian activism. His theological accents are christological, eucharistic and eschatological and focus on the Church's role to continue the mission of Christ to point to, and realize, the kingdom of God through a communal sacramental life that celebrates and is realized in commitment to liberating action for justice. His *Challenges Facing Religious Education in Contemporary Ireland* (2008) explores the idea of imagination in Catholic theology, which he sees linked to a rich doctrine of creation. This is an imagination that is inclusive and comprehensive and that defines in relational rather than oppositional categories. For Lane, Catholic imagination is symbolic and cannot be reduced to propositions; such reduction is a distortion of the divine mystery. As such, Catholic imagination is sacramental, with the materiality of creation and incarnation mediating divine presence. But the Catholic imagination recognizes dissimilarity too and the limits and analogical and symbolic nature of all God-talk. For Lane this opens up an appropriate element of negative or mystical theology.

The theme of imagination is explored in theological analyses of culture and the interface with faith. Donal O'Leary's *Begin with the Heart*, Michael Paul Gallagher's *Clashing Symbols* and the interpretive essay *On the Way to Life* by James Hanvey and Anthony Carroll, commissioned by the Catholic Bishops' Conference of England and Wales from the Heythrop Institute for Religion, Ethics and Public Life, develop an evaluative commentary on contemporary culture, social trends, secularization and modernity and sketch a theological framework in which an accurate understanding of contemporary culture can provide a deeper understanding of how culture shapes a person's grasp on faith. This study of culture and the sacramental imagination probes the points of meeting with or divergence from the gospel and the tasks of proclamation and transmission of faith.

Pastoral theology is necessarily linked to theological formation and education, and here Donal Dorr has developed a contextually sensitive theology and a formation programme exploring different ways of leadership within the faith community, responsive to local needs. His research on the theory and practice of development economics and cultural and religious diversity has led to a series of works exploring globalization and reflecting on the relationship between evangelization, liberation and development. A recurring theme is the training requirements needed to facilitate theological reflection among believers and a critique of the inadequacy of Irish ministerial training in this regard (Dorr 1992, 2000, 2004).

The influence of liberation theology and its analytical tools can also be seen in the work of Sean J. Healy and Brigid Reynolds, who fronted important work for the Irish Conference of Religious (CoRI), enabling the use of social analysis models in transformative grass-roots group work. Their *Social Analysis in the Light of the Gospel* (1983) has been a hugely influential activist's manual, drawing on Joe Holland and Peter Henriot from the Center of Concern in Washington and their *Social Analysis: Linking Faith and Justice* (1980). Their work has been immensely influential in both the Church and political circles, shifting the focus to public policy and providing analysis and informed critical comment to help the Church participate actively in the development of viable alternative political and social options.

A similar synthesis of radical pastoral praxis and theological reflection is to be found in the work of Mary Beasley, a former local authority social worker now wheelchair-bound. Her *Mission on the Margins* (1997) explores her experience among the most marginalized and anonymous men and women in inner-city Birmingham. Her long and creative relationship of dialogue with the Anglican priest and social activist Ken Leech and his work in the East End of London led to ecumenical collaboration in which a network of practitioners helped sustain each other in engaged theological reflection. So too, Austin Smith's *Journeying with God: Paradigms of Power and Powerlessness*

(1990), written out of the experience of many years of inner-city mission in Liverpool, is an extended reflection on what liberation means for those who are powerless in contemporary Britain and how such engagement leads inevitably to a re-conceiving of God; it is a sustained piece of theological retrieval and creativity as the author dwells on the changing context of late modern urban life and confronts its structures, concerns and changing priorities.

Besides the classic social and political frame of liberation theology, the question of sustainability has begun to take a higher profile. The 'greening' of Catholic pastoral theology is found in the work of Sean McDonagh, another returned missionary – from the Philippines. Drawing inspiration from the American 'eco-theologian' Thomas Berry, he has been influential in extending the justice and peace agenda to take account of the integrity of creation. Celia Deane-Drummond is also an influential voice in these ethical debates and a leading figure in forming an ecological spirituality (2008).[13] Today the ecological crisis is becoming increasingly urgent; it motivates the present generation of young adults in the way issues of peace and justice did their parents.

'Spirituality' is a popular topic today – the 'spiritual but not religious' variety – but the rich resources of the Christian tradition are often overlooked; this is a tendency that Catholic writers such as Peter Tyler (see his chapter in this volume) and Philip Sheldrake do much to counteract. *The New SCM Dictionary of Christian Spirituality* (Sheldrake 2005) is now the standard reference book in the subject in the English-speaking world, and an excellent example of theological reflection taking human experience as a starting-point and setting up a conversation with both the tradition and other forms of human enquiry, and including essays on methodology in the study of spirituality; spirituality and culture; spirituality and the dialogue of religions; spirituality, psychology and psychotherapy; spirituality and science; spirituality and social sciences, and spirituality and theology.[14]

Whether in terms of social structures or social and personal relationships, a theological retrieval also functions in the construction of identities with regard to gender. These issues and their pastoral implications are evident in the work of Linda Hogan (1995), Tina Beattie (2003) and other feminist theologians. Ursula King helped a British audience hear the voices of women theologians and practitioners in the developing world with her *Feminist Theology from the Third World* (1994), while her *Spirituality and Society in the New Millennium* (2001) linked the world of spirituality and social, political and pastoral questions.

Catholic pastoral theology has traditionally been linked to moral theology, which has always had a special place within Catholic theology. It is a field where British and Irish theologians have made their mark, with a synthesis of pastoral engagement and acute intellectual enquiry. Kevin Kelly (1999), Jack Mahoney (1987), Enda McDonagh (1972, 1979) and Bernard Hoose (1994) have been at the forefront here. McDonagh's contribution has been especially significant in relation to the Northern Ireland conflict. Beginning in the 1970s, he has explored nationalism and violence. His model of conversion-based discovery within community, with relationship seen as revelatory and emphasizing the importance of the stranger-friend and indeed the importance of the strangeness of God, has been quietly influential within cross-national and party political groups in the North of Ireland that few knew were meeting; all this helped sow the seeds of reconciliation that are being harvested today.

The theology of the Second Vatican Council is concerned above all with the nature of the Church itself, which is reflected in the subsequent work of theologians such as Avery Dulles and Leonardo Boff and in the theology and ecumenical responsibilities of Cardinal Walter Kasper. In the current British scene, the Ecclesiological Investigations Research Network provides both a challenge to and a reflection on pastoral contexts and practice, with Gerard Mannion (2007) and Paul Murray as major Catholic contributors. It is notable also for its engagement with vexed ecumenical issues, a topic on which Durham's Receptive Ecumenism project, led by Paul Murray (2008), has taken the lead.

Pastoral theology is an interdisciplinary exercise, even though a fruitful partnership with the human and social sciences is not always easy, as was signalled by the title of the collected essays of the symposium in Oxford in the late 1970s which addressed these issues – *Sociology and Theology: Alliance and Conflict*. Nevertheless, social scientists have made a notable contribution to pastoral and theological work, especially Michael Hornsby-Smith and his series of landmark sociological studies of the Catholic community (1989, 1991).

Conclusion

Surveying the emergence of Catholic pastoral theology in Britain and Ireland reveals it to be, in the main, the product of a convergence of theological movements from abroad and the reflection by local theologians and practitioners on immediate pastoral and practical issues.

It has been, and continues to be, a dynamic field; and more recently it has been fed by the scholarship of a new generation of British and Irish Catholic systematic theologians. At the same time, this localized Catholic pastoral theology experiences the influence of the practical theology characteristic of the Protestant tradition. The British and Irish Association of Practical Theology (BIAPT) has an ecumenical membership, and its recently re-launched journal *Practical Theology* (formerly *Contact*) has included Catholic members on its editorial board.[15] While it would be true to say that the dominant orientation here has been set by traditions other than the Catholic, there is the potential for mutual enrichment now. The Catholic pastoral theology that leans towards systematic theology and the practical theology of the Reformed traditions that has a strong interdisciplinary linkage with the social sciences have lessons for each other.

For all these prospects to be securely established, however, it cannot be left on the Catholic side to a few people who already have too many pastoral commitments. What is required is an effective network to sustain pastoral theological reflection across colleges, seminaries and universities and relating directly to existing local networks and projects. Theologians can offer a critical but sympathetic space to evaluate and learn from particular local engagements and experience. Such a network could become the living memory of the pastoral life of the Catholic tradition in these countries and provide the basis for a renewed theology responsive to local needs, and yet capable of generating lessons and wisdom for the wider community.

Notes

1 The history of pastoral theology and pastoral practice in Britain and Ireland is a story that ought to be cherished. This chapter gives an overview without claiming to be definitive or comprehensive; such is not possible in a short essay.

2 Originally published as *Grundlegung der Pastoraltheologie als praktische Theologie*, Freiburg: Herder, 1964.

3 The revised papers were produced in P. Corcoran (ed.), 1975, *Looking at Lonergan's Method*, republished in 2007, Eugene, OR: Wipf & Stock.

4 To mention only a few examples of this expanding Catholic presence beyond the religious 'private halls' at Oxford: the prominence of Catholic theologians in the Cambridge and other university faculties; the establishment of Heythrop College in the University of London; the Dominican chaplaincy in Edinburgh and their involvement in New College; the establishment of the Bede Chair of Catholic Theology and the Centre of Catholic Studies at Durham.

5 In 1992 John O'Shea, Declan Lang, Vicky Cosstick and the late Damian Lundy brought out *The Parish Project: A Resource Book for Parishes to Review their Mission*. This was a field-tested resource, with step-by-step help to enable a parish group to reflect theologically on its mission. It used the developed form of Cardijn's see–judge–act method, now known as the pastoral cycle, and became a handbook for grassroot pastoral renewal and local theology.

6 See *A Use of Gift: The Newman Association 1942–1992*. The aims of the Newman Demographic Survey are still pursued by the Pastoral Research Trust and its founder Anthony Spencer, who originally founded the Survey and worked on its staff.

7 Research and publication in this area in Britain and Ireland have been modest, but Amy L. Koehlinger, 2007, *The New Nuns: Racial Justice and Religious Reform in the 1960s*, Cambridge, MA: Harvard University Press, gives an account from the American perspective.

8 To mention just one example: the Hope Community was established by Margaret Walsh, a religious Sister of the Infant Jesus, with her companions in a couple of flats in Heath Town, in inner-city Wolverhampton; the community became deeply involved in what had been a seriously deprived area and something of a human desert. She has written short articles out of this immediate engagement with the people and these social circumstances.

9 To mention a couple of examples: Paul Hypher, who studied with the Rahner brothers in Innsbruck, took up an ongoing watching brief on the changing needs of ministry in contemporary Britain; while working as a parish priest in the diocese of East Anglia he managed to head up serious research on the nature of the Catholic parish and its pastoral needs. So too, David Oakley in the Archdiocese of Birmingham has developed a rich and diverse ministry as well as being pastoral director at Oscott seminary. His doctoral research proposed a rich model to develop the potential of the mystagogical phase of the Rite of Christian Initiation of Adults with a theologically renewed sense of pastoral reflection to go beyond the adaptive social-science-based models in many universities and ministerial training colleges. It is noteworthy that a link is made here between serious pastoral reflection and the liturgical cycle.

10 It produced exceptionally good writing from writers such as Brian Wicker, Adrian Cunningham, Terry Eagleton, Herbert McCabe, Martin Redfern, Lawrence Bright, Nicholas Lash, Rosemary Haughton and others, which set a standard for serious social and theological engagement and inspired a new generation of radical clergy and lay activists.

11 The renewal of the Ignatian tradition was promoted by writers such as, among others, James Walsh, Joseph Veale, Michael Ivens, Gerard W. Hughes, Philip Sheldrake and David Lonsdale.

12 For a fuller account, see Clifford Longley 2000, pp. 284–95.

13 Celia Deane Drummond has taken a year out from her university responsibilities (2009–10) to work as theological resource person for CAFOD and help them network with applied theological practitioners. This is a model of contemporary practical and pastoral theological collaboration.

14 See also the series under the general title of Traditions of Spirituality published by Darton, Longman & Todd, which has opened up current reflection on a broad range of Christian spiritual traditions to a wider readership with

inexpensive books based on the most recent scholarship and written in an easily accessible style.

15 Currently Philip Endean SJ.

Bibliography

Gregory Baum, 1987, *Theology and Society*, New York: Paulist Press.

Gregory Baum with Robert Ellsberg and others, 1989, *Essays in Critical Theology*, Kansas: Sheed & Ward.

Gregory Baum, 1994, *The Logic of Solidarity: Commentaries on Pope John Paul II's Encyclical* on Social Concern, Maryknoll: Orbis.

Mary Beasley, 1999, *Mission on the Margins*, Cambridge: Lutterworth Press.

Tina Beattie, 2003, *Woman*, London: Continuum.

D. Carr, M. Halstead and R. Pring (eds), 2008, *Liberalism, Education and Schooling: Essays by T. H. McLaughlin*, Exeter: Imprint Academic.

Catholic Bishops' Conference of England and Wales, 1980, *The Easter People: A Message from the Roman Catholic Bishops of England and Wales in Light of the National Pastoral Congress, Liverpool, 1980*, Slough: St Paul Publications.

Catholic Bishops' Conference of England and Wales, 1986, *The Common Good and the Catholic Church's Social Teaching*, London: Catholic Bishops' Conference.

P. Corcoran (ed.), 1975, *Looking at Lonergan's Method*, Dublin: Talbot Press.

Celia Deane-Drummond, 2008, *Eco-theology*, London: Darton, Longman & Todd.

Donal Dorr, 1992, *Option for the Poor: A Hundred Years of Vatican Social Teaching*, Dublin: Gill & Macmillan, 1992.

Donal Dorr, 2000, *Mission in Today's World*, Maryknoll, NY: Orbis Books.

Donal Dorr, 2004, *Time for Change: A Fresh Look at Spirituality, Sexuality, Globalisation and the Church*, Dublin: Columba Press.

Michael Paul Gallagher, 2003, *Clashing Symbols: An Introduction to Faith and Culture*, London: Darton, Longman & Todd.

Gerald Grace and Ronald Valenti, 2009, 'Preface and Introduction', *International Studies in Catholic Education* 1:1, pp. 1–4.

James Hanvey and Anthony Carroll, 2005, *On the Way to Life: Contemporary Culture and Theological Development as a Framework for Catholic Education, Catechesis and Formation*, London: Heythrop Institute for Religion, Ethics and Public Life.

Sean J. Healy and Brigid Reynolds, 1983, *Social Analysis in the Light of the Gospel*, Dublin: Columba Press.

Linda Hogan, 1995, *From Women's Experience to Feminist Theology*, Sheffield: Sheffield Academic Press.

Joe Holland and Peter Henriot, 1980, *Social Analysis: Linking Faith and Justice*, Maryknoll, NY: Orbis.

Bernard Hoose, 1994, *Received Wisdom? Reviewing the Role of Tradition in Christian Ethics*, London: Geoffrey Chapman.

Bernard Hoose (ed.), 2002, *Authority in the Roman Catholic Church: Theory and Practice*, Aldershot: Ashgate.

Michael Hornsby-Smith, 1989, *The Changing Parish: A Study of Parishes, Priests and Parishioners after Vatican II*, London: Routledge.

Michael Hornsby-Smith, 1991, *Roman Catholic Beliefs in England: Customary Catholicism and Transformations of Religious Authority*, Cambridge: Cambridge University Press.

Michael Hornsby-Smith (ed.), 1999, *Catholics in England 1950–2000: Historical and Sociological Perspectives*, London: Cassell.

Michael Hornsby-Smith, John Fulton and Margaret Norris, 1995, *The Politics of Spirituality: A Study of a Renewal Process in an English Diocese*, Oxford: Clarendon Press; New York: Oxford University Press.

Gerard W. Hughes, 1985, *God of Surprises*, London: Darton, Longman & Todd.

Kevin Kelly, 1999, *From a Parish Base: Essays in Moral and Pastoral Theology*, London: Darton Longman & Todd.

Patricia O'Connell Killen, 1983, 'Everyday Theology: A Model for Religious and Theological Education', *Chicago Studies* 22 (August).

Patricia O'Connell Killen and David Killen, 1986, 'Theology in its Natural Environment: Issues, Implications and Directions', *New Blackfriars* 67 (June).

Ursula King, 1994, *Feminist Theology from the Third World: A Reader*, London: SPCK; Maryknoll, NY: Orbis Books.

Ursula King (ed.), 2001, *Spirituality and Society in the New Millennium*, Brighton: Sussex Academic Press.

Amy L. Koehlinger, 2007, *The New Nuns: Racial Justice and Religious Reform in the 1960s*, Cambridge, MA: Harvard University Press.

Dermot Lane, 1984, *Foundations for a Social Theology: Praxis, Process and Salvation*, Dublin: Gill & Macmillan.

Dermot Lane, 2008, *Challenges Facing Religious Education in Contemporary Ireland*, Dublin: Veritas.

Nicholas Lash, 1979, *Theology on Dover Beach*, London: Darton, Longman & Todd.

Nicholas Lash, 1988, *Easter in Ordinary: Reflections on Human Experience and the Knowledge of God*, London: SCM Press.

Bernard Lonergan, 1957, *Insight: A Study of Human Understanding*, London: Longmans.

Bernard Lonergan, 1972, *Method in Theology*, London: Darton, Longman & Todd.

Clifford Longley, 2000, *The Worlock Archive*, London: Geoffrey Chapman.

John Lydon, 2009, 'Transmission of the Charism: A Major Challenge for Catholic Education', *International Studies in Catholic Education* 1:1, pp. 42–58.

Herbert McCabe, 1966, 'The Church and the World', in D. Flanagan (ed.), *The Meaning of the Church*, Dublin: Gill & Macmillan.

Enda McDonagh, 1972, *Invitation and Response: Essays in Christian Moral Theology*, Dublin: Gill & Macmillan.

Enda McDonagh, 1979, *Doing the Truth: The Quest for Moral Theology*, Dublin: Gill & Macmillan.

Enda McDonagh, 2007, *Immersed in Mystery: En Route to Theology*, Dublin: Veritas.

Sean McDonagh, 1990, *The Greening of the Church*, London: Geoffrey Chapman.

Sean McDonagh, 2005, *The Death of Life: The Horror of Extinction*, Dublin: Columba.

John Mahoney, 1987, *The Making of Moral Theology: A Study of the Roman Catholic Tradition*, Oxford: Clarendon Press.

Gerard Mannion, 2007, *Ecclesiology and Postmodernity: Questions for the Church in our Time*, Collegeville: Liturgical Press.

David Martin, John Orme Mills and William S. F. Pickering (eds), 1980, *Sociology and Theology: Alliance and Conflict*, Brighton: Harvester Press (re-issued Leiden: Brill, 2003).

Sebastian Moore, 1967, *God is a New Language*, London: Darton, Longman & Todd.

Paul Murray (ed.), 2008, *Receptive Ecumenism and the Call to Catholic Learning: Exploring a Way for Contemporary Ecumenism*, Oxford: Oxford University Press.

Newman Association, 1991, *A Use of Gift: The Newman Association 1942–1992*, produced as issue no. 27 (September 1991) of *The Newman*.

Daniel O'Leary, 2008, *Begin with the Heart: Recovering a Sacramental Vision*, Dublin: Columba.

John O'Shea et al., 1992, *The Parish Project: A Resource Book for Parishes to Review their Mission*, London: HarperCollins.

Karl Rahner, 1964, *Grundlegung der Pastoraltheologie als praktische Theologie*, Freiburg: Herder & Herder; translated as *Theology of Pastoral Action* by W. J. O'Hara and adapted for an English-speaking audience by Daniel Morrissey, 1968, London: Burns & Oates; New York: Herder & Herder.

Karl Rahner, 1969, *Hearers of the Word*, London: Sheed & Ward, revised by J. B. Metz, translated by Ronald Walls.

Philip Sheldrake (ed.), 2005, *The New SCM Dictionary of Christian Spirituality*, London: SCM Press.

Austin Smith, 1983, *Passion for the Inner City*, London: Sheed & Ward.

Austin Smith, 1990, *Journeying with God: Paradigms of Power and Powerlessness*, London: Sheed & Ward.

John Sullivan, 2001, *Catholic Education: Distinctive and Inclusive*, Dordrecht: Kluwer Academic.

James Sweeney, 1994, *The New Religious Order: A Study of the Passionists in Britain and Ireland, 1945–1990 and the Option for the Poor*, London: Bellew.

James Sweeney, 2002, 'The Experience of Religious Orders', in Bernard Hoose (ed.), *Authority in the Roman Catholic Church: Theory and Practice*, Aldershot: Ashgate, pp. 171–80.

Paul Vallely (ed.), 1998, *The New Politics: Catholic Social Teaching for the Twenty-first Century*, London: SCM Press.

James Woodward and Stephen Pattison, 1999, *The Blackwell Reader in Pastoral and Practical Theology*, Oxford: Blackwell.

PART TWO

Fundamentals of a Catholic Pastoral Theology

Introduction to Part Two

Fides quaerens intellectum is theology's classic definition. It is the pursuit of understanding. It accepts the lived experience of faith, and seeks to understand it in many ways and at different levels – in the grasp of the meaning of doctrines and knowledge of the history of salvation. This is theology on home ground, as it were. But the faith (*fides*) that pastoral and practical theology has as its primary focus is located in immediate experience, in practices and everyday reality; and when it comes to understanding such structured contemporary realities theology cannot, given the diversity of human forms of enquiry and knowledge and the proper autonomy of the disciplines of science and the humanities, supply any totalizing or 'ultimate' explanations. The goals of pastoral theology need to be precisely defined.

The Pastoral Theological Approach

Pastoral theology deals with realities rather than texts. There are several notions wrapped up here – reality, context, experience, practices. These signify in various ways the 'immediate' or the 'inner worldly' as a location that is invested with theological significance and constitutes a *locus theologicus*. 'Reality' in its various dimensions has its own authentic voice in the theological enterprise.

This much can be taken as the established, but not unproblematic, starting-point of pastoral theology. What precisely is this *locus theologicus*? It may be human *experience* as an undifferentiated whole; or the *context* – in its socio-political-cultural variety; or the various *practices* we engage in – as human beings, and as Christians. These varied aspects of 'reality' need careful definition in order to articulate whatever theological agenda there might be in relation to them.

Moreover, there is no simple correspondence between 'reality' and the reading of it. Experience does not come to us innocent of any

45

reading; it is always, in some fashion, an already interpreted experience. And a theological hermeneutic is already implicated, in some way and to some degree, in our humanly interpreted experience, even before we take up the formal task of a theological reading. The practices of the Christian life contain an embedded theology; contexts are socially and culturally structured and laden with meaning. The formal theological hermeneutic is always another step in 'making sense' of reality. The theological reading of experience, context or practice does not 'capture' reality in some pure way. In fact, theological readings are chronically open to contest.

Since pastoral theology is concerned with 'reading' contemporary realities, rather than the excavation of historical texts or explication of the meaning of doctrines, its goal can be expressed in terms of 'disclosure': it seeks to uncover and reveal the *significance* of things – of contexts, experiences and practices. Naively put, the theological question would be: 'Where is God in this?' But, of course, to address that question in a formally theological way – as distinct from the immediate faith-apprehension of God – systematic enquiry is required.

This emphasis on the disclosure of the divine is consistent with a discernment model of theology. Discernment in its classical understanding also has the dimension of finding the proper response to the 'will of God' so discerned. In these terms, the goal of practical theology can be seen as bringing about some form of 'transformation'. This is a complex notion; transformation comes in a variety of ways: both active *and* passive, in the world and in the Church, in the life and through the work of Christian believers and communities.

Contents

These are some of the foundational issues that are addressed or implicated in the six chapters of Part Two. That practice now forms part of the theological agenda is not in itself revolutionary – it is in fact a recovery of the traditional understanding – but the way practice is adopted, its place at the heart of theological enterprises, is new and still being worked out. Theology unfolds historically and in correspondence with history.

The centrality of hermeneutics in theology generally and in pastoral theology in particular is underscored in Chapter 3 by Michael Kirwan; he shows the subtleties and complexities of the task of reading the signs of the times. Exploring this headline feature of Catholic pastoral theology, he goes further into the postmodern versus anti-modern controversies described in the earlier chapter by James Sweeney. The actual reading of contemporary realities – the context – is Robert Schreiter's topic. He maps the characteristics of this terrain and describes two different lenses through which they can be read, two understandings of Catholicity. These two understandings are the root of the contemporary bifurcation of Catholic theology, a theme that is picked up in many of the chapters in this volume. The central question of how to conceive of a theology that is pastoral and practical is addressed by Henri-Jérôme Gagey, who traces its genealogy particularly from the French context. He argues that being pastoral and practical has become accepted as an essential feature of all theology; and that to carry it through as practical is a *project* – one in which systematic theology has to work alongside the social sciences, but with the proviso of a proper philosophical understanding of the relationship of the two forms of enquiry in executing the project. Kathleen A. Cahalan makes a similar case, arguing the need for an extension of the scope and professionalism of practical, empirical enquiry within theology; but she takes a somewhat different line from Gagey by espousing practical theology as a special theological sub-discipline, in the manner of what she sees as the emerging sub-discipline of spirituality. The crucial feature of the interrelation of theological principle and empirical reality is addressed in Nicholas M. Healy's chapter on ecclesiology, which is itself a basic building-block of Catholic pastoral theology. Healy is alert to the risk of an ecclesiological perspective that is idealist and uncritical ('blueprint ecclesiologies'); and he argues for an empirical approach to understanding the Church that delivers a practical ecclesiology very much in the line of practical theology. The final chapter, by Martin Poulsom, explores the notion of *praxis* and its use by Edward Schillebeeckx, one of the great Catholic systematic theologians of the twentieth century who took the empirical dimension seriously. In the shift he made in his later work Schillebeeckx sought to overcome any disjunction between a theoretical and a practical theology.

A Catholic Approach?

These essays highlight the prominent notes of Catholic pastoral theology, its main building-blocks as it were, but they also show some unresolved questions about the direction this theological enterprise might take. There is clearly a profound influence that comes from historical systematic theology, and it is this that shapes and determines, in large measure, the make-up of pastoral theology in the Catholic tradition. Revelation and ecclesiology – and, incorporated within those two great systematic theology themes, the doctrine of God, the gospel and context, the signs of the times and the praxis of faith, the relation of church and world – are foundation stones of Catholic pastoral theology. There is wide agreement about this, and Catholic practical theologians find it natural to focus on the social, ecclesial and sacramental dimensions of Christian practice.

At the same time, the question of disciplinary status remains unclear; various proposals have been made about how it should be theorized – as sub-discipline or a theological project. Can practical theology claim to have an identity distinct from other forms of theological enquiry – distinct even from traditional pastoral theology? Or is it simply 'owned' by theology as one of its methods? There may be more to this than intellectual semantics or issues of academic organization. Acknowledgement of its disciplinary independence gives practical theology leverage. This is about agenda-setting within theology, and therefore to some extent it is about power. There is, in addition, the perennial tension between a church orientation and a world orientation; and both paths have their attendant risks – of ecclesial absorption on the one hand, and secularization on the other. But these are risks that pastoral theology must take if it is to be true to itself.

3

Reading the Signs of the Times

MICHAEL KIRWAN SJ

Introduction: The 'Signs of the Times'

This chapter will examine the importance of 'scrutinizing the signs of the times', understood as both an evangelical injunction and an ecclesial duty.[1] In contemporary Catholic theology this is a key mode of approach to current issues and practical-pastoral realities. Insofar as this scrutiny or reading is understood as a 'hermeneutic', then it is the story of a loss of innocence, with the growing pains that such a loss implies. An understanding of pastoral theology as 'hermeneutics' will give some account of this loss and growth. It may even help to ease the pain.

The *evangelical injunction* to 'read the signs' occurs in both the synoptic and Johannine traditions: Jesus urges his listeners to attend to the messianic signs (Jesus' miracles) that herald the advent of the Kingdom. These are as clear as the utterly predictable indicators of seasonal change: fields ripe for harvest, or portents of inclement weather.[2] A generation asking for more than these is 'evil and unfaithful', and will be given only the 'sign of Jonah'. Jonah is evoked by Matthew in order to commend the receptiveness of pagans (such as the Ninevites and the Queen of the South) to God's message, and also to foretell the death, burial and resurrection of Jesus (Matt. 12.38–39). In these texts, no 'scrutiny' of the signs is needed, only a modicum of observational power. Yet too often Jesus' hearers are deaf and blind because of their sinful disposition. Their illiteracy is rooted in a more or less culpable 'hardness of heart', which dulls understanding, rather than any complexity in the signs themselves.

The *ecclesial duty* occurs in *Gaudium et spes*, the Pastoral Constitution on the Church in the World of Today, specifically in Article 4a.[3] According to José Comblin (2005, p. 73) what we have in the Constitution is a conflation of the scriptural usage (the eschatological signs of the presence of God's kingdom) with a more neutral reference to 'signs of the times', simply understood as the changing events and situations of contemporary Western society. The Church acknowledges its responsibility for making a clear-sighted examination of contemporary human reality. This reality is complex and bewildering (in contrast to the biblical signs urged by Jesus); humanity has indeed become 'a question to itself'. Even so, there is every confidence that answers will be forthcoming, that we will 'make a home' for ourselves in understanding.

We shall need to examine the implications of Comblin's suggestion that two senses of 'reading the signs of the times' have become conflated. For now, we can note this alleged tension, and in particular the varying degrees of optimism about whether 'the signs' can be read successfully. Pastoral theology is resourced by scripture and by church tradition, and is here urged by each of these sources to scrutinize what is going on around us. This is to understand pastoral theology as a *hermeneutical activity*, where a readiness and ability to read is essential to its self-understanding.[4] David Klemm offers a succinct definition:

> By 'hermeneutics' I mean the theoretical interest that focuses on the process of understanding meaning in signs and symbols. Interest in hermeneutics begins when we recognize a meaning in human expression and communication that beckons us to understanding and yet withholds the abundance of its sense. Hermeneutical enquiry begins with the advent of meaning: something in the world of a text or actual existence manifests an otherness, a doubleness of meaning.

The summons to understanding is a summons into a presence, an event where our response is repeatedly called forth:

> Hermeneutics has the task of allowing the meanings in texts and existence to speak again. Sacred scriptures, classic literature, and legal codes are texts that carry an intent to speak into a human situation. Because human situations change in unforeseen ways, these texts call for hermeneutics to assist them in speaking again. (Klemm 1986, p. 2)

Hermeneutics requires an attentiveness to the historical and social contextualization of knowledge, as philosophers such as Hans-Georg Gadamer and Paul Ricœur have emphasized. Right understanding is possible only with the overcoming of alienating factors of temporal and cultural distance, as well as 'subjective' blockages. Nevertheless, successful interpretation is possible: for all that we are limited and partisan, human beings are 'at home' in understanding.

This optimism, of course, is open to challenge: for example, in the famous debate of the late 1960s and early 1970s between Gadamer and Jürgen Habermas. For the latter, hermeneutics as a philosophical discipline does not sufficiently recognize the systematic distortions which get in the way of interpretation. Human interest, whether personal or communal, colours all our attempts at knowledge. We think we have made a home for ourselves in understanding, when all too often we have simply erected a makeshift shelter for our neuroses or our alienated consciousness. We delude ourselves and others: the only corrective to this systematic distortion is a systematically organized suspicion, for which the Critical Theory (of which Habermas is a representative) has turned to variations upon the thought of Karl Marx and Sigmund Freud. Paul Ricœur has shown how these objections can serve religious faith, if we are prepared to allow for an honest purification of belief.[5]

Two specific points may be made about the difficulty and promise of hermeneutics for pastoral theology. First, the recognition of ambiguity and resistance: Klemm's definition renders understanding as a kind of 'double-bind', a summons to meaning which withholds the entirety of its sense. Attainment of meaning is only possible after a struggle with what is forbidding or recalcitrant. It is precisely in pastoral realities of extreme suffering, bereavement and so on, that the theologian confronts the possibility that there is no meaning to be won, that senselessness may, after all, be the order of the day. Second, an expansive definition includes interpretation as enactment, as with the actor or musician who 'interprets' a score or a script. In this sense, to 'interpret' the gospel is precisely to enact its demands, to live out the kind of life it demands of us.[6]

Gaudium et spes: The Council Reads the World

To look more closely at the injunction from *Gaudium et spes*. The Constitution addresses all people of goodwill with a declaration of the Church's intention 'to continue the work of Christ with the guidance of the Paraclete', giving witness to the truth in a spirit of service rather than judgement. To this end, an 'Introduction: The Condition of Humanity in Today's World' sets out a programme of dialogue:

To discharge this function, the church has the duty in every age of examining the signs of the times and interpreting them in the light of the gospel, so that it can offer in a manner appropriate to each generation replies to the continual human questionings on the meaning of this life and the life to come and how they are related. There is a need, then, to be aware of, and to understand, the world in which we live, together with its expectations, its desires and its frequently dramatic character. (Article 4)

The subsequent description of the modern world (*GSp*, pp. 4–10) highlights an epoch of profound and rapid change. There is progress, but also uncertainty and paralysis; ambiguities of wealth and poverty, freedom and slavery; a dynamic concept of reality arising from technological and scientific advances, impacted socially by industrialization, urbanization and migration, and religiously, as questions of belief and unbelief become widespread, amid increasing calls for political and economic justice and emancipation. The recognition of these ambiguities of the human condition means that 'humanity is putting questions to itself'. It is here that the root of the problems may be uncovered, for '[t]he imbalances affecting the world today are in fact connected with a deeper imbalance rooted in the human heart where various elements are in opposition' (Article 10). The question 'what is man and woman', and the sense of sorrow, evil and death that holds us back from true fulfilment, find their answer in Christ:

It is the church's belief that Christ, who died and was raised for everyone, offers to the human race through his Spirit the light and strength to respond to its highest calling; and that no other name under heaven is given to people for them to be saved. It likewise believes that the key and the focus and culmination of all human history are to be found in its Lord and master. The church also affirms that underlying so many changes there are some things which do not change and are founded upon Christ, who is the same yesterday and today and forever. It is accordingly in the light of Christ, who is the image of the invisible God and first-born of all creation, that the council proposes to elucidate the mystery of humankind and, in addressing all people, to contribute to discovering a solution to the outstanding questions of our day.

According to Charles Moeller (in Vorgrimler 1969, pp. 77ff.), the *signa temporum* here refer to precisely these defining characteristics of an age – this is the sense in which Pope John XXIII used the term. Reading these signs is a function accorded to the Church, in keeping with the gift of 'discernment' listed by Paul in 1 Corinthians 2.15. Specifically, the 'dramatic characteristics' (*dramatica indoles*) being diagnosed here are a tension between two poles – the 'Hope and Anguish' of this section's title:

> The essence of the dramatic tension in question consists in a transformation, the crossing of a threshold, which more or less implicitly forces itself on the attention. Man's activity and work has given rise to changes which recoil upon man himself, rather like a boomerang. Sartre has described this phenomenon very well in what he calls 'le practico-inerte'. *Gaudium et Spes* points out that these consequences of human action affect man's judgement, his individual and collective desires and his ways of thinking and acting in relation to things and people. The text adds they have consequences too for religious life. (Moeller in Vorgrimler, p. 99)

Of the analysis which follows, Moeller concedes: '[A]ll this, it must be admitted, is not very well put together', compared to one version which was rejected. Joseph Ratzinger, commentating on the following articles (*GSp*, pp. 11–12),[7] sets out the theological contours for the dialogue between Church and world, which has as its prelude a reading of the 'signs of the times'. He notes that the editors of the text rejected as inadequate the Roman proverbial affirmation of 'the voice of the age as the voice of God' (*vox temporis vox Dei*); such an identification runs counter to the message of Matthew 16, where Christ, 'the real sign of the time', is misunderstood and rejected. Instead, the phrase exhorts the Church to 'detect indications of God's presence' in the events, needs and aims of the age. In wrestling with this problem, Ratzinger regrets the fact that 'we still have no rules of kerygmatic hermeneutics' that allow us to appreciate the proclamatory significance of the gospel for the present day. Nevertheless, the Church's tradition of 'discernment of spirits' is cited, making it clear that this is never simply a secular analysis. This is not simply an appreciation of *chronos*, of secular time, but of 'the moment, the *kairos*, in which it must interpret and accomplish the work of the Lord as present'.

Ratzinger goes on to comment on the implications of the model of 'dialogue', implying an inner unity between participants that enables conversation to take place. For Komonchak (2005), following the French theologian Marie-Dominique Chenu, the dialogical structure of *Gaudium et spes* is to be understood as the respectful search for *pierres d'attente* within contemporary culture. These are the 'toothing stones' that allowed a building to be meshed with a future extension. However, such a model is at odds with the 'Augustinian' alternative that Komonchak attributes to Joseph Ratzinger, according to which the Constitution offers only an anodyne sociological analysis, with references to Christ and his work tacked on almost as an afterthought. The idea of an agreed common picture of rational humanity with which the gospel can mesh is a chimera. There are no *pierres d'attente*: the only positives are to be found in evangelical proclamation, and any 'scrutiny of the world' will serve only to reveal the world's poverty and its need of Christ.

Gaudium et spes: Reactions and Misgivings

The current debate with regard to *Gaudium et Spes* concerns its alleged failure to accomplish the tasks that the Council set for itself: 'to elucidate the mystery of humankind and, in addressing all people, to contribute to discovering a solution to the outstanding questions of our day'. We appear to have two options: the first is that this enterprise (of scrutinizing the signs of the times, and of interpreting them in the light of the gospel, so as to respond to the perennial questions of humanity) is fundamentally misguided. This would, however, be a straight denial of the conciliar declaration, that this task has always been a duty of the Church. The second option is to decide that the Council simply made a poor job of its duty in this particular instance, offering a reading of the signs that for contingent reasons was distorted or inadequate.

The two options are not exclusive, of course. An unsympathetic account will accuse the Council Fathers of an overreaching arrogance whose failure to establish the 'relevance' of the gospel in today's world was predictable and deserved. James Hitchcock questions the objectivity and feasibility of the Pastoral Constitution.[8] Not only has the promise of the Council not been fulfilled: its immediate effect was to plunge the Church into a severe internal crisis, provoked by the worldwide transformation of the cultural map that rendered many of the conciliar decrees obsolete. 'The Council fathers apparently had no inkling of that coming crisis; the task of "reading the signs of the times" was apparently far more difficult than was imagined in the euphoric days of the early 1960s.' While Hitchcock cites the antinomianism of the 1960s as the banana skin under the feet of the Council Fathers, Charles Davis indicts the deeper cultural and intellectual shifts that we have learned to call 'postmodernity'. Unlike previous Councils, says Davis, Vatican II was outdated before the ink was dry on the documents; these are 'already now chiefly of interest to the historian'. The Council's central theological co-ordinates – orthodoxy transposed into an anthropocentric key – were soon to be brought into radical question (Davis 1980, p. 1).

We have already noted that José Comblin finds problematic the conflation in *Gaudium et spes* of two senses of 'signs of the times': first, the eschatological awareness of the Gospel texts, such as Matthew 16.4, and a more pedestrian sense in which the Church exhorts itself, quite simply, to 'move with the times'. We also have here a conflation of the signs as *warnings*, and signs as *pointers*. To undertake the task of *aggiornamento* is to accept, in short, that the era of Christendom had come to an end, and the Church needed to open itself to the modern world that it had previously condemned. Comblin provocatively asks about the instinct of institutional self-preservation unconsciously at work here, which is why he is concerned to see a straightforward appeal to institutional 'modernization' being buttressed theologically by the evangelical warnings. 'Would acceptance of and adaptation to the modern world fall within Christian eschatology? In what sense?' (Comblin 2005, p. 73). The temptation for the Council Fathers was to see modernity as such (seen through a Social Democrat or Christian Democrat lens) as the 'eschatological sign'; 'In the end, the teaching on the signs of the times boiled down to acceptance of the modern world' (Comblin 2005, p. 81), thus allowing the Church to become the tool of Western bourgeois society.

From 'left' and 'right', therefore, there are verdicts of dissatisfaction. A Council that saw itself as prophetically reading the present age was caught out by unforeseen cultural shifts, to such an extent that the very enterprise of scrutinizing the signs is seen to be totally discredited: thus Hitchcock and Davis. At stake here is the very legitimacy of 'reading the world' at all, as an activity that an ecumenical Council should be especially concerned about. For Comblin the problem is a twofold hermeneutical naivety: with regard to the 'objectivity' of the signs (the world they were listening to was that of the European bourgeoisie), and with regard to their own unexamined presuppositions, which identified 'the light of faith' with 'their opinion, or their project, the way in which they interpreted Christianity' (2005, p. 81).

Comblin's alternative reading of the 'signs of the times' is the liberationist category of the 'irruption of the poor' into history, specifically the new perception of the poor as subjects and not merely the recipients of developmentalist goodwill. This 'sign', the call to liberation for the oppressed, is occluded: not because it is mysterious, but because human sinfulness does not want to acknowledge a reality that is all too visible to the victims themselves. Only by not reading *this* sign could the Council have opted for such a strikingly optimistic view of the world.[9]

Forty years on, the fault-line remains, and runs through the various retrospectives on the Council. The reticence towards 'scrutiny of the signs of the times' will need to be further articulated within the current debate about the correct 'reading' of Vatican II itself. A debate, for sure, generating more heat than light, as commentators rally around Pope Benedict's assertion of a 'hermeneutic of reform', which needs to be reclaimed over against a false and destabilizing post-conciliar emphasis on a 'hermeneutic of discontinuity and rupture'. What such a debate makes clear, however, is a further twist in the hermeneutical spiral: the Council, which set itself to read and interpret the world, has itself become the object of hotly contested interpretation.

Vatican II: In Search of a Hermeneutic

This contestation – the conflict of meanings of Vatican II itself – is accounted for by a fundamental methodological shift in post-conciliar Catholic theology. John McDade has characterized this shift as a relocation of theology, rather than the generation of new theological themes. Attention to 'the world' as the true *locus* for faith seeking understanding is manifest in the anthropological theologies of Karl Rahner and Edward Schillebeeckx, and among political and liberation theologians. In fact, among prominent Catholic thinkers, Hans Urs von Balthasar is pretty much the exception in his insistence on turning 'inwards', as it were, to the Church's tradition and history as the theatre for theology.

These divergent trajectories are emblematically set up in the theological journals associated with them, *Concilium* and *Communio*. McDade calls the 'worldly' turn of the *Concilium* theologians the *lectio dificilior*, by which we are meant to recognize the dangerous complexities of this way of proceeding. Quite simply, if a systematic analysis of the world is required before theology can begin to do its work, then the possibilities of the theologian going astray are multiplied. Even worse: one's reading of the world will be almost immediately out of date, as analysis becomes superseded by new data and new theories.[10] As we have already observed, this was the ignominious fate of *Gaudium et spes*, according to its critics.

McDade suggests that somewhere in the early 1970s the Council itself ceased to be directly appealed to; what mattered now were the developments arising from the Council, but with their own direction and momentum. Here of course are the seeds of present controversies, about which of these developments are to be cherished as representing the 'spirit' of the Council, or repudiated, because they were not explicitly sanctioned by the Council Fathers.[11] Or – to emphasize the point being made here – the Church gradually became less concerned with reading the world and more with reading itself.

Given the polemics of much of the recent discussion, an outright choice between 'hermeneutics of reform' versus 'hermeneutics of rupture' looks to be an arid one. An interesting refinement on this debate is offered by the German political theologian Johann Baptist Metz, in two articles about his mentor Karl Rahner (Metz 1998). Metz argues that Rahner saw beyond the post-conciliar euphoria to some of our present hermeneutical difficulties. These have indeed arisen out of an imbalanced perspective on the two Vatican Councils. Rahner expressed an anxiety about an immunizing tendency, insofar as 'the Second Vatican Council no longer talked about God, as Vatican I had, but rather confined itself to the God announced in and by the Church'. This 'ecclesiological enciphering' of our talk about God runs directly counter to Karl Rahner's own conviction that (in Metz's words) 'God is a universal theme, a theme concerning all humanity, or it is simply no theme at all'. Rahner has of course alerted us to the proximity of God in every human experience, even those that are avowedly atheistic. Any encryption of our talk about God in exclusively ecclesial or theological terms can only be regretted as sectarian.

The argument goes that a neglect of Vatican I's declaration, that 'God can be known with certainty from created things with the natural light of human reason', has resulted in a reinforcement of precisely this sectarian tendency, so as to privilege the Church's *logos* about God over the 'theological dignity of humankind'.

The matter of which Christianity speaks from its core, even today in the continuing process of enlightenment and in the widely heralded profusion of postmodernism – that is, the God of which it speaks – is a fundamental matter on which everyone can join in the conversation and on which therefore everyone must be heard. So this dogma is not only or primarily trying to impose an obligation on unbelievers, but rather on the church, on theology and on believers themselves. The church and theology must stand ready, in whatever concerns its God, to converse with everyone, to listen to everyone, to argue with every-one who cannot in advance be denied having reason and goodwill. (Metz 1998, p. 111)

Metz (following Rahner) sees in the doctrinal statement of Vatican I a kind of 'declaration of human rights': 'the right of rational persons of goodwill to be heard (and not just to be instructed) when it comes to the God question'. This aptitude of all human beings for God is to be assumed of all who are not irrational or of evil will: anyone not so excluded 'must be heard, must absolutely be heard and taken extremely seriously'.

If this unsettling thesis is correct, that Vatican II did not manage to sustain and reinforce this universal emphasis on the theological author-ity and dignity of humankind, then the search for a 'correct hermeneutic' of the Council is not the primary challenge that faces us – at least not straightforwardly. The struggle for the correct interpretation of either the 'texts' or the 'spirit' of Vatican II can only entangle us further in a disquieting ecclesial encipherment. Paradoxically, if the liberating vista of the Pastoral Constitution is to be recovered, then a 'hermeneutic of continuity' is required, which reconnects us with the universalism of the earlier 'magnificent Council'. For Metz, only such a hermeneutic will enable us to face squarely the God-crisis that we have been avoid-ing with our church talk. It will require us also to break with what Metz calls the 'patronizing caretaker mentality' of the Church, a 'sec-ond immaturity' among its members, which reflects all too accurately the voyeuristic spectator mentality of postmodern culture.

'Apocalyptic' Clarity versus Pastoral Complexity

There is a further theme to be treated, if only *en passant*, which requires us to return to the 'eschatological' dimension of 'scrutinizing the signs of the times'. There is no space here to explore the distinction between eschatology and apocalyptic, but it is not possible to ignore the return of 'apocalyptic' thinking in our post-9/11 political landscape. Intended as a response to the religious extremism of militant Islam, the global War on Terror has fanned into vigorous flame the millenarian tenden-cies within American religiosity. The phenomenal success of the *Left Behind* franchise (over 60 million copies of the 15 novels have been sold) indicates a widespread and feverish willingness to 'scrutinize the signs'.[12]

In such an atmosphere, it is quite conceivable that the responsible Christian reaction is one of refusal, as in Mark 13.21: 'If anyone says to you then, "Look, here is the Christ" or "Look, he is there", do not believe it.' There are, after all, false signs, and false prophets ('refuse to join them'). Precisely this refusal to interpret signs supernaturally is evident in the respectful discussion between Umberto Eco and Cardinal Martini in 1998. The humanist Eco is given the choice of theme.[13] He chooses 'apocalypse', a topic that, he believes, will be of interest to both Christian believer and atheist humanist. Eco expresses anxiety about the 'desperate millenarianism' of contemporary culture, a frenzied living out of our 'terrors of the end', which he can only describe as 'apocalyptic'. In fact, it is Martini who expresses caution about the use of this term, and seeks to defuse it. As the literary critic Frank Kermode warns us, we are 'programmed to prefer fulfilment to disappointment, the closed to the open'. The assumption of meaning, of successful interpretation, is our default position, and we 'prefer enigmas to muddles'.[14]

We have referred above to the dramatic prominence of liberation theology as an attempt to overcome hermeneutical naivety, and such an attempt has encountered opposition, as is well known. The 1984 Congregation for the Doctrine of the Faith (CDF) *Instruction* on 'certain aspects' of liberation theology brought a response from the Uruguayan liberationist Juan Luis Segundo, which is worth citing here. Segundo's 'Warning to the Whole Church' provocatively brings together two conversations: the procedures of liberation theology and the hermeneutical options of Vatican II:

> Let no-one be deceived into thinking that only Latin American theology is involved here. If the analysis I have made is correct, the two parts [of the 1984 Instruction] despite their differences, are united by one point that affects the entire Church: *the negative evaluation of Vatican II and of the post-conciliar period*. . . . [T]he same Spirit who helped the Council speak the truth also helped it to speak clearly. Fidelity to that Spirit does not allow the opposite to be spoken on the pretext of explaining the Council better or of preventing it from being misunderstood. (Segundo 1985, pp. 155–6; emphasis in original)

Whatever the justification of Segundo's assertion, we have seen enough to recognize that this appeal to clarity is something of a two-edged sword. For a start, it can be the rallying cry of traditionalists, citing post-conciliar 'confusion' as evidence of Vatican II's inauthenticity. There is no register here of the concerns expressed by Metz, citing

Rahner, concerning Vatican II's 'ecclesial encipherment'. Most dramatically, Segundo's appeal runs counter to the withering critique of his fellow liberationist Comblin, who understands the clarity of the Council Fathers not as the voice of the Spirit, but as the unanimity of a false consciousness: their acquiescence in a Western bourgeois consensus. Even if we decide that Comblin overstates his case, the challenge is implicit: with the loss of our hermeneutical innocence, are we no longer entitled to 'clarity'?

If a hermeneutical pastoral theology has any specificity at all then it must surely include a readiness to stay with 'muddles' rather than enigmas. We are used to the idea that pastoral theology responds to the messiness of human situations, and *in extremis* to situations that seem devoid of meaning altogether: bereavement, breakdown, every kind of estrangement and cruelty. Here the pastoral theologian will simply be the one who accompanies those who wrestle, like Jacob with the angel, in hope of blessing.

What I have sought to make explicit in this essay is the theoretical underpinning for such apparently hopeless straining after a meaning that beckons and withholds. To hand oneself over to the risk of hermeneutics is to acknowledge uncertainty, plurality and even conflict of interpretations, and the real possibility of distortion and miscommunication. The unavoidable self-implication of the interpreter is one part of the burden of modernity that the Fathers of the Second Vatican Council took upon themselves. 'They were their situation', and the Council that sought to scrutinize the world is itself the object of scrutiny, requiring a 'hermeneutic'.

But if there is embarrassment at Vatican II's alleged 'strained optimism', that the 'signs of the times' could be read off like a thermometer, then perhaps hermeneutics comes to our aid once again, by insisting on generous retrieval as well as suspicion and critique. Paul Ricœur speaks of the need for a 'second naivety', a fresh engagement with religious texts and symbols after critique has done its work: 'beyond the desert of criticism, we yearn to be called again' (Ricœur 1967, p. 351). Or, to throw one last metaphor into the mix: Louis Marie Chauvet uses a striking image when discussing the sacramental dimension of the 'pastoral interview' (Chauvet 2001). A pastoral conversation, between the minister or pastoral agent and persons requesting sacramental initiation, can be itself a grace-filled event (a fusion of horizons?) – provided there is, on both sides, a renunciation of the 'bad faith' of power play and deception that too often mars such encounters. This means a recognition that 'both are at sea in the same boat' – even if it is still the job of the pastor to see the boat safely to shore. We must learn, in other words, to be satisfied with the firm grip of our hand on the tiller, and not grieve overmuch for the loss of solid ground under our feet.

Notes

1 We seem to have several options for translating the phrase that appears in *Gaudium et spes* as *signa temporum perscrutandi*; the usual term 'reading the signs of the times' seems a weak rendition of *perscrutandi*, as does the Tanner use of 'examining'. Vorgrimler's account of the text's redactions has *diagnoscendi*. My default translation in this chapter is 'scrutinizing'.

2 Matthew 16.1–4; see also Mark 8.11–13; and Luke 11.29–32 and 12.54–56.

3 Citations of *Gaudium et spes* (*GSp*) are taken from the Tanner edition (1990).

4 For an account of pastoral theology as hermeneutics, see Farley 1999.

5 Paul Ricœur, 1987, 'Hermeneutics and the Critique of Ideology', in *Hermeneutics and the Human Sciences*, Cambridge: Cambridge University Press, 1981 [1987], pp. 63–100.

6 Such a description can be usefully set alongside the definition of practical theology offered by the Jesuit theologian Karl Rahner, as 'that theological discipline which is concerned with the Church's self-actualisation here and now – both that which *is* and that which *ought to be*'. Rahner 1972, p. 102.

7 Vorgrimler 1969, pp. 115–23.

8 In a feature article in *The Catholic World Report* entitled 'The End of *Gaudium et Spes*?' Professor Hitchcock's analysis is quoted approvingly on a traditionalist Catholic website, as a radical questioning of *Gaudium et spes* and of Vatican II itself (Hitchcock 2003).

9 Perhaps more than any other contemporary style of theology, the theology of liberation has attempted to overcome hermeneutical naivety. Indebted especially to radical educational theorists such as Paulo Freire, liberationists stress the location of the reader as the starting-point in the struggle for an effective theological literacy. For an extensive exploration of the questions of method, see Clodovis Boff 1987; for the adoption of a liberationist template in the task of pastoral theology, see Stephen Pattison 1994.

10 McDade's choice of phrase is interesting for another reason. In biblical exegesis the *lectio dificilior* means that where there is a clash of meanings, there may be good grounds for preferring the unexpected or problematic reading over the obvious one!

11 In his Christmas Address to the Roman Curia in 2005, Pope Benedict decries the divisiveness of the 'hermeneutic of discontinuity and rupture' in its appeal to the 'spirit' of the Council, to impulses that are not contained in the texts themselves – leaving a wide margin for interpretation that was to prove disastrous.

12 For a resurgence of the theme of apocalypse in political theology, see Robert Hamerton-Kelly 2007.

13 See Eco and Martini 2000.

14 In an essay entitled 'The Man in the Macintosh, the Boy in the White Shirt' (Kermode 1979, pp. 49–73). The 'Man' in the title is a mysterious character in a macintosh, who pops up randomly in the pages of Joyce's *Ulysses*; the 'boy' is the young man who runs away naked in Mark 14.51–2. In each case there have been many ingenious attempts to identify and explain the character. Only as a last resort, as it were, do we contemplate the possibility that these may be entirely fortuitous presences!

Bibliography

Benedict XVI, 2008 [2005], 'A Proper Hermeneutic for the Second Vatican Council', in Matthew L. Lamb and Matthew Levering (eds), *Vatican II: Renewal within Tradition*, Oxford: Oxford University Press, pp. ix–xv.

Clodovis Boff, 1987 (1978), *Theology and Praxis*, Maryknoll, NY: Orbis.

Louis Marie Chauvet, 2001, *The Sacraments: The Word of God at the Mercy of the Body*, Collegeville, MN: Liturgical Press.

José M. Comblin, 2005, 'The Signs of the Times', *Concilium* no. 4, pp. 73–85.

Charles Davis, 1980, *Theology and Political Society*, Cambridge: Cambridge University Press.

Umberto Eco and Carlo Martini, 2000 [1996], *Belief or Nonbelief? A Confrontation*, London: Continuum.

Edward Farley, 1999, 'Interpreting Situations: An Inquiry into the Nature of Practical Theology', in James Woodward and Stephen Pattison (eds), *Blackwell Reader in Pastoral and Practical Theology*, Oxford: Blackwell, pp. 118–27.

Robert Hamerton-Kelly (ed.), 2007, *Politics and Apocalypse*, East Lansing, MI: Michigan State University Press.

Adrian Hastings (ed.), 1991, *Modern Catholicism: Vatican II and After*, Oxford: Oxford University Press.

James Hitchcock, 2003, 'The End of *Gaudium et Spes*?', in *The Catholic World Report*, May 2003: http://www.wf-f.org/JFH-GaudiumEtSpes.html.

Frank Kermode, 1979, *The Genesis of Secrecy: On the Interpretation of Narrative*, Cambridge, MA: Harvard University Press.

Fergus Kerr, 2007, *20th Century Catholic Theologians*, Oxford: Blackwell.

David E. Klemm, 1986, *Hermeneutical Inquiry*, vol. I: *The Interpretation of Texts*, Oxford: Oxford University Press.

Joseph Komonchak, 2005, 'The Church in Crisis: Pope Benedict's Theological Vision', *Commonweal* vol. 132, no. 11 (3 June).

Matthew L. Lamb and Matthew Levering (eds), 2008, *Vatican II: Renewal within Tradition*, Oxford: Oxford University Press.

John McDade, 1991, 'Catholic Theology in the Post-Conciliar Period', in Adrian Hastings (ed.), 1991, *Modern Catholicism: Vatican II and After*, Oxford: Oxford University Press, pp. 422–43.

Albert Melloni and Christoph Theobald (eds), 2005, 'Vatican II: A Forgotten Future', *Concilium* 4.

Johann Baptist Metz, 1998, 'Karl Rahner's Struggle for the Theological Dignity of Humankind', *A Passion for God: The Mystical Political Dimension of Christianity*, New York: Paulist Press, pp. 107–20.

John Milbank, 1990, *Theology and Social Theory*, Oxford: Blackwell.

Stephen Pattison, 1994, *Pastoral Care and Liberation Theology*, Cambridge: Cambridge University Press.

Karl Rahner, 1972, *Theological Investigations* vol. IX, London: Darton, Longman & Todd, p. 102.

Paul Ricœur, 1967, *The Symbolism of Evil*, New York: Harper & Row.

Juan Luis Segundo, 1985, *Theology and the Church: A Response to Cardinal Ratzinger and a Warning to the Whole Church*, London: Geoffrey Chapman.

Norman Tanner (ed.), 1990, *Decrees of the Ecumenical Councils*, vol. II: *Trent to Vatican II*, London: Sheed & Ward.

Christoph Theobald, 2005, 'The Theological Options of Vatican II: Seeking an "Internal" Principal of Interpretation', *Concilium* 4, pp. 87–107.

Herbert Vorgrimler (ed.), 1969, *Commentary on the Documents of Vatican II*, vol. V: *Pastoral Constitution on the Church in the Modern World*, London and New York: Burns & Oates.

James Woodward and Stephen Pattison (eds), 1999, *Blackwell Reader in Pastoral and Practical Theology*, Oxford: Blackwell.

4

Pastoral Theology as Contextual: Forms of Catholic Pastoral Theology Today

ROBERT SCHREITER CPPS

Introduction

One of the important areas to explore in the investigation of distinctively Catholic features of a pastoral or practical theology is that of context. Just what constitutes the context, how that context interacts with both the gospel message and the tradition of the Church, and what one seeks as outcomes of that interaction, are all points that must come into consideration. Added to this is a second set of considerations relevant to this volume, namely, discerning the specifically Catholic contributions to the shaping of a pastoral theology.

Yet, however complex this matter may seem to be, it is a necessary one to investigate. That is so because pastoral theology is the site where the Church lives out its beliefs; it is the point where discipleship and following in the way of Christ is at its most evident and at its most urgent. If pastoral theology is to be more than simply paring down such intricate doctrines as the Trinity or the meaning of Christ's redemption to recipe-like programmes for application, then we must honour the site where that happens – in the world in which Christians find themselves. To honour that site means not only to enter into the arena of the world itself, but also to plumb the meaning of context, both as a theological *locus*, and as the site of interaction of the gospel and the Church in a reflective and responsible way.

This is not only a problem for Catholics; the same holds for Protestants as well (the situation of Orthodox and Oriental faith will not be taken up here). Protestants share these same concerns and, as do Catholics, will vary the emphasis on context or Church in a considerable fashion. Let me just take two points from Protestant discussions to help illustrate the ground that a discussion from the Catholic side will in some ways mirror. Perhaps one of the first ways to understand the place of context in practical theology (and in other types, for that matter) for Protestant theology was to construe theology as the outcome of the interaction between 'text' (that is, the Bible) and 'context'. Context would be read here as a text, much as is the Bible. The governing assertion here was Karl Barth's remark that, in order to do theology, one must have the Bible in one hand and the newspaper in the other. This is of course reminiscent of Augustine's comment about reading the book of nature and the Book of the Word of God. In this reading of the two 'texts' one would look for correspondences between the two. This kind of approach to the matter of context has prevailed on the more liberal end of the Protestant spectrum.

On the more conservative end, there has been a preference for translation models, that is, where one-to-one equivalents to the Bible are sought in the local context.[1] Here the Bible clearly has the upper hand. The context must be made to conform to the text, rather than entering into the discussion with more or less equal footing.

I note these two different approaches within Protestant reflection on context to indicate that there is no single 'Protestant' line on reflecting on context in a practical theology. And so we should not expect to find a single, unified Catholic voice on this topic either. Twentieth-century Catholic theology was first emancipated from its Neo-Scholastic straitjacket by the historical research of the *ressourcement* movement of French and German scholars. By their first resorting to historical context, it became possible for those of us in later generations to consider contemporary contexts as well. Especially the Pastoral Constitution *Gaudium et spes* set the scene for what we are able to talk about in Catholic pastoral theology today.

So just what are the distinctive elements that contribute to a Catholic pastoral theology today? This will involve engaging the qualifier 'Catholic'. Following Timothy Radcliffe and others, I would agree that at this time in the early twenty-first century, we are seeing two distinctive approaches within the Roman Catholic Church about what makes the Church 'Catholic', and that both see themselves as representing the best of that Catholic tradition. These voices are often these days placed at odds with each other. Radcliffe portrays them as '*Gaudium et spes* Catholics' versus '*communio* Catholics', respectively.[2] Others have suggested *Concilium* versus *Communio* Catholics, after the two journals by those names. Like any description of something as large and extensive as is the Roman Catholic Church, labels capture only the high peaks of a variegated terrain.

Even the now time-worn 'progressive' or 'liberal' versus 'conservative' or 'traditional' labels are wearing thin, especially among young Catholics, for whom the Second Vatican Council is an event that happened before they were born. So we find ourselves at a time when our nomenclature only partly illuminates the phenomena we are studying, but also divides them in an unhelpful manner.

In order to look at the contextual nature of a Catholic pastoral theology, I will begin by looking at its 'Catholic' nature, and then at its 'contextual' qualities. That will involve looking at the current Catholic theological landscape through two conceptions of the theological idea of catholicity. The conceptions I will use are very familiar historical ones: they have defined that mark of the Church for us since the early second century, when the term was introduced. They lie beneath the current discussion of catholicity within the Roman Catholic Church. My point is not to put them into opposition with each other. They have survived side-by-side throughout history (albeit with shifting emphases in priority) for a reason: they represent different faces of the kind of catholicity the Church hopes to embody and attain. Rather, I will portray them in conversation, especially how the strengths of the one help illuminate the limits of the other. Together they argue strongly for a multivalent understanding of the catholicity of our Church.

Having laid that groundwork, I will then turn to what context means in each of these approaches. Context can play a number of different roles at once in its interplay with theological tradition. I will explore five dimensions of context as they impinge upon a Catholic pastoral theology, namely: (1) the meanings of context and culture, (2) their approach to pluralism and modernity, (3) the formation of Catholic identity, (4) what the transformation of context entails, and (5) what the practice of a Catholic pastoral theology looks like. In the conclusion, I will point to where these reflections on the role of context in a Catholic pastoral theology urge us to go as next steps for dialogue within the Roman Catholic Church itself on this matter, as well as with the practical theologies found among Protestant theologians today. Needless to say, in a presentation of this length, these areas can only be sketched out. But my hope is that this sketch will be suggestive of some constructive ways to go forward.

Two Forms of Catholicity

In looking for developing the resources of a genuinely Catholic pastoral theology, one must necessarily begin by examining what it means to be 'Catholic'. There are of course a number of ways into that discussion. I choose here the two understandings of catholicity that have shaped the Church's self-understanding of this concept as early as Ignatius of Antioch, who introduced the term. Since labelling is so unsatisfying, I will call them simply the 'first' and 'second' understandings, respectively. This use of cardinal number terms does not indicate priority of place (although perhaps it does in terms of historical appearance).

The first approach, derived from Ignatius of Antioch, sees the Church as *kath'holou*, that is, to be found throughout the whole world. This is catholicity that is defined principally by its extension throughout the world.[3] That extension embraces both its role and its mission. The Church, as bearer of the Good News of Jesus Christ, is not something unto itself, but is the agent of the *missio Dei*, the mission of the Trinitarian God, in the world. Thus its mission is to extend itself throughout the entire world, bringing the gospel of healing, redemption and reconciliation to every creature (Matt. 28.19–20). In order to do so, the Church focuses not so much on itself but, in the kenotic fashion of its Lord, upon the world it was sent to redeem. It engages that world by listening to it carefully, sharing its joys and hopes, its suffering and fears, as was so eloquently stated at the very beginning of the Pastoral Constitution *Gaudium et spes*. The Church exists for this mission of bringing all things and all people together in Christ. That listening or watching of the world is captured especially in the watchword of 'reading the signs of the times'. The world is seen as graced, although at the same time broken and sinful. Yet grace continues to build upon that nature. One can see why Radcliffe and others have referred to this first approach as a *Gaudium et spes* approach, since it seems to draw its strength so much from that important document.

The second approach has as its point of departure the other principal understanding of catholicity; namely, catholicity as the fullness of faith.[4] The Church is the depository and guarantor of the full and living faith that has been passed down by Christ to the apostles and through them to the Church in the course of history, down to the present time. It is that *regula fidei* to which the Church conforms itself and from which it draws its identity and purpose. There is therefore much more a focus on the Church in the Church-and-world economy than in the first approach, which has the world as its central concern. Some of the proponents of this position today describe themselves as Neo-Augustinians, growing out of Augustine's reading of the Christian tradition through a Neoplatonic lens. The theology that emerges from this forged a powerful identity that shaped much of Western Christian theology. The 'neo' in this Augustinian theology finds its origins especially in the works of Bonaventure, who hesitated at Aquinas's embracing the newly discovered works of Aristotle to achieve a new synthesis of faith for the changing world of the thirteenth century. Bonaventure's darker vision of history saw the world not as expanding as a graced reality, but as a world in crisis. Here the touchstone is Augustine's *De civitate Dei*, the *City of God*. The context in which the latter part of this great work was written lay in the shadow of the sack of Rome by the Vandals in 410. In the ruins of the earthly city, it was the Church that maintained God's Word, and the world can only be saved by entering the Church.

To be sure, not everyone who finds themselves in this second approach has a deeply dark vision of the world. But this second approach is much more critical of the world. It is one that sees the world in crisis, and the Church as holding the answer to that crisis.[5] From an ecclesiological point of view, it draws theological strength from some of the images of the Church found in the Dogmatic Constitution *Lumen gentium* – especially the Church as Light to the Nations, and *sacramentum mundi*. The Church both is able to discern the divine plan for the world, and embodies its most complete presence within that world. The Church is truly engaged with the world around it, but does not take its direction from that world. Rather, it offers the world the possibility of entering that divine economy, the City of God.

These are but rough and incomplete sketches of two approaches to catholicity, taking as their starting-points the two understandings of catholicity that have been part of the Church's heritage since antiquity. As we turn now to understandings of the contextual in Catholic pastoral theology, there will be an opportunity to expand on both of these as I try to read the role of context in the pastoral theologies likely to emanate from these two views of Church and world.

Pastoral Theology as Contextual: Reading through the Two Lenses

What are the particular understandings of context and the contextual that arise out of the two approaches to catholicity that live inside the Church today? In order to understand this, I have suggested approaching the question from five different angles: context, pluralism, identity, transformation, and practices. This seems necessary to me since all involved in this discussion will admit that all pastoral theology (or any other kind of theology, for that matter) occurs in a context. Where paths differ is how to construe the role of the context – how salient it is for theology, how it is to be approached and understood, what place it has in the outcomes of pastoral theology. All of these angles begin with the concept of context itself, and all five contribute to understanding the salience and role of context in pastoral theology.

Context and Culture in Pastoral Theology

This first angle of entry takes up how context is valued in and of itself for pastoral theology. Key to that understanding also will be how context is construed as a (somewhat) configured whole – namely, culture. Let us look at context and culture through the lenses of the two kinds of catholicity.

In the first approach, context is a site of exploration and discovery. It is not presumed that we know what is within the context ahead of time. We must listen and look carefully and respectfully to the context. In other words, the context has its own integrity and its own agency, apart from our pastoral gaze. The context reveals to us a world that is at once whole and autonomous, yet also broken and needful of care and redemption. It is our task to enter into that world in a sympathetic and compassionate way, accompany that world in its struggle for its own liberation and emancipation in order to overcome oppressive and unjust realities.

From the perspective of culture, modern and postmodern concepts of culture give the best picture here.[6] Culture is something constantly under construction as groups interact and borrow from others, and struggle to deepen their humanity. Those cultures may have greater or less coherence (hence, modern or postmodern), depending upon the larger social conditions around them. As people migrate from their home territories and settle in great conurbations, postmodern understandings are likely to take on more salience.

Theologically, this first approach of catholicity by extension in the world proceeds from the Trinitarian *missio Dei* to that world. We do not so much bring Christ to the world but discover the *semina Verbi*, the seeds of the Word already there. This is a world from which a certain knowledge of God can be had apart from divine revelation; natural theology, therefore, plays an important role in this understanding of context from this first approach. Culturally, it sees human beings as co-creators of the world as one of the implications flowing from our being made in the image and likeness of God (Gen. 1.27–8). Recognizing at the same time the sinfulness of the world, there must be a struggle to bring out the justice of God in this world, that a genuine *shalom* of God might come to reign in creation. Thus, a concern for pursuing justice and building peace are seen as central for the transformation of the world into something closer to God's intentions for creation.

In order to do this, one must learn to read the 'signs of the times'. This means, following Augustine, reading both the book of nature and the book of God's Word. Both are given roughly equal importance, since God is present in the world as well as in the revelation entrusted to the Church.

The second approach accords context and culture great importance as well. It reads these from the *regula fidei*, a God-given economy of truth by which the world, created by that same God, is to be understood. Approaching the context requires more of a diagnostic than an analytic approach. One finds this expressed, for example, in the language of *Evangelii nuntiandi*, where the approach to the context is one of purifying it from sin through the introduction of gospel values, and elevating its most noble dimensions by means of those same values. If the first approach to context was discovery and affirmation, the second leans more to diagnosis of ill and transformation.

Culture is viewed more through a classical lens, although modern elements are not missing. Here culture is seen as a normative set of values and practices into which one tries to grow. This is captured especially in the German idea of *Bildung*, or formation. Modern elements of culture are introduced here insofar as the artists and intellectuals of any given society are culture-makers, and have a responsibility to help in this process of cultural purification and elevation.

From a theological point of view the Church, as the depository of God's revelation and the manifestation of the City of God on earth, has a responsibility to share this treasure given to it, and to invite human beings into the divine economy that makes the life of the Church, especially in its worship and its heritage. That divine economy is the economy of Christ. While the Church works for the purification and elevation of culture, the Church itself is a kind of culture into which one can come and in which one can live. If justice and peace are the principal hallmarks of concern for context in the first approach, it is holiness and truth – which together issue forth in beauty – that most characterize the second. To be sure, both approaches care about the virtues of the other. But the distinctive characteristics are nonetheless in evidence.

The 'signs of the times' are of great importance in the second approach as well. But rather than reading them through the lens of God's work in the world as we best understand it, the second approach lies closer to the occurrence of that term in Matthew's Gospel (16.1–6; par. Luke 12.4–56).[7] The signs of the times are read in an apocalyptic-eschatological economy. Those signs are read through the lens of crisis, the lens of how the City of God sees the world in its entrapped situation, a situation from which it cannot extract itself by its own power. The splendour of the City of God, the light to the nations, helps the world see the crisis into which it has fallen, and points the way out of that crisis toward the Heavenly City.

Pluralism and Modernity

A second angle of entry for understanding context in Catholic pastoral theology is by looking at pluralism and the relation to modernity. By pluralism here is meant both intellectual and cultural pluralism – the pluralism of ideas and values that mark contemporary (especially urban) societies, and the pluralism of values and practices as people migrate into different contexts and come into contact with one another.

For the first approach, one deals with pluralism first of all by acknowledging and then engaging difference. It is the different that the other represents in our midst that is for us the most enigmatic and perhaps the most challenging dimension. Only by beginning with that otherness can we hope to build the kind of conversations that will lead to a harmonious society where difference is recognized and even celebrated as a gift for the enrichment of human society.

Modernity is an imperfect form of society, but the best yet found to tolerate the presence of differences. Embracing modernity is central to the message of *Gaudium et spes* for engagement with the world. Modernity needs to be critiqued, especially in its atheistic and relativist tendencies. But it is a natural development out of Christianity itself, and therefore has to be shaped and nurtured accordingly.

The second approach comes to pluralism by starting with the unity that underlies difference. This approach seeks what John Paul II called the 'truth of the human being'. Difference may be at first the most salient phenomenon encountered in pluralism, but it is not its most essential aspect. On this view, to become overly fascinated with difference can result in the promised engagement with the 'other' never really occurring. Difference is peripheral to a deeper oneness, and to dwell only on difference can result in people living in parallel worlds that never touch each other. God is one, and the world God created mirrors that divine unity. That should be the starting-point lest we fall, as Benedict XVI has so famously said, into the 'dictatorship of relativism'.

Modernity is a deeply ambivalent phenomenon for this second approach. It often appears naive in its cult of progress and its sunny optimism about the perfectibility of the human condition. Some in the second approach (as can be found among some of the progenitors of the Radical Orthodoxy movement) hold that modernity is indeed an outgrowth of Christianity, but as a heresy. *Gaudium et spes*, for all its enthusiasm about the world, failed adequately to account for the fallen character of humanity and for the consequences of human sinfulness.[8] What is needed in the pluralist situation of modernity is not so much a deeper involvement in understanding the other as a pedagogy that helps people in pluralist society find the truth about the human being that underlies apparent difference and that then helps them conform themselves to that truth.

Identity

The last point about pedagogy and formation leads us to another dimension of context; namely, how persons and societies form their identities in a pluralist society. The first approach emphasizes the fact that cultures and the identities that are formed within them are the outcome of a constructivist project. Cultures and identities are constructed things rather than something given (hence, a preference for modern and postmodern concepts of culture in this approach). Given especially the multiplicity of cultures that much of the world's population now encounters, and the speeding-up of that process by globalization, we are more aware than ever before of the always provisional quality of our identities. Indeed as Amartya Sen has persuasively argued, it is important today that human beings realize they need to rely on multiple identities (in the sense of multiple identifications) in order live non-violently in the world (Sen 2006). A too narrowly based identity can create occasion for forms of identification that become intolerant or even lethal to oneself and to others.

Theologically, this approach to identity is based on chapter 2 of *Lumen gentium*, where the Church is presented as the pilgrim people of God. Our task is to take our part in building the Reign of God as a people underway, together, to the Heavenly City, the New Jerusalem. As a pilgrim people, we must be prepared to encounter many new and different things along the way and, like the itinerant mission of Jesus in Galilee, meet these situations as they come to us. At the same time, we do our part in helping bring about the Reign of God. Our identities are therefore ec-centric, in the sense of focused outward on the realization of God's Reign. That is completely consistent with the understanding of encountering our context as outlined above.

Identity is also a central category for the second approach, and perhaps the angle of vision that it contributes to most significantly in a theology of context. Identity involves, to use the title of the first volume of Hans Urs von Balthasar's *The Glory of the Lord*, 'seeing the form' (Balthasar 1983). The formation of our identity comes less from turning toward seeing God's work in the world than from turning inward – to the Church and to oneself – to discover the form of Christ. It is to this form, this archetype of true and full humanity, that we most conform and adhere. As we advance in this conforming ourselves, in this becoming truly holy, we have an identity that allows us then to engage a broken and sinful world, a world that misreads at times its own self, and bring it too into the pedagogy of Christ, the Great Teacher. The centre of this identity formation is therefore not outward, but inward. That inwardness should not be mistaken for turning in on oneself in a selfish way; it is an inwardness for the sake of a subsequent outward movement. In this it mirrors the *exitus–reditus* movement of Neoplatonic philosophy and the theologies of John Scotus Eriugena and Pseudo-Dionysius.

This creates a powerful sense of identity and offers a clear pedagogy on how to achieve it. It is nurtured in the liturgy of the Church and in the spiritual and mystical traditions of the Church.

Transformation

Both approaches witness to the sinfulness of the world and realize that, if the Church is in a context and nothing is transformed, then the gospel has not been preached and the Church has not witnessed to its crucified and risen Lord. Yet how the transformation is understood has distinctive elements, both flowing from views of catholicity.

The first approach sees the world in need of transformation. The baseline from which such transformation works, as it were, is the platform of creation itself. God created the world and saw that it was good (Gen. 1.25, 32). At the same time, this world has been disfigured by sin. The transformation of the world beyond its sin, using any and all of the terms the Church has used for that process – redemption, salvation, liberation, justification – never utterly destroys that platform of creation. Rather, according to a time-honoured Catholic principle, grace builds upon nature. If one returns to the controversies about the relation between nature and grace in Catholic theology from the 1930s through the 1950s, one comes out here somewhat with Karl Rahner. Grace cannot be seen as extrinsic to nature, but is given to us already with our encounters with nature.

In terms of how this transformation takes place, the dialectics of change may be seen as operating somewhat symmetrically; that is, nature and grace, world and church work on a roughly equal basis, since both are graced by God, and both carry sin in their members. Thus one cannot be completely nullified by the other. Another, important consequence in this more symmetrical approach is that transformation is not simply about the transformation of individuals, but the transformation of institutions and societies as well. This pertains not only to cultural and social structures in the world, but to the structures of the Church as well. The Church may be seen as the spotless Bride of Christ, but its participation in sin cannot be overlooked either.

In the second approach, the need for transformation is seen perhaps even more strongly than in the first approach, albeit from a different angle. The intensity of this need creates a greater focus on sin in the world than the first – so much so, that one can speak here more in terms of an Augustinian dialectic of sin and grace, rather than the Thomistic dialectic of nature and grace. In its extreme (non-Catholic) types, found in some strains of Calvinism, sin has so utterly destroyed human nature that God's redemptive power must utterly reconstitute us. While there is nothing of that extreme in Catholicism, it does denote that there is no symmetry in the world–church dialectic. The Church clearly has – and must have – the upper hand. This is so because of the faith entrusted to the Church. The economies of grace that can be traced out in the Church's faith are the roadmaps for the transformation of the world.[9]

Because of the asymmetry between world and church in this view of the dialectic of transformation, the reform of the world's structures provides a less promising way of bringing about transformation toward the Reign of God. The focus is first on the individual sinner who must repent and grow into holiness. Thinking that reforming sinful structures will make much difference belies an optimism about human progress that the sinful history of the world does not support. The Church, as holding the fullness of faith as a sign of its catholicity, cannot be measured against the admittedly imperfect standards of the world. Because it holds the fullness of faith, the Church cannot be held to be sinful; only individuals within the Church are such.

Practices

So where do all these dimensions of context come together as approaches to a Catholic pastoral theology? For the first approach, what the pilgrim people of God do, on their way through this world toward God's final Reign, is construct a narrative of God's working in the world. They have gone out in mission (Matt. 28.19–20), preaching Good News to the poor, and liberty to captives (Luke 4.18–19). They work toward the transformation of the world as their preparation in the unfolding mission of the Triune God in the world. Their identities are embedded in the narrative of salvation history – a history of how God has sided with the poor and oppressed, how justice has been done, and a greater goodness is coming about. It is a narrative about care – for those least privileged, for the marginalized, and for the earth. It is a narrative about how God's justice becomes more and more manifest in this world. It is a narrative where there is place for the stranger. The narrative continues to grow as more people are included in God's own story. That story is never far from the concrete and particular contexts in which God's people operate. And it moves toward a narrative of reconciliation when God 'will be all in all' (1 Cor. 15.28).

This narrative structure creates an identity by linking together the stories of how God is transforming the world. It is an account of the moments of redeeming and liberating grace found in history. The pilgrim Church, with a strong sense of mission as participating in the *missio Dei*, finds its concrete expression in the building of God's reign in justice, peace and reconciliation. It is, in Graham Ward's telling image, a pastoral 'theology at the western door'; that is, standing on the threshold in the main doorway of the Church facing outward toward the world with the message of God's grace. It is a pastoral theology that takes as its foundational words, the final words of the Eucharist: '*Ite, missa est*' (Ward 2005, p. 59).

For the second approach, the practices of pastoral theology begin within the liturgy and prayer of the Church, and its spiritual and mystical traditions. Formed in this pedagogy to be conformed with Christ, the followers of Christ can then turn to their contexts. Amid the sinfulness and brokenness of those contexts, they can come to discover the outlines of God's plan for the world in action as they have seen it mirrored in the economies of divine grace. The story of the world must be conformed into the pattern of Christ's death if it is to come to know the power of the resurrection (Phil. 3.10–11). Mission has an outward movement; but it is an outward movement in order to bring people into the sacred space of the Church, the City of God. Up until the late sixteenth century, the most commonly understood biblical motive for mission was precisely this: not Matthew 28.19–20 ('Go out to all the nations') but Luke 14.23 ('Make them come in'). This pastoral theology looks through the western door of the Church as well, but from the perspective of the sanctuary where the divine mysteries are celebrated, rather than from the threshold of the door itself. The beauty of the liturgy draws in those yearning for the splendour of the truth. The Church's liturgical practices and mystical traditions provide the lens that brings the crisis of the world into focus.

Conclusion: The Contextual Character of Catholic Pastoral Theology

My intent here has been to explore Catholic pastoral theology as both catholic and pastoral. Catholicity, as a contested concept within contemporary Catholic theology, yields two sets of understandings of the catholicity of the Church. These two understandings are not antithetical, although they are sometimes made so in the contemporary debate. There is always the danger of proponents of one side caricaturing the views of proponents of the other. I have tried to avoid that as much as possible, but I surely have not escaped it. I think both approaches yield important insights into the contemporary context of Catholic living. In speaking here of context, I will restrict myself to the context of the North Atlantic.

The first approach takes otherness more on the terms in which the 'other' wants to present itself. For that reason, it fits into modern understandings of tolerance and living with pluralism. It has an epistemological humility vis-à-vis the other, understanding that encounter as a continuing act of discovery and disclosure. It gives, in its initial encounter at least, a greater sense of 'recognition' of the other, an important concept for multicultural interaction. It admits the instability and even fragility of identity in a pluralistic world, and supplements the lack of clarity with a strong sense of compassion and empathy. It sees the world in need of transformation, and constructs its projects of transformation in categories of justice, inclusion, peace and reconciliation.

The second approach finds its strength in its own interiority rather than outward movement. It draws a strong sense of truth from that interiority that it consciously uses as a lens to view the world. Its approach to the world is more diagnostic than phenomenological. It sees the world not in the labour pains of a new creation (Rom. 8.22) but as a world in crisis, a world that has lost its way. Pluralism is more apparent than real; what matters has to do with a deeper truth. It has an epistemological confidence about the cogency of its vision, and the therapeutic power of its prescriptions. Consequently, it imparts a strong sense of identity – not as something constructed along the way, but as something that is given to the Church by its Lord. Justice for a broken world is important, but will only come about through a prior commitment to holiness, to a conforming to the divine will. That identity is strengthened not so much by a cumulative narrative of God's action in the world as by the repeated action of the liturgy, an action that reveals the divine economy of the world. Its commitment to social action is always embedded in the understanding that the human being's capacity for sin, the human being's incapacity to do good unaided by divine grace, will trump every utopian project and dream of a better world.

In a confusing (or confused) world, which view of catholicity best informs a Catholic pastoral theology? One sees glimmers of past experience and history in both approaches. The first approach clearly had the upper hand in the years immediately following the Council. The second approach is much in evidence at the present time, some forty years on. It has powerful advocates in high places in the Church today.

A final note: are both of these approaches really contextual? There is a tendency to read the first approach as a thoroughgoing contextual approach that is inductive from a methodological point of view, and the second as at least incipiently deductive as it approaches its context. That, I believe, is too simple a distinction. As Protestant theologians have already made clear in contemplating the theory–praxis nexus in practical theology, all praxis is theory-laden and all theory finds its roots in some prior praxis.[10] One could argue that the praxis proposed in the second approach to a Catholic pastoral theology is simply more aware of its presuppositions about context and culture than is the first. Indeed, the second approach, in its argument about culture, sees the first approach as naive and insufficiently philosophical in its understanding of the nature of culture. However this is ultimately to be construed, the presence of these two approaches reminds us that Catholic pastoral theology, as it continues to be explored and debated in the coming years, has multiple proposals about its Catholic character as well as a range of construals of what makes it contextual.

Notes

1 Bevans 2002 explores the relative strengths and weaknesses of the translation model.

2 See Radcliffe 2006. The choice of *communio* for the designation of the second group is somewhat infelicitous, given that all Catholics embrace *communio* as a definition of the Church, especially in light of the 1985 Extraordinary Synod of Bishops. To be sure, they assign the term different meanings.

3 *Smyrn.* 8.2: 'wherever Jesus Christ is, there is the Catholic Church'. Scholars believe that 'Catholic' here refers to the Church's universality.

4 'The Church is Catholic or universal because it has spread throughout the entire world, from one end of the earth to the other. Again, it is called Catholic because it teaches fully and unfailingly all the doctrines which out to be brought to men's knowledge, whether they are concerned with visible or invisible things, with the realities of heaven or the things of the earth.' Cyril of Jerusalem, *Catech.* 18, 23f.

5 For two views of this from the point of view of people who would identify themselves with the first approach, see Komonchak 2005, pp. 11–14; Boeve 2007, pp. 205–27.

6 For the conceptions of culture at play here – classical, modern, and postmodern – see the helpful discussion in the first part of Kathryn Tanner's *Theories of Culture* (1997).

7 For an illuminating discussion of the theological meanings of 'signs of the times' as they were seen at the time of the Second Vatican Council and continue to play themselves out today, see Ruggieri 2006, pp. 61–70; and Theobald 2006, pp. 71–84.

8 This is an objection that Cardinal Ratzinger raised on a number of occasions in the past.

9 Graham Ward refers to the two types of dialectic – symmetrical and asymmetrical – as supplementary and complementary, respectively: Ward 2005, pp. 53–4.

10 Don Browning, one of the progenitors of the practical theology movement in the English-speaking world, makes this point clearly already in his *A Fundamental Practical Theology: Descriptive and Strategic Proposals* (1991).

Bibliography

Hans Urs von Balthasar, 1983, *The Glory of the Lord: A Theological Aesthetics*, vol. I: *Seeing the Form*, Edinburgh: T&T Clark.

Stephen B. Bevans, 2002, *Models of Contextual Theology*, Maryknoll, NY: Orbis Books.

Lieven Boeve, 2007, 'Europe in Crisis: A Question of Belief or Unbelief? Perspectives from the Vatican', *Modern Theology* 23, pp. 205–27.

Don Browning, 1991, *A Fundamental Practical Theology: Descriptive and Strategic Proposals*, Minneapolis: Fortress Press.

Joseph Komonchak, 2005, 'The Church in Crisis: Pope Benedict's Theological Vision', *Commonweal* 132 (3 June), pp. 11–14.

Timothy Radcliffe, 2006, *What's the Point of Being a Christian?* London and New York: Continuum.

Giuseppe Ruggieri, 2006, 'Zeichen der Zeit. Herkunft und Bedeutung einer christlich-hermeneutischen Chiffre der Geschichte', in Peter Huenermann (ed.), *Das Zweite Vatikanische Konzil und die Zeichen der Zeit heute*, Freiburg: Herder, pp. 61–70.

Amartya Sen, 2006, *Identity and Violence: The Illusion of Destiny*, New York: W. W. Norton.

Kathryn Tanner, 1997, *Theories of Culture*, Minneapolis: Fortress Press.

Christoph Theobald, 2006, 'Zur Theologie der Zeichen der Zeit' and 'Bedeutung und Kriterien heute', in Peter Huenermann (ed.), *Das Zweite Vatikanische Konzil und die Zeichen der Zeit heute*, Freiburg: Herder, pp. 71–84 .

Graham Ward, 2005, *Cultural Transformation and Religious Practice*, Cambridge: Cambridge University Press.

5

Pastoral Theology as a
Theological Project

HENRI-JÉRÔME GAGEY

'All meaningful reflection is for the sake of action and all meaningful action is for the sake of friendship.' (John Macmurray[1])

The Contemporary Project of Practical Theology

Practical theology can, in principle, lay claim to a long tradition as a field of study and research. Some scholars go back elegantly to its ancient roots, such as *The Praktikos and Chapters on Prayer* by Evagrius Ponticus (345–99 AD) or the *Catechetical Lectures* of Cyril of Jerusalem. They refer to Duns Scotus and the break introduced in theology by William of Ockham, and then to modern practices of pastoral training for Catholic and Protestant clergy.[2] However, all such attempts to establish ancient lineage fail to reveal a picture of a well established discipline; and it is noticeable that many Catholic authors in the 1960s greeted its appearance as a recent fact rather than the continuation of a long line of research – for example, Marie-Dominique Chenu:

> The awakening of pastoral theology and the foundation in Faculties and Seminaries of special chairs are so many admirable signs of the renewal of theology itself, which has always found truth and life by being the clear and constructive expression of the church in action. The pastoral sector is undoubtedly the most active place where there is currently progress in theological knowledge.[3]

Similarly, Pierre Adnès of the Gregorian University maintained at the end of the 1960s that pastoral theology 'still remained at the stage of promises and infancy', even though he saw its birth or profound renewal as the most characteristic feature of the renewal of theology at present.[4] In the wake of the Second Vatican Council, pastoral or practical theology appeared by and large as something new and promising, but even its most committed supporters did not try to hide their uncertainty about its epistemological status. J. Audinet, former director of the Institute of Catechetical Theology at the Institut Catholique de Paris, and one of the pioneers of French-speaking practical theology, gave this odd answer to a question during a conference in 1972:

> If you ask me whether I really believe there is a pastoral theology distinct from other forms of theology, [I would answer that] I do not know. I would tend to say that I do not believe so. I believe there are many ways to deal with Christian reality, whether by means of praxis, or its symbol system, or its history.[5]

Audinet acknowledged that despite increasing interest in practical theology across the world it remained difficult 'to grasp and locate it among all the disciplines that up to now are recognized as components of theology'.[6] Similar views were expressed on the Protestant side by Isabelle Grellier of Strasbourg. She confessed that 'at the crossroads of these several types of approach, where there is a more or less coherent gathering of fields that at first glance seem very heterogeneous, practical theology is not easy to define'. But she saw this positively: 'perhaps the fact that these questions remain unresolved still contributes to the interest of this discipline as always in search of itself and thus on the move'.[7]

When theorists and experts speak with less uncertainty than this, it is usually quite easy to guess why. Very subtle attempts to define epistemological status, whether during conferences or in publications, witness, first and foremost, to the need to sustain the academic legitimacy of specialized faculties and departments of practical theology!

The best way to grasp practical theology is probably as a 'project', as outlined in a very enlightening essay by the Jesuit theologian Rene Marlé, *Le projet de théologie pratique*.[8] This characterization is both negative and positive. Negatively, it marks the difficulty of seeing practical theology as a homogeneous disciplinary field, defined by the unity of its object and methods. Positively, it stresses the good reasons why from the mid-twentieth century so many theologians have engaged in such a demanding conversation across the various disciplines that analyse and interpret the diverse fields of human action and behaviour. Their strong feeling was that this dialogue was inescapable if they were to overcome the double break that theology experienced during the century. First, the break from the merely pragmatic purposes of traditional 'pastoral theology' as taught in both Catholic and Protestant seminaries; and second, the break with neo-scholasticism, which was proving less and less able to address the new questions arising from the development of historical consciousness in modern times. Taken more as a project than a complete achievement, practical theology arises in the wake of a double evolution and crisis: the internal evolution and crisis of pastoral theology, and the internal evolution of systematic theology. We examine these two points in that order.

A Disciplinary Field in Need of Legitimacy

Practical theology is, in the current literature, a disciplinary field in need of legitimacy. Let us examine, first of all, the most obvious feature of this search for legitimacy – the refusal to reduce practical theology to the unsatisfactory status of an 'applied theology'. In her presentation of the current tasks of practical theology, Grellier opposes the traditional picture of it as putting into practice a timeless knowledge deduced from the Bible and Christian tradition. This would make it a second – not to say secondary – discipline, applying to the life of the Church, and to the practice of pastoral ministry, doctrines in the development and interpretation of which it itself played no part. This leads to normative conclusions – practical theology has to say what is to be done or avoided. Grellier's refusal of such a secondary role for practical theology is commonplace in the second half of the twentieth century. As Bernard Kaempf wrote:

> The danger of such a position is that the practical level is very likely to be considered the second rank compared to 'genuine' theology which occupies an almost totalitarian position, regarding practice as the simple transmission of professional 'know-how'. Until now, practical theology has not entirely recovered from this implicit or explicit designation, in particular in the French-speaking countries. As a result, practical theology within the University and especially in Faculties of Theology has not obtained the more solid and stable status it needs.[9]

Similarly, many insist on not reducing practical theology to a narrowly pastoral and ecclesial theology, stressing the need for it to be open to new actors and other fields and not restrict its reflection to religious activities and concerns.

> If the mission of the Church constitutes the framework of practical theology, then it will have to be concerned not only with worship, organization and the functioning of the Church, such as the transmission of the gospel to children from Christian background and training of ministers, but also with the announcing of the gospel to those who do not claim to be Christian, as well as with all actions of solidarity carried out in the name of the gospel, or with all the fields of diakonia, whether cultural, social, material, etc.[10]

The contemporary quest for a practical theology is firmly opposed to this classical model of 'pastoral' or 'practical' theology as a long matured wisdom derived from experience, providing helpful advice for future ministers in the various aspects of their pastoral activity. Granted this opposition, the next task is to trace the genealogy of practical theology as an authentically scientific discipline.

The Usual Genealogy

Beyond the rhetorical references to Evagrius Ponticus and the *Catechetical Lectures*, Schleiermacher is commonly acknowledged as the 'father of practical theology'. In his famous *Brief Outline of the Study of Theology*[11] he was the first explicitly to locate practical theology in a general syllabus of theology. The practical theologian who finds it difficult to define his disciplinary status finds in Schleiermacher a prestigious ancestor who provides legitimacy and the blueprint of a programme to be achieved. Consequently, many imagine that it suffices 'to pursue Schleiermacher's concern and reflections in order to show how perfectly scientific practical theology's methodology is, so that, from this point of view, it has no cause to be envious of the other theological and scientific disciplines'.[12] More accurately, however, Jean-François Zorn, professor of practical theology in the Protestant department of theology in Montpellier, praises Schleiermacher for having introduced practical theology into the university system; it is thanks to him that practical theology has escaped the status of simple pastoral counselling and has developed with the assistance of the tools of the social sciences. But Zorn stresses that:

regrettably during the nineteenth century, practical theology remained an 'applied science' with professional aims limited to helping pastoral leaders in charge of pastoral care. An applied science: that is, practical theology applies to church life, according to a deductive method, truth claims established elsewhere, in the Bible, reason or history; and the professional aim: the concept of pastoral leadership narrowly focused on pastoral care. It is clear that it is not necessary to over-estimate the role of Schleiermacher in the emergence of the contemporary project of practical theology.[13]

In fact, it was not in defining practical theology itself that Schleiermacher was most creative and influential. What is memorable in his *Brief Outline of the Study of Theology* is its overall definition of theology as both a positive and a critical discipline responsible for the faithfulness and well-being of a historical tradition. Theology is not a neutral enquiry about religious experiences but a commitment with responsibility for a community. And that is the reason why, according to Schleiermacher, theology is primarily the concern of those charged with church leadership. As the Swiss Protestant theologian Pierre Gisel stresses, from this point of view Schleiermacher shares a lot of generally unsuspected common ground with the dialectical theology of Karl Barth. What renders Schleiermacher's text out of date and, so to say, pre-modern, is that it still defines practical theology as a sort of applied theology, so that the practice does not produce a feedback effect on philosophical or historical theology.[14] For that reason, the practical theology he inspired risks being quite conservative because it tends to support already established practices without opening the way to invent or adapt them according to changed times.

Having considered French-speaking Protestant practical theologians, we can recall the previous reflections of the Dominican theologian Pierre-Andre Liégé, very influential in France and particularly at the Institut Catholique de Paris in the 1970s. According to Liégé, practical theology until the twentieth century limited itself to the training of ministers in charge of pastoral care within the Church. In his genealogy, pastoral theology entered the University in 1777, when the Empress Maria Theresa undertook the reform of the German universities. At that time, the aim of practical theology was to train clerics, without any doctrinal concern. Liégé recalls that during the Catholic Counter-Reformation pastoral theology already appeared as a pragmatic attempt to train 'good priests fulfilling with dignity the tasks of their ministry'. It is only in the middle of the nineteenth century that a genuine project of pastoral theology emerged in Catholicism, in the Tübingen School which, under the influence of Schleiermacher, attempted for the first time a systematic reflection on the future of the Church considered as the sacrament of salvation. But, Liégé says, these efforts almost failed and had little influence on scholastic theology.[15]

In short, the usual genealogy of practical theology celebrates both Schleiermacher and the Catholic School of Tübingen. However, there is no real continuity between them and the 1950s practical theology project, which made a real break with the agenda of 'applied' theology.[16] Such a break only happened when scholastic theology became more and more ineffective for theologians who saw the necessity to take seriously the crisis of faith in the context of modernity. According to Liégé it was only in the wake of the Second World War that there appeared in Germany a charismatic and kerygmatic theology concerned for the *praxis* of the Church. The first attempts did not prove very fruitful, although they expressed a new aspiration for a theology inserted into the current reality of the Church as the universal sacrament of salvation. They opened the way for more effective attempts that developed in the 1950s in both Germany and France.[17]

A Focus on the Church as the Medium of the Faith

Practical theology, therefore, is not, in the current meaning of the term, the child of traditional applied pastoral theology, but the result of a deep break which made the timeless conception of Christian life, as presented by neo-scholastic theology in contrast to patristic theology, unsustainable. From that moment, the project of practical theology emerged as reflection on the effective enactment of the mystery of faith and focused on Christian community life and its construction as the Body of Christ.

The focus on the Church as the medium of the faith became more and more pronounced in the Catholic Church at Vatican II, which was called precisely because of the collapse of the Christendom system as established in the wake of the Counter-Reformation and renewed in the nineteenth century. As Liégé writes, the break with Christendom required 'a theological criticism able to accompany the necessary renewal of Christian practices so that the experiment would not break with standard patterns nor be confused with improvisation'.[18] It is in this context of crisis that a global definition of pastoral theology emerged, stated by Liégé this way: a theology that 'resolutely chooses to concentrate on the Church, where it finds God and Christ in the act of revelation and salvation'. Here, Liégé quotes Rahner:

> In the broadest meaning, pastoral theology (or better, 'practical theology' or the theology of church practices) is a theological reflection about the upbuilding of the Church through its own practices understood as the embodiment of God's work in and for the world, so that this deed does and must accomplish itself according to the permanent nature of the Church and according to the contemporary situation of the world and of the Church. It is this situation that pastoral theology must elucidate theologically.[19]

But, Liégé continues, 'Such a pastoral theology is still only carried out in a fragmentary way', and in the rest of his article he expounds what ought to be its further development.

Why was it so important at that time to reflect on the activity of the Church in its double structure of social practice and God's work? Because of the painful experience that things were not going the way they should! In short, if church practice became 'a theological place' – a *locus theologicus* according to the phrase then in vogue – it was precisely because the practices seemed to be failing! In a context of crisis, practical theology claimed a reforming purpose, to give back to practices the potential they had apparently lost. At this point, practical theology comes to be defined as 'a *critical* discipline of the practices of the church'. I underline here *critical*. Rahner, quoted by Liégé, puts it clearly:

> The moment has come for us to create a 'practical theology' that cannot be identified with seminary pastoral teaching which gives guidelines for pastoral action to beginners. It must take for its object the whole current reality of the Church and must basically re-examine the present situation of the Church, coldly and from a genuinely theological point of view as well; it must have its starting-point in ecclesiology, to come to this very simple question which summarizes everything: 'what must the Church do today?' (quoted by Liégé 1971, p. 65)

A Critical Examination of the Church's Practices

Even if it is programmatic, the contemporary definition of practical theology that emerges from this survey of the literature paints a quite coherent picture of a thinking process in four steps: (1) it refers to the various practices connected with the Church, (2) using diverse disciplines such as church history and the social sciences, (3) in an ongoing dialogue with philosophy, and (4) supported by the resources of, and responding to issues and questions in, systematic theology. Taking these four points in order.

1 Practical theology that deals with the various practices connected with the Church, although its aim is not only to train future ministers, submits these practices to critical analysis to reveal what is at stake in them, and to readjust them in their basic principles and reinterpret them.

2 Practical theology can be defined as a theology in dialogue with the social or human sciences because its object is social practices, not 'texts' as in the case of traditional systematic theology.

3 The conditions for this dialogue must be set in such a way that practical theologians (if such theologians exist) do not simply fall under the control of the conscious or unconscious assumptions of the social sciences. Here, it is philosophy that provides the conceptual tools. (I should emphasize that this articulation of theology with the social sciences mediated by philosophy is much better understood today than in the 1970s when the social sciences tended to exercise the role of a new metaphysics.[20])

4 But if the first task of practical theology is to reconsider the mission of the Church as the milieu of faith, that can only be done in close dialogue with systematicians, as Grellier notes.[21] Here we reach a delicate point, well clarified by the Protestant theologian Paul Keller, who states that the rise of practical theology is rooted in the shift from the beginning of the nineteenth up to the end of the twentieth century from a metaphysical to a historical comprehension of reality.[22] It is only because this shift occurred within systematic theology that practical theology could emerge. I put it more radically: as a condition for the appearance and development of the practical theology project, systematic theology had to discover its own fundamentally practical orientation.

We now explore this by reference to Walter Kasper's analysis of the current situation of theology in *Theology and the Church*. Referring explicitly to the long intellectual tradition of his own university of

Tübingen, he shows how the rupture with neo-scholastic metaphysics and the acceptance of the new way of questioning that came with the development of the historical sciences led dogmatic theology to assume its own practical orientation and concerns.

The Practical Orientation of Theology

The end of the scholastic and the irruption of historical questions

Without claiming to be original, Kasper presents the collapse of neo-scholasticism as a historical break. The neo-scholastic onto-theology, constructed during the nineteenth century as a fortress to resist the timeless rationalism of the Enlightenment, eventually broke down, since its debate with the Enlightenment turned out to be more and more historical and focused on issues such as the evolution of dogmas, the shift from the historical Jesus to the Christ of faith, and so on. All that led theology back to its sources – Scripture, patristic theology, liturgical documentation, and so forth – which became subject to critical histori-cal enquiry. As a result, it became impossible to deny the irreducible diversity, across time and place, of Christian doctrines, rites, moral patterns, etc. This was a paramount intellectual experience that brought to ruin the sense of the unity and coherence of the Christian faith as had seemed obvious for centuries. The role and significance of metaphysics, which was for theology the science of last principles giving reality its ontological grounds, was radically threatened. Its universal categories provided the theological tradition with the tools to take account of the reality of God as the unique being encompassing and determining the whole while at the same time exceeding it. According to Kasper, the true and main crisis of current theology derives from the fact that we currently lack such a metaphysics.[23] As a result, the monolithic unity of theology came to an end, and this paved the way for a plurality of disci-plines and methods highly specialized and differentiated, as well as for a pluralism of theological orientations according to cultural contexts. However, for Kasper:

> The move back to the ghetto of the old handbook theology is out of the question, for, in the long term, the evolution of the last decades provides too many positive and promising new starting-points. And in any case it is not possible to flee the present situation and its chal-lenges. It is even a question of life and death for catholic theology

to release itself completely from the prison of the neo-scholastic system.[24]

While underlining the highly critical character of the situation of pluralism for theology, Kasper claims that it is impossible to go back. Conversely, he outlines three principles for rebuilding a unitary theology.

1 The 'principle of ecclesiality' establishes that the truth of faith is given in a living process of tradition interpreting and actualizing the unique Gospel of Jesus Christ.[25] The negative opposition between sub-jectivist and objectivist comprehensions of truth is overcome: it is the comprehensive 'we' of the Church that is the subject of faith and the place of truth. Kasper supports an existential and historical definition of faith, and consequently relativizes the vision of faith as adhesion to an abstract doctrinal system. Of course the role of doctrine is not denied. Kasper carefully defines it, but stresses that doctrine has to be understood as a normative ecclesial interpretation of Scripture, and so must be interpreted from the Scriptures. Over and above doctrine, the tradition of faith exists in multiple forms: the liturgy above all, and the testimony of faith lived in daily life.[26]

2 The scientific principle: this rests on the fact that faith is not only the 'external faith in the Church' but faith in God's self-revelation requiring an obedience that is internal (in conformity with reason) and not external to the mystery. Consequently, theology must accept being in dialogue with other instances of reason.

3 Kasper's third paramount principle of catholic theology today is its orientation to practice. This orientation is rooted in the very nature of faith, which itself is practice-oriented. 'Theology must not only communicate a theoretical and speculative knowledge: it aims at the practice of faith, hope and charity.'[27] Theology is practical because it is concerned with the personal and social practices of life, with daily experiences and problems. In addition, if theology deals with the con-temporary culture in which it is immersed, then it has a critical task to discern how it is always at risk of being misguided by the dominant assumptions of its time as well as dominated by the interests of peculiar social groups. From this perspective, the practical responsibility to pave the way for the Church to fulfil its mission according to the historical context falls with theology as a whole (systematic theology included) and not only with moral and pastoral theology.

However enlightening and open-minded, this definition of the 'practi-cal' inner orientation of systematic theology could still be misinterpreted as a new version with only minor changes of practical theology as applied theology. To escape this, it is necessary to stress that when applying itself to the practical level, systematic theology engages in a process of verification of its own major assumptions. With this aim in view I will now consider a famous paper by the French Jesuit Henri Bouillard entitled 'the current task of fundamental theology'.[28]

From apologetic to fundamental theology

Bouillard's paper is a vigorous plea for the apologetic function of fundamental theology dedicated to expressing Christian truth claims in an understandable way. However, as he emphasizes, fundamental theology can no longer achieve this in the same way as traditional Catholic apologetics in the past. Usually, apologetics was limited to the treatises on revelation and ecclesiology, on the assumption that it was possible for theologians to establish the fact of divine revelation without seriously examining its contents. They claimed to prove the divine authority of the magisterium without having to consider the meaning of its statements. However, it is a hopeless task to try to establish the credibility of a magisterium that presents the Christian message if one does not express the meaning and internal credibility of the message itself and its contents. For this reason, it was necessary for fundamental theology to encompass the whole field of dogmatic theology. Signs and evidence of credibility are signs and evidence not of credibility in general but of the content of the faith. For that reason, apologetics and dogmatics have to co-operate in order to check the validity of their claims while confronting them with daily life as experienced in our historical situation.

Bouillard summarizes the mission of fundamental theology today: 'It is a matter of checking the meaning and the reference of the word "God" as it appears in Christian speech.' But he immediately adds that the meaning of this word 'God' can only appear in the language game to which it belongs. In itself, the word 'God' is meaningless, because it is impossible to show the being it indicates. Consequently the famous rule that Wittgenstein defined in general for every word has particular theological relevance: the meaning of 'God' is its use in language.[29] However, it is Christian faith as experienced and not only as confessed that defines the language game through which the word 'God' is concretely embodied: 'the meaning of the word [God] appears only at the core of the constellation of significations it organizes and coordinates: faith, human existence, creation, man and woman as image of God, sin, grace, revelation, redemption, Christian community, fellowship with humanity, resurrection and eternal life'. But if it is in the Church, and through Jesus, that we meet God the Father, he who is from the beginning our creator and present to us through the history of salvation orienting us toward eternal life, so the task of fundamental theology is not only to establish the 'fact of revelation', but also to discover in the Christian fact as a whole the actualization of the idea of God and of his relationship with humanity. Then, according to Bouillard, theology has the task 'of verifying the meaning and the reference of the word "God" as it appears in the language of faith, among the constellation of many terms which it coordinates' (Bouillard 1972, p. 35). But, as Bouillard asks, how to verify this?

Theology as verification

Bouillard's answer is close to the correlation theology of Tillich. It is a matter of establishing that the statements of the Christian message are positively related to our universal experience of reality, so that they appear as the answer to the radical question implied in this experience, to the question that the human being is to, and for, him- or herself. Thus it will appear that these statements are meaningful for us and deeply concern us because they reveal our own reality and embody or actualize our own truth:

> Therefore verification consists in the discernment and expression of the relationship, the internal bond, between the question of existence, as revealed by a philosophical analysis, and the answer given by the Christian message. In other words, it consists in relating to each other, without confusion, a hermeneutics of human existence and an evangelical hermeneutics of the message. (Bouillard 1972, p. 34)

Here, in addition to Tillich, Bouillard positions himself with Blondel, Bultmann, Ebeling and Ricœur,[30] while echoing the warning of Balthasar that he summarizes as follows:

> Beware of anthropological reduction; the internal measure of the human spirit must not become the measure of the divine revelation. Above all contemplate the figure of Christ in order to discern in it the radiance of the splendour of God and of his love for human beings.[31]

In other words, apologetics must not frame or enclose revelation in the limits of the pre-understanding or assumptions of an alleged pure reason because revelation releases reason from its own limits while opening it to new possibilities far beyond these limits.

Thus, it is only at the core of experienced faith that the meaning and the reference of the language of revelation can be verified. But while quoting the Belgian philosopher Jean Ladrière, Bouillard actually goes further:

> The reality to which the language of the faith refers 'is not given elsewhere than in this language itself' and 'does not take shape except through it'. This reality 'cannot be revealed but by this language, insofar as it is itself an act allowing the believer to welcome the very reality it speaks about'. For that reason the word of faith must contain within itself the criteria of its own truth. It is itself the process of its own verification, and this verification is an unceasing ongoing process. (Bouillard 1972, p. 38)[32]

Put differently, the truth claimed by the message is not the object of some kind of informative knowledge. It is not to be completed by more information. It is to be fulfilled (performed, realized, accomplished) in the life of the one who welcomes it. Consequently, this truth is not only announced in words claiming intellectual assent. It communicates itself through all the mediations (narrative, symbolic systems, ritual, social, etc.) that give shape to the existence of those who believe in the gospel.

In the words of the French philosopher André Dartigues, who radicalizes Bouillard's statement, because revelation occurs within history, 'God, who is the object of it, cannot be envisioned as a reality facing the mind of the theologian in the manner of an *ob-jectum*.'[33] Revelation communicates much more than a true idea of God, it allows participation in God's life. As a result, God's self-communication necessarily goes along with a transformation of humankind and of the world that receives him. Apart from this transformation – which only allows us to know him as we become as he is – we can have no access to his mystery. In other words, to enter into the knowledge of God means, for human beings, to engage in their own achievement of fullness. The revelation that is achieved through its multiple mediations (that is the faith-word and practices enacted in the medium of the Church) is not reduced to the communication of truths to be known. It constitutes the disclosure as well as the enactment of the new possibilities that are opened to humankind through Christ, so that henceforth, but within an eschatological horizon, they receive the new identity promised by the Son to those who welcome him. This goes far beyond the positivist conception of revelation of Vatican I.

If, according to Bouillard, the task of the theologian-philosopher consists in discerning 'how the Christian message, in its various elements, answers the radical questions implied in human existence', then this discernment and the verification necessarily comprises a practical orientation. It needs to discern the conditions under which the mediations of faith that the tradition of the Church unfolds can be enacted and embodied in the present so as to give a practical answer to the radical issues challenging human existence within history and society.[34] The verification of the truth claimed by Christian faith, which defines the task of fundamental theology, is therefore a practical one. The '*intellectus fidei*' is necessarily a practical intelligence – of the mediations through which faith is embodied in the life of the believing community. From this point of view, the shift from a narrowly apologetic theology to contemporary fundamental theology as defined by Bouillard inescapably involves a similar shift from a fundamental theology to a practical one; 'practical', that is, according to Kasper's formula: 'a theology related to its conditions of determination as well as to its own capacities of determination'.[35] Within this framework, practical theology has not only to think of how to enact concretely what Christian faith has always (allegedly) known about itself, but to question critically and reinterpret and express anew the self-consciousness of faith. In this way there is real feedback and mutual influence between the theoretical and the practical – which is precisely what was missing in Schleiermacher's definition of practical theology.

Conclusion

Starting from epistemological reflections on the status of practical theology in the French context, we eventually come to see that if the project of practical theology exists it is as an evolution internal to systematic theology when challenged by the crisis of the Church. Indeed, by being required to think historically about revelation and its communication, systematic theology was inexorably brought to recognize practice as a *locus theologicus*, and to discover its own self as practice with its own orientations and concerns. Must the conclusion, then, be that now practical theology has to design, at least in broad terms, a new way of theologizing in general, since it is impossible to think theologically of Christian truth claims without thinking of the church practices that enact and embody them? Things are not so simple. Alongside systematic theology, whose starting-point is located in Christian truth claims in order to check their truthfulness and the accuracy of their interpretation through history, there is still place and need for another way of theologizing primarily focused on church practices (catechesis, liturgy, counselling, etc.) rather than texts. For this, the first intellectual partners are the social or human sciences that facilitate the analysis of practices, rather than history or philosophy, which are the usual partners of systematic theology. However, this does not mean that 'theologizing about practices' constitutes a full theological speciality to be developed by 'practical theologians'. Rather, it requires the creation of interdisciplinary spaces of research in which theological questioning and enquiry can work in partnership with the numerous procedures of objectification enacted by the social and human sciences.[36]

Notes

1 John Macmurray, 1957, 1995, *The Form of the Personal*, vol. II: *The Self as Agent*, London: Faber & Faber, p. 15.

2 Bernard Kaempf, 1997, 'Histoire de la théologie pratique', in Bernard Kaempf (ed.), *Introduction à la théologie pratique*, Strasbourg: Presses Universitaires de Strasbourg.

3 'Le réveil de la théologie pastorale, la fondation dans les Facultés et les Séminaires de chaires spéciales, sont autant de signes admirables du renouveau de la théologie elle-même, qui toujours a trouvé vérité et vie à être l'expression, éclairée et construite, de l'Église en acte. Le secteur pastoral est sans doute le lieu le plus actif des progrès actuels du savoir théologique.' Marie-Dominique Chenu, 1957, *La Théologie est-elle une science?*, Paris: Fayard, p. 110.

4 'La théologie pastorale avoue n'en être encore qu'au stade des promesses et des balbutiements. En tout cas, rien n'est plus caractéristique de la théologie contemporaine et de ses orientations que la naissance ou la profonde rénovation de cette discipline.' Pierre Adnes, 1967, *La Théologie catholique*, Paris: Presses Universitaires de France, p. 106.

5 Jacques Audinet, 1976, *Les Déplacements de la théologie*, Paris: Beauchesne, p. 93.

6 Joseph Doré, 1991, *Introduction à l'étude de la théologie*, vol. III, Paris: Desclée, p. 521.

7 'Lieu carrefour de plusieurs types d'approches, rassemblement plus ou moins cohérent de domaines qui peuvent, à première vue, paraître très hétérogènes, la théologie pratique ne se laisse pas facilement définir. Mais peut-être le fait que la question reste ouverte contribue-t-il à l'intérêt de cette discipline encore (toujours ?) en recherche d'elle-même et donc en mouvement.' Isabelle Grellier, 1997, 'Les démarches de théologie pratique', in Bernard Kaempf

(ed.), *Introduction à la théologie pratique*, Strasbourg: Presses Universitaires de Strasbourg, pp. 42–3.

8 René Marlé, 1979, *Le Projet de théologie pratique*, Paris: Beauchesne.

9 'Histoire de la théologie pratique', in Kaempf 1997, p. 28. The same orientation has been developed by the Swiss Calvinist theologian P. Gisel: 'L'enseignement dit de "théologie pratique" ne saurait justement se contenter d'être la pure application d'une théorie élaborée par ailleurs. Non seulement un tel enseignement n'aurait en effet plus rien d'universitaire – il pourrait sans dommage et même avec profit être alors transféré au niveau des étages pratiques ultérieurs, dépendants d'autres "intérêts" et d'autres instances institutionnelles – mais, surtout, l'organon de la théologie comme telle s'en trouverait déséquilibré, j'entends: la constitution de la théologie comme discipline spécifique, faite de diverses approches intrinsèquement articulées. Dès lors, ce ne serait pas que la "pratique" qui serait affectée par une telle vision – ravalée qu'elle se verrait au rang subalterne d'application – mais, par contrecoup, la " théorie" se trouverait elle aussi gravement touchée, succombant notamment à l'illusion d'un discours dont la vérité tiendrait à sa seule cohérence propre, sans confrontation avec la réalité et sans attention accordée à l'histoire.' 'Pratique et théologie: Introduction', in S. Amsler, Kl. Blaser et al., *Pratique et théologie*, Geneva, Labor et Fides, 1977, p. 11.

10 Grellier 1997, p. 45.

11 Friedrich Schleiermacher, 1850, *Brief Outline of the Study of Theology*, Edinburgh: T&T Clark.

12 Kaempf 1997, p. 28.

13 In an unpublished note of 1998 written for the French section of the ECTA.

14 See on that point: J. Burkhart, 'Schleiermacher's Vision for Theology', in Don S. Browning (ed.), 1983, *Practical Theology*, San Francisco: Harper & Row.

15 S. Browning, *Practical Theology*, p. 57.

16 As written by Jean-François Zorn (see n. 13 above): 'Aujourd'hui nous ne pouvons plus nous contenter d'une telle définition de l'objet de la théologie pratique, même si, je dois le dire, nous continuons par la force de choses et le poids des traditions à travailler selon ces orientations'. He gives three reasons for this dissatisfaction: 'nous avons aujourd'hui une nouvelle perception des rapports entre la théorie et la pratique: Le réel résiste aux affirmations de la théorie. Aussi, plutôt que d'être un lieu d'application de théories, on . . . considère aujourd'hui le réel comme un lieu de vérification d'hypothèses. La méthode utilisé en théologie pratique ne sera plus la déduction mais la corrélation, c'est à dire la recherche d'articulations, dans un va et vient, de la théorie et de la pratique, sachant que la pratique informe tout autant la théorie que le contraire.'

17 In France the *Institut Supérieur de Pastorale Catéchétique* created in 1956 within the Institut Catholique de Paris was a place of great importance for the development of this new style of practical theology supported by Liégé, who was one of its pre-eminent professors with J. Audinet and R. Marlé quoted above.

18 Liégé 1971, p. 59.

19 Karl Rahner, 1970, 'Pastorale', in *Petit dictionnaire de théologie catholique*, Paris: Seuil.

20 For a general view on how theology can legitimately use human sciences see Louis-Marie Chauvet's chapter in this volume. See also Jean Joncheray, 1995, 'Comment peuvent travailler ensemble des sociologues, des théologiens, des pasteurs ?', *Revue des sciences religieuses* no. 3, pp. 322–33; and Jean Joncheray, 1993, 'Le rapport sciences humaines/théologie en théologie pratique', in Bernard Reymond et Jean-Pierre Sordet (eds), *La Théologie pratique: statut, méthodes, perspectives d'avenir*, Le point Théologique, 57, Paris: Beauchesne, pp. 61–74.

21 Grellier, 1997, p. 45.

22 Paul Keller, 1988, 'La pratique, un lieu pour la théologie', *Études Théologiques et Religieuses*, no. 3, p. 405.

23 Walter Kasper, 1990, *La Théologie et l'Église*, Paris: Cerf, pp. 10–15.

24 Kasper 1990, p. 13.

25 Kasper 1990, p. 22.

26 Kasper 1990, p. 15.

27 Kasper 1990, p. 22.

28 Henri Bouillard, 1972, 'La tâche actuelle de la théologie fondamentale', 1972, *Recherches Actuelles*, vol. II, Paris: Beauchesne.

29 Schubert M. Ogden, 1967, *The Reality of God*, London: SCM Press, p. 35.

30 Ogden 1967, p. 34.

31 Ogden 1967, p. 38.

32 Here, Bouillard refers to J. Ladriere, 1970, *L'Articulation du sens*, Paris: Cerf, pp. 238–41.

33 André Dartigues, 1996, 'L'histoire comme lieu théologique de la modernité. Effets de modernité dans la théologie des années soixante aux années quatre-vingt', in Pierre Gisel and Patrick Évrard (eds), *La Théologie en postmodernité. Actes du 3ᵉ cycle de théologie systématique des Facultés de théologie de Suisse romande*, Geneva: Labor et Fides, p. 121.

34 Gisel and Évrard, 1996, p. 42.

35 As Walter Kasper puts it, 1990, p. 18.

36 Within the Faculty of Theology and Religious Sciences of the Institut Catholique de Paris, both the Institut Supérieur de Liturgie, and the Institut Supérieur de Pastorale Catéchétique may be considered as good examples of such interdisciplinary spaces of research where the prospect for practical theology is put into practice. However, professors there do not use the designation 'practical theologians'.

Bibliography

Gilbert Adler, 1995, 'Théologie pratique et/ou pastorale', *Revue des Sciences Religieuses* no. 3 (July).

E. Arens (ed.), 1993, *Habermas et la théologie*, Paris: Cerf, pp. 103–22.

Jacques Audinet, 1992, 'La diversité pratique des théologies pratiques', in Joseph Doré (ed.), *Introduction à l'étude de la théologie*, vol. II, Paris: Desclée, pp. 521ff.

Jacques Audinet, 1995, *Ecrits de théologie pratique*, Montreal–Paris–Brussels–Geneva: Novalis–Le Cerf–Lumen Vitae–Labor et Fides.

Jacques Audinet and Henri Bouillard (eds), 1977, *Le Déplacement de la théologie*, Le Point Théologique, 21, Paris: Beauchesne.

Henri Bouillard, 1972, 'La tâche actuelle de la théologie fondamentale', in *Recherches Actuelles*, vol. II, Paris: Beauchesne.

Don S. Browning (ed.), 1983, *Practical Theology*, San Francisco: Harper & Row.

Georges Casalis, 1973, 'Théologie pratique et pratique de la théologie', in M. Carrez (ed.), *Orientations*, Le Point Théologique, 5, Paris: Beauchesne, pp. 85–105.

Marie-Dominique Chenu, 1957, *La théologie est-elle une science?* Paris: Fayard.

M. Despland, 1987, 'Passé ou futur de la théologie ? La signification de la *Kurze Darstellung* pour les tâches de la théologie aujourd'hui', *Laval théologique et philosophique* 43.2, pp. 141–53.

Joseph Doré, 1992a, 'Théologie et pratique pastorale', in *Introduction à l'étude de la théologie*, vol. II, Paris: Desclée, pp. 575 ff.

Joseph Doré, 1992b, 'La responsabilité et les tâches de la théologie', in *Introduction à l'étude de la théologie*, vol. II, Paris: Desclée, pp. 345–428.

Pierre-Luigi Dubied and Bernard Reymond (eds), 1994, 'La théologie pratique dans ces dernières décennies', *Foi et Vie* 93 (July), pp. 59–74.

Henri-Jérôme Gagey, 2002, 'La tâche clinique de la théologie', in François Bousquet and Henri-Jérôme Gagey (eds), *La Responsabilité des théologiens*, Paris: Desclée, pp. 357–66.

Pierre Gisel, 1989, 'Pratique et Theologie', in S. Amsler et al., *Pratique et Theologie*, Pratiques, 1, Geneva: Labor et Fides.

Pierre Gisel and Patrick Évrard (eds), 1996, *La Théologie en postmodernité: Actes du 3e cycle de théologie systématique des Facultés de théologie de Suisse romande*, Geneva: Labor et Fides.

Isabelle Grellier, 1997, 'Les démarches de théologie pratique', in Bernard Kaempf (ed.), *Introduction à la Théologie Pratique*, Strasbourg: Presses Universitaires de Strasbourg, pp. 41–57.

Jean Joncheray, 1993, 'Le rapport sciences humaines/théologie en théologie pratique', in Bernard Reymond and Jean-Pierre Sordet (eds), *La Théologie pratique: statut, méthodes, perspectives d'avenir*, Le Point Théologique, 57, Paris: Beauchesne, pp. 61–74.

Jean Joncheray, 1995, 'Comment peuvent travailler ensemble des sociologues, des théologiens, des pasteurs?', *Revue des sciences religieuses*, no. 3, p. 322–33.

Bernard Kaempf (ed.), 1997, *Introduction à la Théologie Pratique*, Strasbourg: Presses Universitaires de Strasbourg.

Walter Kasper, 1990, *La théologie et l'Église*, Paris: Cerf.

Paul Keller, 1988, 'La pratique, un lieu pour la théologie', *Études Théologiques et Religieuses* no. 3, pp. 403–14.

Georges W. Kowalski, 1991, 'La praxis comme lieu théologique', *Revue de l'Institut Catholique de Paris* no. 40 (October–December), pp. 168–80.

Bernard Lauret and François Refoulé (eds), 1987, *Initiation à la pratique de la théologie*, vol. V, *Pratique*, Paris: Cerf.

Henri de Lavalette, 1961, 'Réflexions sur la théologie pastorale', *Nouvelle Revue de Théologie* 83 (1961), pp. 593–604.

Pierre-André Liégé, 1971, 'Positions de la théologie pastorale: une théologie de la Praxis de l'Église', in *Recherches Actuelles*, vol. I, *Le Point Théologique*, 1, Paris: Beauchesne.

René Marlé, 1979, *Le Projet de théologie pratique*, Le Point Théologique, no. 32, Paris: Beauchesne .

René Marlé, 1982,'Théologie pratique et spirituelle', in Bernard Lauret and François Refoulé (eds), *Initiation à la pratique de la théologie*, vol. V, Paris: Cerf.

Félix Moser, 1995, 'Quelques repères pour arpenter le territoire de la théologie pratique', *Etudes théologiques et religieuses*, no. 1, pp. 47–59.

J. G. Nadeau (ed.), 1987, *La praxéologie pastorale*, 2 vols, Montreal: Fides.

Schubert M. Ogden, 1967, *The Reality of God*, London: SCM Press.

Bernard Reymond and Jean-Pierre Sordet, 1993, *La théologie Pratique: statut, méthodes, perspectives d'avenir*, Le Point Théologique, 57, Paris: Beauchesne (congrès international oecuménique et francophone de théologie pratique).

Marcel Viau, 1987, *Introduction aux études pastorales*, Montreal: Éd. Paulines.

Marcel Viau, 1993, *La Nouvelle théologie pratique*, Paris: Les Éditions du Cerf.

A. Visscher (ed.), 1990, *Les Études pastorales à l'Université: Perspectives, méthodes et praxis*, Ottawa: Presses de l'Université.

Jean-François Zorn, 2001, 'La théologie pratique, de la maison de ses pères à aujourd'hui', *Hokhma* 77, pp. 75–93.

6

Pastoral Theology or Practical Theology?
Limits and Possibilities

KATHLEEN A. CAHALAN

Catholic theologians and theological educators have often dismissed practical theology as a Protestant category not applicable to the Catholic setting, but there are many reasons why Catholics should join efforts in a renewed practical theology. Practical theologians today are examining what constitutes a Christian way of life in our time, and the negotiations entailed in embracing religious practice within diverse social, cultural and interreligious contexts. Furthermore, practical theology remains attentive to the study of the practices of ministry and their relationship to communities of practice. In terms of the former, Catholics have something to gain and contribute to the rich ecumenical conversation about Christian identity and practice. In terms of the latter, Catholic approaches to the teaching and study of ministry seem woefully inadequate to the challenges facing the Church and its ministers.

The most common way to place practical theology is as a discipline within Protestant theological education that has long been associated with areas of study related to the practice of ministry. In the Catholic lexicon, 'pastoral theology' is the name given to the curricular area pertaining to the practice of ministry. Catholics have been slow, and somewhat averse, to adopting practical theology in place of pastoral theology. But there are serious problems regarding pastoral theology that Catholics have been even slower to address: it has few identifying markers of a discipline; it has never gained much of an identity or status in Catholic theological education; it suffers from low regard and lack of doctoral trained faculty in full-time, tenured positions. But does adopting practical theology in place of pastoral theology solve a problem for Catholic theological education?

Practical theology needs to be considered anew in Catholic theological education, not for legitimacy in the academy, but because practical theology is a creative theological enterprise that is ambitiously exploring issues related to the lived Christian faith and the practice of ministry. Catholics can ill afford to endure the current limitations of pastoral theology if such a discipline is to give concerted attention to the practice of ministry. But Catholics may be suspicious. Is not all theology, in one way or another, 'pastoral' in terms of its concern for faith in the community and the world? Should we not turn our attention to reviving pastoral theology as a discipline? Before advancing why Catholics should seriously consider today's proposals for practical theology, I consider, in the first half of this chapter, the history and place of pastoral theology in Catholic theological education, and explore whether it can be revived or should be relinquished. I opt for the latter, and in the second half of the chapter I take up a proposal for considering practical theology in the Catholic context and how it might move beyond pastoral theology and its problematic legacy.

Pastoral Theology: Discourse, Field or Discipline?

As the study of spirituality gained legitimacy in the academy in the 1980s and 1990s it became necessary to define spirituality as an academic discipline. Sandra Schneiders, one of the early scholars in the area, argued that the discipline of spirituality could be distinguished from a discourse or a field about spirituality. A discourse is 'an ongoing conversation about a common interest' that includes professionals, specialists, teachers and practitioners of all sorts. Because discourse is widespread it 'risks becoming a catch all term for whatever anyone wants', as witnessed in the 'spirituality' section of major bookstores. A field pertains to 'an open space in which activities which have something in common take place'. A discipline, however, is distinct from either discourse or field, insofar as it pertains to 'teaching and learning, including research and writing, on subjects specified by the material and formal objects of Christian spirituality in the context of the academy' (Schneiders 2005, pp. 6–7).

Schneiders' distinctions are helpful in identifying how the category of 'pastoral theology' has been used in Catholic ecclesial and theological discourse since the Second Vatican Council. The Council was pivotal in claiming 'pastoral' as an ecclesial discourse pertaining to the Church's relationship to the world, most notably in *Gaudium et spes*, the only constitution given the title 'pastoral'. As the document notes, 'pastoral' means 'resting on doctrinal principles' that 'seeks to set forth the relation of the Church to the world and to the men of today' in order to address social issues and 'to enter into dialogue with it about all these different problems' (*Gaudium et spes*, no. 3). As one commentator notes, 'If there was one sentence repeated more often than any other at the Second Vatican Council it was: 'This council is pastoral in its scope, objectives, and aims' (Fearns 1968, p. 36). Certainly, *Gaudium et spes* meant to broaden the idea of 'pastoral' beyond its traditional association with ordained ministers to embrace the way in which the whole Church witnesses and transforms the world. All theology was charged with becoming more open and directed to social and cultural realities, more *pastoral*, rather than closed within traditional scholastic categories. For example, theologians defined pastoral theology as a 'self conscious perspective on the contemporary life of the Church and the living out of Christian faith in today's world' (Imbelli and Groome 1992, pp. 133–4).

Pastoral theology is also a *field* pertaining to the teaching and practice of pastoral ministry. In theological education, pastoral theology is a field that includes pastoral ministers as well as theologians, bishops and episcopal conferences, all who write and speak about issues of faith and ministry. For instance, a good deal of pastoral literature is generated outside the academy by the Vatican and bishops' conferences, such as the United States Catholic Conference of Bishops. Since 1971 the National Catholic News Service in the USA has published *Origins*, which includes official statements, speeches and documents pertaining to the Church and ministry. Since the Council an explosion of information in all areas of ministry has taken place, including the development of professional organizations, conferences, journals and continuing education for ministers.[1] In this sense, professional, educational and ecclesial activity exists within a field of activity and thought related to ministry, mutually influencing thought and practice.

But pastoral theology in theological education is not without its problems. According to Peter Phan (1994, pp. 5–6), 'It is common knowledge that the nature and task of pastoral theology is highly controverted.' The category has at least four meanings, often creating confusion about its purpose and scope. It refers, first, to the 'theoretical and practical training of the clergy' especially in regard to their 'shepherding' or 'pastoring' role in relationship to the local community, a position advocated by the Protestant theologian Steward Hiltner in the 1950s (1958, pp. 15–23). Second, it is commonly used in reference to pastoral care, particularly clinical pastoral education methods of training and supervising student chaplains, which is the primary way

Protestants use the term. Pastoral theology is also associated with that which pertains to 'practical disciplines of theology' such as ascetical and spiritual theology, in contrast to historical and dogmatic theology, traditionally the 'speculative branches' of theology. Finally, pastoral theology is associated with the widely accepted method and process of theological reflection in ministry education as it relates to human experience, advocated by Patricia Killen (1994) and Robert Kinast (1996).

Pastoral theology in terms of ministry education, then, is a very large field. Training for pastoral ministry has expanded beyond Catholic seminaries to include colleges, universities and dioceses.[2] Of course, religious women and men had been seeking ministry training prior to the Council, but in the post-conciliar era many schools began adding faculty, courses and degree programmes that emphasize one or more of these four areas of pastoral training. The expanding forms of ministry training, as well as the specialization and professionalization of areas of ministry, was certainly unforeseen in the wake of the Council, and yet these changes mark one of the most significant developments in post-conciliar theological education. It is easy to conclude from a brief glance at the past 40 years that the *field* of pastoral theology is everywhere.

The third category, the discipline of pastoral theology, is more difficult to identify. It can be located in its parts but not as a whole. In other words, the sub-disciplines of liturgy, religious education, pastoral care or homiletics each operate independently from any common connection to a discipline called pastoral theology. And this level of specialization, which Edward Farley (1995, p. 133) claims is the 'most powerful structure at work in faculty life', operates independently of any overarching discipline. Specialization determines faculty identity and loyalty to such a strong degree that faculty can be suspicious of the academic content and rigour of other disciplines. In fact, pastoral theology has never actually existed as a discipline, and is a quite recent addition to seminary curricula.[3] It functions, not as a discipline, but as a way to describe courses in the curriculum that pertain to ministry, merely a course catalogue heading.

Despite the Council's vision of the pastoral stance of the Church toward the world and the expansion of areas of pastoral ministry in theological education, pastoral theology as a theological discipline can be found nowhere. There are no academic journals for pastoral theology, no professional organizations, and no graduate programmes for a doctorate in pastoral theology; few theologians would identify their 'teaching, research and writing' in the discipline of pastoral theology. In a study of Catholic theological education, Katarina Schuth points out that pastoral studies is 'subdivided into distinct areas of study and in many cases employs part time faculty engaged in the ministry associated with their particular discipline. Perhaps for that reason, pastoral studies are emphasized less than Scripture, systematic, moral or sacramental theology'. Overall, Schuth has found wide variance in seminary courses in pastoral studies: 'canon law and homiletics have uniformly moderate requirements, pastoral care and counseling has uniformly minimal requirements, and religious education has the least requirements'. Of all the curricular areas, ministry has the 'most varied requirements, ranging from no credits to as many as fourteen, and including courses as disparate as the practice of collaborative ministry, social analysis, ministry to families, leadership in parish settings, and ministry to the multicultural community . . . In almost all theologates, pastoral field education . . . carries the burden of providing the knowledge and skills necessary for ministerial service' (Schuth 1999, p. 187).

One dimension of disciplinary status is certainly missing. Catholic universities have not developed doctorate programmes in pastoral theology. Again, doctorates can be obtained in spirituality, liturgy or religious education, but not in pastoral theology. If graduate students seeking doctoral training wanted to become pastoral theologians, would they be encouraged to consider such a career? They would most likely select an area within pastoral theology, or opt to attend one of the new programmes in practical theology at Protestant theological schools.

Schuth (1989, p. 171) reports a perception of a regrettable 'erosion of the academic' due to the increase in pastoral studies courses. The attitude that pastoral theology has weakened the academic integrity of theology arises from the sense that pastoral theology is 'not academic', which usually translates as interpersonal and process-oriented, in opposition to the rigorous, scientific or theoretical. The view is due in part to the perception that pastoral theology contains little theological substance itself, but instead is an application of the ideas established in other areas. Pastoral theology has come to be, according to Imbelli and Groome (1992, p. 129) an 'administrative convenience' and a 'delivery system for the more prestigious theology'. They point out that pastoral theology is deemed less demanding, rigorous and serious, 'relegated to part time personnel teaching at odd hours, consisted of various courses that lacked clear cogent integrated vision. One consequence was that the substantive fields were let off the hook from pastoral questions and could maintain an objective stance in relation to contemporary concerns. Catholic theological educators have been slow to give up the notion that theology is essentially a theory-to-practice enterprise, but it seems that a diminished notion of the practical persists today. Given the situation, are attempts to make pastoral theology into a viable discipline remote? Can 'pastoral theology' convey the current hope to improve and strengthen 'teaching and learning, research and writing', about ministry?

One disadvantage to 'pastoral' is its root 'pastor', not because a pastor's work is unworthy of study, but because it portrays the field too narrowly. In the past, pastoral theology attended to the tasks of the ordained pastor, but today most ministers are not pastors and function in diverse ecclesial settings and ministries; 'pastor' only captures one role in the entire spectrum of ministry. Furthermore 'pastor' has strong connotations with male ministers, and in the USA today, of all people engaged in Catholic ministry, the majority are women. Another disadvantage is that 'pastoral' is limiting insofar as it pertains to the shepherding function of the pastor, which is one aspect of ministry. Several European Protestant theologians argue for retaining pastoral theology: Heitink (1993, pp. 310ff.) advocates pastoral theology as part of practical theology that would focus on the professional training for pastors, and Elaine Graham also favours 'pastoral theology' over 'practical theology' (2002, pp. 11–12).

But in the USA it is obvious that pastoral theology is at the same time everywhere and nowhere. Because of its widespread use as discourse and field, is there merit in creating a discipline? Are the widespread perceptions about pastoral theology in fact true? Is one reason that pastoral theology has such low status in theological education precisely because it never became a discipline and did not develop standards of research and performance commonly adjudicated through academic journals and professional societies? What would it take to strengthen the 'teaching and learning, research and writing' about the practice of faith and ministry into a disciplined search for knowledge that is informed by practice for the sake of practice?

Can Catholics Claim Practical Theology?

An interesting proposal for Catholic pastoral and practical theology was put forth in the 1960s by Karl Rahner and Heinz Schuster, who proposed that pastoral theology should attend to the contemporary realities of the Church as it is in the present moment living into the future. In their view pastoral theology was a young discipline that was conceived to 'fill a gap in clerical training' but was not intended to make a contribution to theology as a whole (Schuster 1965, p. 6). And that view of pastoral theology, according to Rahner and Schuster, was too narrow given the realities of the post-conciliar Church.

Similar to the Protestant proposals for practical theology in the 1980s, these two Catholic theologians advanced a much more *practical* and *action-oriented* theology. For Rahner and Schuster, pastoral theology attends to the 'action of the Church' in the concrete existential conditions of the 'here and now' (Rahner 1968, p. 25). Pastoral theology should be an 'existential ecclesiology' that examines 'precisely and comprehensively exactly what should become "present" in today's Church'. They acknowledge both the existential and historical as starting-points of pastoral theology, in order to overcome the traditional biases in Catholic theology focused on ontological and ahistorical understandings of the human person and the Church.

What do the authors mean by the 'action' of the Church? Pastoral theology can no longer pertain *solely* to the practices of ministry as carried out by clergy, though that is one of its areas of concern. Influenced by the understanding of 'pastoral' in *Gaudium et spes*, pastoral theology examines how the Church, understood as the whole people of God, carries out its mission in concrete historical local communities. Pastoral theology should address four areas of church 'action': (a) the functions and positions of all members the Church as they 'co-operate in the Church's fulfilment'; (b) all the activities that the Church engages in to fulfil its mission, including activities of the clergy such as preaching, liturgy and worship, the sacraments, but also 'the Christian life of the individual faithful' and the 'practice of Christian love'; (c) the 'communal and sociological aspects' of the Church; and d) all the 'formal' means by which the fulfilment of the Church's life and mission are achieved, including 'piety, sexes, moral theory and practice, provision, and administration' (Schuster 1965, p. 10).

Pastoral theology is not to be confused with the Church's action; rather it is the determination theologically of the Church's 'principles and prescriptions for the Church's present action'. In that sense pastoral theology is 'theological' and 'theoretical'. It is a 'precondition' to church law, and it is contingent, since it identifies plans and strategies that are finally submitted to the 'hidden providence of God'. Rahner and Schuster identified a gap between the ideal, essential systems defined by ecclesiology and systematic theology and the actual way in which the Church lives out its essence, 'its beginning' in the concrete realities of history and existence.

A few years later, Schuster argued against using 'pastoral theology' as the new approach, and opted for 'practical theology' because it 'provides a basis for a scientifically responsible self awareness of the Church as she has to act here and now'. Practical theology 'can work out principles and decisions for the contemporary fulfilment of the Church', which in his estimation is not 'yet the pastoral concern and activity of the Church proper' (Schuster 1965, p. 13).

Interestingly, Rahner and Schuster argued for a *pastoral* and *practical* theology that never came to be in Catholic theology. But their proposal is not radically different from the way practical theologians today are conceiving of practical theology in relation to both the lived Christian faith and the practice of ministry.

A Proposal for Practical Theology

One of Rahner's and Schuster's key insights that is relevant to practical theology today is the claim that the Church and its faith cannot be explained solely through the formal categories of systematic theology, but are also living realities that are expressed and embodied in a variety of particular circumstances and influenced by a range of historical and contextual factors. Practical theologians, with the aid of historians and social scientists, seek to understand faith as it is actually lived and how it becomes a way of life for people of faith in a given context. It is also normative insofar as the description of particular aspects of lived faith are evaluated for inadequacies, distortions and missing features, and constructive proposals are advanced to enable fuller, more 'abundant ways of life' fitting to the situation.

In a recent essay, 'Mapping the Field of Practical Theology,' James Nieman and I define six features of the field and discipline of practical theology (Cahalan and Nieman 2008, p. 66). As a field we view practical theology as a creative and interdisciplinary exchange among practitioners and scholars interested in exploring issues related to the practice of religious faith, community building and leadership; some scholars within the field will also have a serious commitment to tending the issues related to practical theology as a discipline. We claim that:

- Practical theology engages Christian ways of life and therefore takes as its basic task the promotion of faithful *discipleship*.
- Practical theology offers leadership for such discipleship by giving sustained attention to various forms of *ministry*.

- Practical theology brings wisdom to the formation of ministers and the study of ministry in its approach to *teaching*.
- Practical theology as a discipline involves the relationship between several distinctive domains of *research*.
- Practical theology focuses in every instance especially upon the *current events* and the *concrete settings* that must be faithfully encountered.
- Practical theology employs that focus in order to *discern* existing situations of life and *propose* eventual directions for action.

Our definition highlights several distinctive points. First, it acknowledges that practical theologians attend both to the lived faith of Christians in the Church and the world and to the leaders, or ministers, of Christian communities. Both realms of Christian life and practice are part of the field of practical theology, though certainly not all practical theologians attend to both. Second, practical theologians will teach in a variety of contexts, some teaching undergraduate students in colleges and universities, and some teaching in particular areas of ministry in seminaries and graduate theological schools. Third, within the broad field of practical theology, some will attend to the theoretical and scholarly aspects of the discipline, working out definitions, and intersections with other disciplines, and pursuing research and publication. Fourth, regardless of context or focus, practical theologians share a common commitment to understanding the contemporary facets of Christian and ministerial practice, and strive to be constructive and strategic as they serve Christian communities as well as the academy.

Practical theologians, then, share a common focus and task, not merely a method or starting-point. Practical theologians attend to the immediate realities of the Christian life as it is being lived in particular social and historical contexts and examine the normative claims of how to live more faithfully in the near and distant future. Practical theologians study what is and what is coming to be in order to articulate a theological understanding of how the Christian community, individually and as an ecclesial body, lives and can live more faithfully. Practical theologians pay close attention to the particular, local, contextual, existential, actual, and specific dimensions of lived Christian faith. Attending closely to any one aspect of discipleship means that practical theologians are especially attentive to culture and context, not as something added to the dynamics of faith, but as constitutive of discipleship.

Rather than arguing for Catholics to create an entirely separate discipline of practical theology or a Catholic practical theology it may be enough for Catholics to acknowledge that the field and discipline already exist and encourage more colleagues to join its efforts.[4] Within that larger effort, of course, Catholic practical theologians will take up particular issues and questions pertinent to the Catholic community. But what might be gained by such a move? How would practical theology in fact aid Catholic theological educators in strengthening the 'teaching and learning, research and writing' about ministry?

Practical theology offers at least three important insights that are currently underdeveloped in Catholic ministry education. First, practical theology brings resources about the nature of practice to its understanding of ministry as a practice. Second, practical theologians are identifying the distinctive qualities of teaching a practice, in this case, teaching a practice of ministry. Third, scholarship related to the practice of ministry, as well as to congregational life and dynamics, needs far greater attention.

First, how do Catholics understand ministry as a practice? Catholics have given considerable attention to a theology of the *minister*, but scant attention to a theology of *ministry* (McBrien 1987, pp. 11–14; O'Meara 1999, p. 141; Cahalan 2006, p. 120). Historically, Catholics understood ministry in relationship to a theology of priesthood, the sacrament of ordination, and the sacramental character, often referred to as 'substance ontology'. Practice did not receive much attention in this perspective, primarily because the intention was to define the sacrament in terms of the ontological change that brought about a new relationship to Christ and empowered the priest for sacramental ministry.

Much discussion about the identity of priesthood and the meaning of the sacrament of ordination has pointed to the inadequacies of the substance ontology approach. Today ecclesiologists and sacramental theologians focus on a relational ontology: how the sacraments of baptism and ordination place a person into a new ecclesial relationship. Through a process of 'ecclesial repositioning' ministers stand in relationship to the community in a new way. The theology of ordered communion takes account of the diversity of ministers serving the Catholic community (for example, ordained ministers, including bishops, presbyters and deacons, and lay ecclesial ministers who are either installed or commissioned ministers). Susan Wood, Richard Gaillardetz and Edward Hahnenberg argue that rites of ordination, commissioning and installation reposition the baptized believer in relationship to the community as minister. The concept of 'ordered ministries' is a way both to explain the unifying basis for all ministry and of acknowledging a variety of ministries and ministers (Gaillerdetz 2003, pp. 31–5;

Wood 2003, pp. 259–63; Hahnenberg 2003, pp. 176–84). The ideas of relational ontology and a theology of ordered communion have been important in advancing an understanding of the identity and place of the minister as existing in a new set of relationships in the community and with Christ. However, as helpful as this theological work has been, it continues the long-standing Catholic interest in a theology of the minister without corresponding attention to ministry as a practice.

Catholic theologians are generally averse to 'functional' understandings of ministry. Numerous examples of this sentiment abound. Susan Wood (2000, p. 119) writes:

> If a presbyter is identified by what he does, this identity is potentially threatened with the change of activity. More profoundly, however, these functions or ministries become an extension of the general ministry of the congregation, a phenomenon known as congregationalism. In congregationalism ritual forms are regarded as the product, creation and property of the congregation and lack their own symbolic density, authority, and objectivity. There is no essential difference between a lay and an ordained minister. They are merely differentiated by what they do rather than what they are. Since what the presbyter does is becoming more and more interchangeable with what the lay people do, this results in an identity crisis for the ordained minister.

In relationship to the diaconate, William Ditewig says (2007, p. 23):

> In our Catholic understanding of sacramental theology, we have come to understand that ordination to the priesthood has a sacramental meaning that goes beyond the specific function of the priest. As a result of ordination, we realize that there is more to 'being' a priest than simply 'doing' priestly things. Similarly, then, ordination to the diaconate involves more than simply doing the 'functions' of the deacon. We can begin to see that there is more to 'being' a deacon than simply 'doing' diaconal things.

Many claim that the ordained minister cannot be defined by what he does but only by his sacramental identity. Because priests, deacons and lay ministers do many of the same things, defining them by 'function' confuses 'identity'. Furthermore, if a minister is defined by what he or she does, how do we understand their identity when they are not 'doing' ministry? Unfortunately, the 'being' of the minister continues to be defined over against the practice of ministry, which is conceived through an impoverished notion of 'doing' and 'function'. Such a dichotomy has helped neither the identity *nor* the practice of ministers, and it certainly has not contributed to theological education for ministry. Without an adequate way of understanding the relationship between ontology and function, being and doing, and identity and practice, Catholic understandings of the minister will remain divorced from a well grounded theology of ministry as practice.

Ministry, as Thomas O'Meara has claimed, is a verb, it is an intentional action and activity. As I have argued, ministry is not just any action or act by a minister, but is best understood as action in relationship to six fundamental practices: teaching, preaching, presiding at worship and prayer, pastoral care, social and prophetic service, and administration. Because each practice has a biblical, Christological, pneumatological and ecclesial basis, they are not merely functions. They are enduring practices of the tradition of ministry: practised in all times and places where Christian communities have gathered. None of these is an action or a function that can be considered after the identity of the minister is determined. Rather as practices, they are embodied forms of expression and ways of knowing, communal and social forms of engagement that have a history and bear the tradition; they are intentional actions engaged to shape disciples and communities for faith and witness. As practice, they are integral to the formation of identity: in other words, the identity of ministers is not something that happens prior to their practice, but in and through their practice.

When ministry is viewed as a practice, the question of how to teach a practice becomes central for theological educators. Recently, practical theologians have given greater attention to what is distinctive about teaching in the practical fields and what it means to teach a practice (Miller-McLemore 2008, pp. 172–4). In teaching students to preach or to offer pastoral care, practical theologians must teach a body of knowledge about the practice (its history, theology and theory), but they also must teach certain competencies and virtues in order that 'students see how that knowledge, competency and virtue is carried out and enacted, how it is "performed"' (Witvliet 2008, pp. 140–3). The kind of teaching practical theologians aim for is one that promotes a way of knowing as a form of 'phronesis', or pastoral wisdom, that helps students become not just competent but wise practitioners who are able to develop a 'pastoral perception' and 'pastoral imagination'.

These are clearly not where students begin, so teaching a practice must have a beginning phase, a time when basic skills are practised again and again, much as a musician or a nurse learns scales and procedures. As with any practice, there are phases of learning that require appropriate pedagogy for the beginner, the advanced beginner, the competent and the expert minister. The seminary or graduate school is one educator on an entire spectrum of formation and education: students come already formed in the practices of faith and ministry and they will continue to learn in the practice of ministry post-graduation and ordination (Scharen 2008). Teaching for ministry, then, demands highly competent teacher scholars, who bring an expertise in practising a practice as well as studying and researching a practice. As Bonnie Miller-McLemore notes, by being a teacher of practices, the practical theologian is 'implicated' in the classroom: the teacher cannot just teach about the subject matter, but their own practice is revealed to students and mirrored back to them: we teach teaching by teaching, we teach preaching by the way we preach, and we teach something about care in the way we relate with students (2008, p. 173). As noted in the first half of the chapter, Catholic pastoral theology has not provided a disciplined body of knowledge about the practice of ministry or high standards for what teaching and scholarship in relationship to ministry mean.

Finally, research and scholarship about the practice and the context of ministry has grown significantly in the past few years. Such research includes historical studies, contextual analyses, with particular attention to questions about congregational life, vitality, mission and leadership. Catholics do not lack sociological descriptions of our situation, including important studies of priests and lay ecclesial ministers (Dolan 2002; Steinfels 2003; D'Antonio 2007; Schuth 2006). But we have been slower to develop the analyses of how ministry is being practised today and practical theological resources for ministers to respond to the situation so thoroughly described to us by sociologists: How is ministry carried out in a clustered parish? What are ministers doing about the declining rate of Catholic attendance in the liturgy? What are the most effective methods of catechesis in the post-denominational reality Catholics are quickly facing? And so on. Practical theology pursues research in a collaborative way: the questions practical theologians pursue cannot be answered without insight and conversation with ministers and other researchers. At present, Catholics lack a critical mass of theologians pursuing this approach to the study and research of the practice of ministry.

What needs to happen to make practical theology a disciplined form of theology that attracts more Catholics from seminaries, theological schools and departments of theology? Perhaps we can learn a lesson from scholars in the field of spirituality. About 15 years ago a community of scholars at professional meetings began a conversation about spirituality (though in the beginning there was not agreement about the term or subject matter) and began producing a publication out of their conversation. The group became the Society for the Study of Christian Spirituality (1992) and their publication, the *Christian Spirituality Bulletin* (1993). Scholars interested in spirituality found that the term had multiple and diffuse meanings, especially in the broader culture where 'spiritual' was being attached to every book title and popular fad. Interest in spirituality also faced a prejudice in the academy as being 'naïve and intellectually shallow' (Burton-Christie 2005, p. xxi).

Its emergence as a respectable discipline seems to be related to several key moves: scholars from a variety of disciplines and traditions became interested in a similar set of phenomena; they met to discuss their ideas and through a journal 'devoted to critical reflection on an entire range of texts, traditions, and questions' were able to foster a 'common discourse'; through this discourse a 'range of questions that belonged within the discourse of spirituality and the distinctive methods and approaches' to answer those questions began to meet with consensus. No one could have imagined 15 years ago that today spirituality would be viewed as an important academic area that no curriculum, Catholic or Protestant, would lack and that now features several doctoral programmes at prominent institutions.

Practical theology exists as an ecumenical interdisciplinary field of enquiry that needs more Catholic involvement and that Catholics might, surprisingly, find quite interesting. For example, 25 of the 400 members in the Association of Practical Theology are Catholic. In the International Academy of Practical Theology, about one-fourth of the members are Catholic. Likewise, rigorous Catholic scholarly attention needs to be advanced in practical theology and held to the standards of excellence through common avenues of discourse and judgement. This may be the way in which doctoral studies, particularly in areas related to ministry, might be challenged to expand and improve. Why wouldn't Catholics embrace a practical theology that studies communities of Christian discipleship and ministry in order to advance our efforts in 'teaching and learning, research and writing in the academy' in such an important area of faith and theology?

Notes

1 Academic disciplines have risen in relation to each area of ministry, so that catechesis, liturgy, pastoral care and preaching each constitute a respectable discipline.

2 The Center for Applied Research in the Apostolate in the USA studies Catholic ministry formation programmes that prepare men and women for ministry as priests and deacons and in lay ecclesial ministry.

3 Did pastoral theology exist prior to the Second Vatican Council? Prior to the 1960s Catholic theology operated primarily (though not exclusively) within seminary education, whose sole purpose was the education of priests. The duties of the priest were taught as an aspect of moral theology since the purpose of moral theology was to guide priests in their sacramental ministry, particularly as confessors in the sacrament of penance. Moral theology, in addition to canon law, offered priests a way of thinking pastorally about concrete situations in believers' lives. After the Council, moral theology retained its pastoral focus in the seminary, though there was a decided shift away from the neo-Thomist manualists' approach. Outside the seminary, moral theology advanced in the academy in a non-pastoral direction, taking up social questions of bio-ethics, population, and sexual ethics.

4 I think it is best to claim that there are Catholic approaches to issues in practical theology, but not a 'Catholic practical theology'. One reason is that any attempt to define a Catholic practical theology is necessarily dependent on the tradition of practical theology, which is largely Protestant. It is more fruitful for Catholics to join with Protestant colleagues in discussions about the nature of practical theology, bringing resources from the Catholic tradition to that conversation, and taking up questions pertaining to the Catholic community as practical theologians. This was borne out several years ago when members of the Practical Theology Group of the Catholic Theological Society of America took up the question of Catholic practical theology. Ray Webb (2006, p. 107) defined practical theology as the 'theological discipline distinctive for its engagement of specific life situations with the Tradition'. He proposed a framework for Catholic practical theology that would be (1) immersed in Catholic theology, (2) theoretical and scientific, (3) practical, and (4) full of challenge and opportunity. Webb's description of practical theology is largely informed by Don Browning's approach, and in fact he is identifying distinctive Catholic resources in doing practical theology in a Catholic context. Robert Schreiter (2003) also defined a Catholic approach to practical theology that includes four areas: (1) interaction with culture; (2) the place of the Church in practical theology; (3) theological presuppositions behind the doing of practical theology (incarnation, nature and grace, and analogical imagination); and (4) concepts of universality. In essence, both Webb and Schreiter described Catholic approaches to practical theology but not a distinctively Catholic practical theology.

Bibliography

Dorothy C. Bass (ed.), 1997, *Practicing our Faith*, San Francisco: Jossey-Bass.

Tom Beaudoin, 2003, *Consuming Faith: Integrating Who We Are with What We Buy*, Lanham, ML: Sheed & Ward.

Don S. Browning, 1983, *Practical Theology: The Emerging Field in Theology, Church, and World*, San Francisco: Harper & Row.

Douglas Burton-Christie, 2005, 'Introduction: Beginnings', in Elizabeth A. Dreyer and Mark S. Burrows (eds), *Minding the Spirit: The Study of Christian Spirituality*, Baltimore, ML: Johns Hopkins University Press, pp. xxi–xxiii

Kathleen A. Cahalan, 2004, 'Married in Ministry: Theological and Spiritual Considerations', *New Theology Review* 17/3 (August), pp. 61–71.

Kathleen A. Cahalan, 2006, 'Toward a Fundamental Theology of Ministry', *Worship* 80/2 (March), pp. 102–20.

Kathleen A. Cahalan and James R. Nieman, 2008, 'Mapping the Field of Practical Theology', in Dorothy C. Bass and Craig Dykstra (eds), *For Life Abundant: Practical Theology and the Education and Formation of Ministers*, Grand Rapids, MI: Eerdmans, pp. 62–85.

William V. D'Antonio, 2007, *American Catholics Today: New Realities of Their Faith and Their Church*, New York: Rowan & Littlefield.

William T. Ditewig, 2007, *The Emerging Diaconate: Servant Leaders in a Servant Church*, New York: Paulist Press.

Jay P. Dolan, 2002, *In Search of an American Catholicism: A History of Religion and Culture in Tension*, New York: Oxford University Press.

Michael Downey, 2003, 'Ministerial Identity: A Question of Common Foundations', in Susan K. Wood (ed.), *Ordering Baptismal Priesthood*, Collegeville, MN: Liturgical Press, pp. 3–25.

Craig Dykstra and Dorothy C. Bass, 2002, 'A Theological Understanding of Christian Practices,' in Miroslav Volf and Dorothy C. Bass (eds), *Practicing Theology: Beliefs and Practices in Christian Life*, Grand Rapids, MI: Eerdmans, pp. 13–32.

Edward Farley, 1995, 'Why Seminaries Don't Change: A Reflection on Faculty Specialization', *Christian Century* 114 (5 February), pp. 133–43.

John M. Fearns, 1968, 'Pastoral Formation and Seminary Training', *NCEA Bulletin* (August).

Austin Flannery (ed.), 1987, *Vatican Council II: The Conciliar and Post Conciliar Documents*, New York: Costello.

Richard R. Gaillardetz, 2003, 'The Ecclesiological Foundations of Ministry within an Ordered Communion', in Susan K. Wood (ed.), *Ordering Baptismal Priesthood*, Collegeville, MN: Liturgical Press, pp. 26–52.

Mary L. Gautier, 2006, *Catholic Ministry Formation Enrollments: Statistical Overview for 2005–2006*, Washington, DC: Center for Applied Research in the Apostolate.

Elaine L. Graham, 2002, *Transforming Practice: Pastoral Theology in an Age of Uncertainty*, Eugene, OR: Wipf & Stock.

Edward P. Hahnenberg, 2002, 'Hard to Find: Searching for Practical Faculty in the 1990s', *Auburn Center Background Report* 8 (January), pp. 3–7.

Edward P. Hahnenberg, 2003, *Ministries: A Relational Approach*, New York: Crossroad.

Gerben Heitink, 1993, *Practical Theology: History, Theory, Action Domains*, Grand Rapids, MI: Eerdmans.

Steward Hiltner, 1958, *Preface to Pastoral Theology*, New York: Abingdon Press.

Robert P. Imbelli and Thomas H. Groome, 1992, 'Signposts Toward a Pastoral Theology', *Theological Studies* 53, pp. 127–37.

Patricia O'Connell Killen and John de Beer, 1994, *The Art of Theological Reflection*, New York: Crossroad.

Robert Kinast, 1996, *Let Ministry Teach: A Guide to Theological Reflection*, Collegeville, MN: Liturgical Press.

Richard P. McBrien, 1987, *Ministry: A Theological, Pastoral Handbook*, San Francisco: Harper & Row.

Bernard L. Marthaler, 1976, 'A Discipline in Quest of an Identity: Religious Education', *Horizons* 3/2, pp. 203–15.

Bonnie J. Miller-McLemore, 2008, 'Practical Theology and Pedagogy: Embodying Theological Know-How', in Dorothy C. Bass and Craig Dykstra (eds), *For Life Abundant: Practical Theology and the Education and Formation of Ministers*, Grand Rapids, MI: Eerdmans, pp. 170–90.

Earl C. Muller, 1997, 'Afterword', in Patrick W. Carey and Earl C. Muller (eds), *Theological Education in the Catholic Tradition: Contemporary Challenges*, New York: Crossroad.

National Catholic Education Association, 1992, *The Recruitment and Retention of Faculty in Roman Catholic Theological Seminaries*, Washington, DC: NCEA.

Thomas F. O'Meara, 1999, *A Theology of Ministry*, 2nd edn, Mahwah, NJ: Paulist Press.

Peter Phan, 1994, 'Karl Rahner as Pastoral Theologian', *Living Light* 30 (Summer), pp. 3–12.

Karl Rahner, 1968, *Theology of Pastoral Action*, New York: Herder & Herder.

Howland Sanks, 1984, 'Education for Ministry Since Vatican II', *Theological Studies* 45, pp. 481–500.

Christian Scharen, 2006, *One Step Closer: Why U2 Matters to Those Seeking God*, Grand Rapids, MI: Brazos Press.

Christian Scharen, 2008, 'Learning Ministry Over Time: Embodying Practical Wisdom', in Dorothy C. Bass and Craig Dykstra (eds), *For Life Abundant: Practical Theology and the Education and Formation of Ministers*, Grand Rapids, MI: Eerdmans, pp. 265–88.

Sandra M. Schneiders, 2005, 'The Study of Christian Spirituality: Contours and Dynamics of a Discipline', in Elizabeth A. Dreyer and Mark S. Burrows (eds), *Minding the Spirit: The Study of Christian Spirituality*, Baltimore, ML: Johns Hopkins University Press, pp. 3–21.

Robert Schreiter, 2003, 'Catholic Practical Theology: A Contextual Approach', unpublished paper, Catholic Theological Society of America.

Heinz Schuster, 1965, 'The Nature and Function of Pastoral Theology', in *The Pastoral Mission of the Church*, vol. III, Glen Rock, NJ: Paulist Press.

Katarina Schuth, 1989, *Reason for the Hope: The Future of Roman Catholic*

Theologates, Wilmington, DE: Michael Glazier.

Katarina Schuth, 1997, 'Theological Faculty and Programs in Seminaries', in Patrick W. Carey and Earl C. Muller (eds), *Theological Education in the Catholic Tradition: Contemporary Challenges*, New York: Crossroad.

Katarina Schuth, 1999, *Seminaries, Theologates, and the Future of Church Ministry*, Collegeville, MN: Liturgical Press.

Katarina Schuth, 2006, *Priestly Ministry in Multiple Parishes*, Collegeville, MN: Liturgical Press.

Peter Steinfels, 2003, *A People Adrift: The Crisis of the Roman Catholic Church in America*, New York: Simon & Schuster.

Terrence W. Tilley, 2001, *Inventing Catholic Tradition*, Maryknoll, NY: Orbis Books.

Raymond J. Webb, 2006, 'The Development of a Catholic Practical Theology', *Chicago Studies* 45/1 (Spring), pp. 105–17.

Barbara G. Wheeler, Sharon L. Miller and Katarina Schuth, 2005, 'Signs of the Times: Present and Future Theological Faculty', *Auburn Studies* 10 (February).

John D. Witvliet, 2008, 'Teaching Worship as a Christian Practice', in Dorothy C. Bass and Craig Dykstra (eds), *For Life Abundant: Practical Theology and the Education and Formation of Ministers*, Grand Rapids, MI: Eerdmans, pp. 117–48.

David Wood, 2008, 'Transition into Ministry: Reconceiving the Boundaries between Seminaries and Congregations', in Dorothy C. Bass and Craig Dykstra (eds), *For Life Abundant: Practical Theology and the Education and Formation of Ministers*, Grand Rapids, MI: Eerdmans, pp. 290–304.

Susan K. Wood, 2000, *Sacramental Orders*, Collegeville, MN: Liturgical Press.

Susan K. Wood, 2003, 'Conclusion: Convergence Points toward a Theology of Ordered Ministries', in Susan K. Wood (ed.), *Ordering the Baptismal Priesthood*, Collegeville, MN: Liturgical Press, pp. 256–65.

7

Ecclesiology and Practical Theology

NICHOLAS M. HEALY

In order to discuss the relation between ecclesiology and practical theology, it will be useful to consider them as part of what seems to be a more general turn to the concrete in theological enquiry that began in its present form about three or four decades ago. During the intervening time, theologians of diverse perspectives – liberationist, feminist, political, moral, pastoral and practical, even doctrinal – have argued in various ways that theology, especially since the Enlightenment, has been too focused on doctrine in abstraction from experience, practice and the particular. Christianity is not properly understood as a set of beliefs, a system of doctrine or a religious theory about the way things are. It is, rather, a way of life experienced concretely in and through one's beliefs, practices and attitudes as these are formed by one's church, one's social, cultural and political situation, and personal history. Experience is always contextual, and the context particular, so Christianity can be adequately understood only if one gives an account of its local, concrete forms to complement broader, more generalizing descriptions.

The turn to the concrete has encouraged the use of critical disciplines in theological enquiry – not only history, but also social-scientific accounts of the lived experiences of Christian communities within their various contexts. Thus the field of practical theology draws from many sources: social psychology, organizational and network theories, phenomenology, leadership and educational theories and much more, in order to develop rich, critically informed descriptions of church life that point to areas for improvement – better leadership, more appropriate practices, more engaged and fruitful internal social dynamics, greater openness to other churches or the surrounding society, or growth in membership.

Most practical theology uses some form of the revised correlation method, whether explicitly or not.[1] This differs from the earlier Tillichian version in that the focus is more on the local situation and concrete experience than on working up a systematic proposal about the fundamental elements of contemporary society and the primary meaning of Christianity. It is also more explicit in acknowledging the interpretive and contextual nature of its enquiries. The approach usually begins by developing a critical account of the concrete situation, using empirically oriented disciplines, brings this into conversation with a critical interpretation of the Christian tradition, revising the latter as appropriate, and concludes with proposals for practical change. Significantly, unlike more traditional Catholic theology, doctrine is not permitted to guide the enquiry directly, for the approach moves from empirical accounts of present practice through critical reflection to better practice. Doctrine is considered in the light of the interpretation of the situation and as part of an interpretation of the Christian tradition. The desired outcome of the enquiry for practical theology is better practice, the criteria of which do not necessarily derive from an analysis of doctrine or from a theological account of the Church.[2]

For its part, Catholic ecclesiology as such has generally been rather slower to make its turn to the concrete, a hesitation that is perhaps reflective of the history of this variable sub-discipline of systematic theology. For most of its history – since, say, the death of Augustine – the Church was so taken for granted as a major aspect of ordinary life that its nature and function needed little theological explication. When they discussed the Church, theologians usually did so in relation to doctrines they understood to be more central, such as soteriology, Christology or the doctrine of the Trinity, and their remarks were often brief and in passing. It was only with the Reformation challenge to prevailing assumptions about the Church that Catholic theologians turned to ecclesiology more extensively and systematically. It was a major component of the controversial theology of the Counter-Reformation period, in which its function was primarily to support claims about the soteriological necessity of the Catholic ecclesiastical structures and the Church's function as the sole guardian and authoritative teacher of revealed doctrine and practice.

The heavy emphasis on the visible aspects of the Church persisted through into the era of the theological manuals. It shifted to some degree as church authorities took on the challenges of the Enlightenment, presenting the Church as the superior alternative to modern society, a *societas perfecta* (a society sufficient in itself). The apologetic emphasis declined considerably (or, one might also say, took on a very different form) with the work of the *ressourcement* theologians, especially Yves Congar and Henri de Lubac. They led Catholic theologians to recover a far more 'theological' view of the Church as a mystery of salvation made possible in and through its relation to the triune God. Yet even as they turned attention to the Church's 'invisible' theological depths, their influential historical writings displaced the earlier focus on the static and structural aspects of the visible Church to acknowledge and appreciate the rich variety of the Church's history as the visible expression of its depths.

In the second half of the twentieth century, theologians further explored the Church's theological aspects, often by using a particular image or concept as a normative model. 'Body of Christ', 'People of God', 'sacrament' and, somewhat more recently, 'communion' or *koinonia*, were especially favoured by Catholic theologians.[3] Each refers to the essential aspect of the Church, and often of Christianity itself, from which all other aspects can be delineated normatively in a full-scale systematic treatment. While by no means ruling out reflection on the concrete, the method tends to privilege the invisible essence of the Church in (subsequent) discussions of its visible life, so that doctrine remains primary and normative. That is not to say that the practical agendas drawn from the concrete life of the Church do not contribute to the selection of the model. For example, if one believes that overcoming modern individualism and reasserting communal authority will be beneficial, one might affirm the essential nature of the Church as 'communion' or 'Body of Christ'. However, the same concept or image can be used to model alternative, even conflicting ecclesiologies. Thus 'communion' could support an ecclesiology giving priority to face-to-face communion, and thus to individual congregations and grassroots communities.

At least on the face of it, though, many of these ecclesiologies derive their models from doctrinal and scriptural analyses rather than critical accounts of ecclesial experience, whether local, regional or universal. Nor, in many cases, does history factor in – empirical history, that is, in distinction from the history of theology. Often divorced from the confusions and sinfulness of ordinary Christian life, model ecclesiologies can be essentialist, abstract and idealistic. They are 'blueprint ecclesiologies' in that they present descriptions of the Church that may be appealing in their conception and design, but have limited practical utility since they fail – theologically as well as otherwise – to address the realities of church life in the concrete. While it may well be useful on occasion to present ideal accounts of the Church, these should be complemented by sufficient theological attention to what the Church can do and become, here and now, in this particular situation, given these empirical factors. Otherwise ecclesiology may look a little too much like the enthusiastic but ultimately obstructive and tragically destructive five-year plans of the Soviet era. Furthermore, included among the empirical factors are theological and ideological beliefs and attitudes of varying degrees of consonance with the God of Jesus Christ. The more an ecclesiology stays with the ideal and fails to address the concrete, the more difficult it will be to demonstrate that a sought-after practical outcome is a consequence of a theologically appropriate model, and not an ill-formed fruit of unacknowledged and unwarrantable ideology. At the least, it is difficult to see among blueprint ecclesiologies any place for empirical reality to exert some normativity on the interpretation of doctrine, and there is little evidence of self-reflection with regard to context and ideological presuppositions.

For these and other reasons, some theologians have sought ways to bring the methods and material of empirical research into ecclesiological enquiry. A pre-eminent ecclesiologist, Joseph Komonchak of the Catholic University of America, has made a strong case for the use of social science in ecclesiological enquiry.[4] Catholic ecclesiologists have recently become involved in extensive discussions and a number of projects with practical theologians and social scientists interested in the Church.[5] This activity reflects an increasing overlap of interest and, to some degree, methodology among practical theology and what might be termed 'practical ecclesiology'. The latter can be defined as a form of ecclesiological enquiry in which empirical accounts of the Church's concrete life contribute vitally to the development and the formulation of a systematic-theological account of the Church. Unlike practical theology, then, practical ecclesiology's direct objective is not a practical proposal, but a proposal about the nature and function of the Church that will have practical, perhaps even 'prophetic' consequences.

Yet there remains a distinct hesitation on the part of theologians of the Church to adopt the empirical methods and material of practical theology. No doubt this reflects both the history of ecclesiology as well as unease about challenging the institutional structures and centralized authority in the face of a certain defensiveness among church authorities. A more significant concern may well have to do with the role and authority of doctrine in relation to empirical methods. This issue has surfaced in some of the reactions to Roger Haight's recent three-volume ecclesiology,[6] an exercise in practical ecclesiology that makes at least four moves in common with practical theology. First, the object of Haight's enquiry is the empirical Church rather than doctrine about the Church (1.35). He distinguishes between an 'Ecclesiology From Above', which begins with normative doctrine, and an 'Ecclesiology From Below', which is based upon an account of the empirical Church, its history and contemporary forms and issues. An ecclesiology from above 'mediates an understanding of the church in a distinctive, revealed, supernatural, and doctrinal language that in some measure sets the church apart from the secular world' (1.21). If its 'historical consciousness is controlled by doctrinal understanding' the Church may appear to be 'the summit of all religious forms' (1. 22). Second, Haight's concern is practical in that he seeks to change the Church in such a way that it will more readily join with the world's projects as a partner and equal. Third, he adopts the correlation method (1.26) and, fourth, uses empirical disciplines – history and social theory – to arrive at a description of the Church in its various historical contexts.

Haight's objective in the third volume is to arrive at a normative ecclesiology, noting (rightly, in my view) that 'a theological understanding of the church would be purely dogmatic and uncritical without reference to the church of history, and a description of the historical church without any reference to its theological self-understanding would not correspond to the actual, true church' (3.31). He draws from the Church's historical experience (described in the first two volumes) a set of 'ecclesiological principles' upon which to build what he calls a 'transdenominational ecclesiology', that is, an experientially grounded ecclesiology sufficiently rich and flexible that it can be appropriated over time by all denominations in their own distinctive ways. It is thus from within the Church's variegated history, in the implicit as well as explicit ecclesiology developed and operative within particular ecclesial experiences, that Haight derives his critical, normative and practical ecclesiology.

There is far too much to Haight's ambitious and brilliantly executed project to do it justice here. I have sketched a few of its elements only to give an idea of what a practical ecclesiology might look like if it adopted something like the methodology of practical theology. Haight's work differs from practical theology, to be sure – especially in the project's scope, which covers a massive amount of material from the full length of the Church's history. To render this material coherent and ecclesiologically useful, he must select and omit, take the more general view rather than tease out the many ambiguous and conflicting particularities of local church experience, smooth out exceptions in favour of the general rule. This is entirely reasonable, of course, since Haight's goal is not that of a practical theologian. He seeks to develop a theological understanding of the Church as a whole, an understanding that will permit and foster significant changes in practice.

Haight's project has thus far received mixed reception among those engaged in Catholic ecclesiology, an often expressed concern being the place of doctrine vis-à-vis non-theological disciplines. With his rejection of the 'from above' approach, Haight appears to derive ecclesiological principles and ideals solely from descriptions of the Church's historical experience, aided by social theory. Doctrine – in the form of the ecclesiological principles – is normative, but only after it has been purged by the critical fires of non-theological disciplines. It cannot have a normative function in the initial historical description of the Church except as 'historical theology', the description of the history of theologically informed ideas and practices in their contexts. If used initially, 'from above', it will distort our understanding of the empirical Church, bringing with it unchallenged beliefs about the nature of the Church and society.

One can certainly understand Haight's concern. Doctrine is too often used uncritically and ideologically, not least within the Catholic Church. However, one difficulty with the approach 'from below' may be that it replaces one dubious authority by another. History and social science are academic disciplines that insist upon a religiously neutral position. Such critical disciplines and viewpoints (*pace* John Milbank) are vitally important for our understanding of the Church's life in its fullness. But ecclesiology cannot accept their aid on the assumption they offer more accurate descriptions of the way the Church really is (even when all appropriate hermeneutical reservations are duly acknowledged). If it did, it would effectively render its theological perspective secondary and dependent, whether or not the description made frequent reference to the Church's self-understanding. Haight gives the impression (to me at any rate) he is contending that the theological perspective – one normed by doctrine – can be critical only *after* it has been brought into another framework and revised to some greater or lesser degree to fit it. The problem, to repeat, is that any non-theological framework is likely to have doctrines of its own about the nature and function of religion, religious communities and religious doctrines and practices, which may conflict with what Christians and the churches might reasonably believe to be true.

It may be that somewhat similar remarks can be made with regard to some forms of practical theology, too. Unless doctrine contributes from the very beginning of the enterprise, and does so in a way that critically informs and guides the analysis of the situation in some way while at the same time leaving the empirical critical disciplines unimpeded, then it is difficult to see how practical theology can be critical in a *theological* sense – as an exercise in theology. Some forms of practical theology, especially (but not only) those that claim it should become the normative theological form, give clear evidence that theological and non-theological assumptions – doctrines, in effect – are operative from the beginning, yet remain largely unexpressed and thus not subjected to critical reflection. Sometimes, these unexamined doctrines rely upon a grand narrative of enlightenment that makes questionable assumptions about many things: about the nature of their work, the Church, Christian doctrine, the community vis-à-vis the individual, the relation of ideas to actions, the role of the modern university, and its relation to government and funding sources, to name just a few.[7] One cannot do everything all at once, of course, and practical theology has, as I noted, a legitimate agenda distinct from that of practical ecclesiology. But it may be that one of the functions of practical ecclesiology may be to help practical theology by addressing such issues more directly from a doctrinal perspective, all the while with the concrete Church very much in view.

In the remainder of this chapter, I want to sketch out just a few elements of a somewhat different approach to practical ecclesiology that may complement Roger Haight's approach, and possibly that of practical theology, too. Perhaps the key difference from both is that I propose a negotiation between doctrine and the empirical in which both are normative, though in quite different ways, from the very beginning of the enquiry. There are three main elements to the proposal (the first two of which are concurrent rather than sequential): the doctrinal basis; the empirical enquiry; and the subsequent theological proposal (with its practical corollaries).

First, then, the doctrinal basis. I want to say that all reflection on the Church that seeks to be theological should be informed by doctrine, for the very enterprise of being the Church, as well as critical enquiry into its self-understanding, is grounded in a set of beliefs. These beliefs are doctrines not only because they are part of the catholic tradition, they are also too theo-logically necessary to be optional, even though they may be cast in a fairly wide range of forms. They can be stated in roughly the following way.

First, the Holy Spirit works in a special way in the Church, to the extent, at least, of making it possible for it to *be* the Church. Although the Church is a thoroughly human institution, it is different from any other group of people in this regard. It may well be the case that the

Holy Spirit works among other groups, even all of them in one way or another. But for this group alone can it be said the Spirit brings its people together as the Church. From this belief it does not follow – on doctrinal and scriptural grounds as much as any other – that the Church is superior to other groups. It just means its members have a distinctive relation to God; other people and groups might have their own distinctive relation, too. Second, the distinction rests on the belief that the Church and its members are called by the gift of faith to love and serve Jesus Christ. Again, this does not indicate any special status, even though this belief has been used to claim it. It is just that the members of the Church have been given this distinctive relation to Jesus Christ through grace. (To some degree this is also empirically evident: no other group tries to follow Jesus Christ.) Third, the Church believes that God has freely chosen its members to live in a way that displays to all the faith and love of God for all humanity embodied in Jesus Christ, and thereby to witness to him in the power of the Spirit. Our election is not on the basis of any merit since, fourth, the Church also believes (though it could acknowledge it far more often) that it is sinful and confused, and often follows Christ poorly or works against him. However, fifth, in hope it believes that it is maintained in the truth of the gospel by the Holy Spirit to the extent that it can trust it will follow Christ and witness to him, even if at times in spite of itself.

The failure to acknowledge fully what might be termed the 'ordinariness' of the Church – its location within and as part of the world with all its confusions and sinfulness, not above or distinct from it – is primarily a failure of doctrinal theology: the uncritical, self-serving and ideological use of basic and rather formal doctrines like these. In my view (and here I may differ from both Haight and many practical theologians), it is not a solution to rely on other disciplines to correct the Church's self-understanding, though such disciplines may often play a vital supporting role in that self-criticism. The failure arises when the Church forgets these doctrines, all of which point to its fundamental giftedness, its inability to function as it should without grace. Lacking faith in its Lord, the Church turns to some created thing it can possess: apostolic succession; a revelatory tradition; a centralized, bureaucratic and authoritarian hierarchy; a supernatural liturgy; its status as a *societas perfecta*; an infallible pope. It holds and teaches the false doctrine that one or a combination of these renders it something approaching a *tertium quid* between God and the rest of creation. Its failure – its sin, more frankly – is not primarily to forget history or acknowledge some social-scientific critique, even though these are almost always contributing causes, but its failure to trust, love and hope in the triune God.

These doctrines are true, I venture to say (in faith). I do not use 'true' here in the sense of being held by Christians merely 'as if' they are true, nor in any sense that would permit us to say they are expressions of experiences that can be described in better ways by more general language. Nor, on the other hand, do I mean they correspond directly to reality. Obviously doctrinal 'truth' is a notion requiring substantial nuance, discussions of analogical language, the contextualization of experience, a sophisticated hermeneutic theory and so on. However, unless these doctrines reflect the way things are in the relation between the Church and God in some real way, and provide the best guides for our efforts to live in accord with Jesus Christ, who is the truth, it is difficult to see the point in being a Christian and a church.[8] Why follow Jesus of Nazareth unless he is something like the Gospels say he is? And why work at following him better unless the Church's endeavours to do so are more or less on track?

With this doctrinal basis in view, I turn, second, to the critical analysis of the concrete Church. While this may be done at a broader level, as Haight does, it is also necessary for those engaged in practical ecclesiology to have on hand good empirical accounts of particular congregations, for it is in these that the full complexity of the Church's concrete experience comes to light. These accounts should, of course, be developed by those with the appropriate training, who will often be non-theologians. This is a good thing since, as far as possible, no theological presuppositions or doctrines should be permitted to inform the empirical analysis, either by suggesting things to look for, or setting out some kind of heuristic structure or agenda. That would be to bypass the local experience too quickly and undermine the critical and concrete nature of the enquiry.

Instead, the doctrines noted above do two things. First, to repeat, they render the enterprise a theologically valid one by underwriting the possibility and the significance of attempting to reform our lives to become more consonant with Jesus Christ. Second, they guide us in deciding upon the kind of empirical investigation to engage in. For example, they indicate the need to privilege the congregation's own language in its self-description, since the Holy Spirit works not just in the leadership or in larger ecclesial forms but within congregations and among individuals, enabling them to figure out how to follow and witness to Christ. If the Church is not quite like other social groups, nor one congregation quite like another, it is also doctrinally reasonable to think that individual believers are not quite like one another either.

As Jeff Astley convincingly argues, each Christian engages in what he calls 'ordinary theology'.[9] We are all – prior to any critical investigation by others – already attempting to find a way of being Christian that is appropriate for us in our context and with our personal history. We do so by a kind of negotiation, an often piecemeal effort of testing, reflection and renegotiation that is far too dialectically complex, unsystematic and concrete to be thought of as a correlation between the situation and its questions and an interpretation of the Christian tradition. To be sure, much ordinary theology is confused or worse, but it is certainly a part of the concrete Church and is informed by the working of the Spirit. So it may be that in looking deeply into the lives of congregations we may find something valuable not often present elsewhere and worth making widely known. Living Christian lives within the world gives opportunities for broader experiences than are available to some academics and church leaders and thus, it may be, enables more fruitful negotiations.[10]

The kind of enquiry useful for practical ecclesiology is thus one that simply gives an account of what is going on in a congregation, using the members' own language(s), with minimal theorizing and generalization, and maximum attention to detail and complexity. The account should attend to the variations in ways of Christian living at both the congregational and the individual levels. Although generalizations brought from observations of other kinds of groups, whether non-religious or other congregations, may sometimes be very helpful in later reflection on the empirical descriptions, they should initially be used very sparingly and self-critically. Most suitable for practical ecclesiology, in my view, is an ethnographic approach, using participant observations and primarily qualitative research methods.

It is then, third, the task of practical ecclesiology to reflect upon what such empirical studies might have to say for the theology of the Church. It may be that the realities of church life are such that we will need to renegotiate our understanding or placement of doctrine. The doctrines mentioned above all remain intact, but what they and other ecclesiological doctrines mean and how they are cast within the larger web of Christian belief and practice may need reconsideration in light of the concrete Church. The work of practical ecclesiology is dialectical and complex in a way rather similar to (though usually more rigorous and sophisticated than) that of 'ordinary theology'. Its function is to negotiate, as it were, a more adequate understanding of the Church that is then tested by experimentation in church life, where further negotiations will occur concretely, to become known through subsequent empirical accounts and be brought into critical engagement with doctrine once again, and so on.

I conclude by giving two brief examples – or merely hints, really – of this negotiation. Both examples suggest the possibly radical implications of engaging doctrine and the concrete Church. One of the most emphasized doctrines of the Roman Catholic Church asserts the church leadership's teaching authority over its members. This doctrine has arguably been in effect from the very beginning, though it has been interpreted in diverse ways over the centuries. The church authorities have increasingly centralized their role, demanding conformity and issuing threats to those who challenge their teachings. The blame for the present 'crisis of authority' in the Church is often asserted to lie with some aspect of contemporary society – the culture of narcissism, individualism, consumerism, and the like, and so-called 'cafeteria Catholics' are treated patronizingly or with derision. Yet it may be the crisis is due more to the failure of the authorities to acknowledge and adequately address the way the Christian life is actually lived. One of the benefits of detailed and non-generalizing descriptions of congregational life is that they reveal the plurality of ways of living and thinking as Christians. Ethnographers have noted how even within a single congregation there can be so much diversity that it is very difficult to give an account of the congregation's 'identity' without occluding exceptions and conflict or denying the significance of its less noticed members.[11] If such pluralism is an unavoidable aspect of living the Christian life (a consequence of engaging in ordinary theology and enabled by grace), the authorities need to find far more sophisticated ways to address it than they have used thus far. We should not abandon the doctrine of teaching authority, but – to state the obvious – it needs massive reconsideration. It may be that the doctrine is at present distorted by an assumption that the Holy Spirit works to bring conformity rather than rich complexity and experimentation. It may be that the hierarchy of truths is at present disordered, failing to privilege the work of the Spirit sufficiently. Greater trust in the movement of grace throughout all levels of the Church may encourage the introduction of new practices of theological discussion among the laity and with their leaders that will help everyone engage in more fruitful ordinary theology.[12]

The second example draws upon the finding of some ethnographic studies that congregational boundaries cannot be clearly marked out.[13] A congregation may be affected, even partly constituted, not only by those who are active members but by those who exist on its margins, perhaps as family members, those who work in organizations connected with the congregation, those who live in a community in which the congregation is active, or those, say, who use the church hall for AA meetings. This penumbra around congregations and the larger ecclesial forms suggests that ecclesiology should expand to include reflection on this phenomenon.[14] The notion of clear and distinct church boundaries still informs much ecclesiology and may distort the discussion of issues such as the relation of church and culture, church and society, or indeed church and church, by construing each couple as two clearly separable entities, rather than as variably mixed.

How negotiations like these might be pursued in practice is another matter. Here I have tried only to suggest that doctrines are of more significance and critical value in reflecting upon the concrete Church than is acknowledged by some kinds of practical theology and by Haight's version of practical ecclesiology. I think it not unreasonable to privilege doctrine from the beginning of both forms of enquiry, provided neither it nor non-theological assumptions and agendas intrude on the empirical analyses, and provided doctrine is used self-critically rather than apologetically. In this way, it may be possible to avoid too heavy reliance on historical and social-theoretical explanatory analyses that conform to their own doctrines and presuppositions. As an alternative approach that to some degree complements practical theology, ethnographic participant-observer descriptions of the particularities of congregational life might have profoundly critical and constructive implications for both doctrinal and practical-theological reflection on the Church.[15]

Notes

1 Some of the classic expositions of practical theology, such as Don S. Browning 1991, refer to David Tracy's account of the correlation method laid out initially in Tracy 1975, which advances on Paul Tillich's original method.

2 I have relied on influential expositions of practical theology in this summary description, for example, besides Browning 1991, also Edward Farley 2003. There are other forms, of course, to which some of my points will not apply.

3 The 'models approach' is described by Avery Dulles, SJ, 1974/1987. I have offered criticism of the models approach in Healy 2000. Here I draw mostly pp. 25–51 for this and the next paragraph.

4 See Joseph A. Komonchak 1995. My own book, Healy 2000, is similarly concerned.

5 For instance, the second Receptive Ecumenism conference, organized by P. D. Murray and held at Ushaw College, January 2009; the Ecclesiological Investigations group, led by Gerard Mannion and Paul Collins; the conferences

on Ecclesiology and Ethnography held at Yale University in 2007 and Oxford in 2008, to mention just a few.

6 Roger Haight's three-volume *Christian Community in History* (2004–8) is part of a larger project that earlier treated grace and (controversially) Christology.

7 The bearing of funding on research has been noted frequently, for example, by Stanley Hauerwas 2007, pp. 82–8; Arthur Farnsley 2004, pp. 32–7.

8 I do not mean to suggest that anyone I have mentioned in this chapter would disagree.

9 Jeff Astley 2002 is an example of a practical theologian whose work is not at all susceptible to my critical comments. Perhaps that reflects his location in the UK: see the editorial essay in Guest, Tusting and Woodhead 2004, pp. 1–19, for a discussion of the differences between congregational study in the USA and the UK.

10 John T. Noonan has shown how ordinary Christians have frequently led the way in major moral shifts, including the rejection of slavery and the acceptance of religious freedom, while professional moral theologians have been hampered by their training, isolating culture and concern for precedent. Noonan 2005, *A Church that Cannot Change*.

11 See Frances Ward 2004, 'The Messiness of Studying Congregations using Ethnographic Methods'.

12 I discuss the relation between ordinary theologies, academic theology and official theologies in Healy 2009, pp. 24–39.

13 See especially Timothy Jenkins 1999.

14 An insight of Harald Hegstad in a paper entitled 'Ecclesiology and Empirical Research on the Church' that he delivered at the Ecclesiology and Ethnography Conference in Oxford, 2008.

15 Some of the material in this chapter draws upon papers I presented at the Oxford conference on Ecclesiology and Ethnography and at the second international conference on Receptive Ecumenism and Mutual Learning at Ushaw College in January 2009 (both papers will eventually be published).

Bibliography

Jeff Astley, 2002, *Ordinary Theology: Looking, Listening and Learning in Theology*, Aldershot: Ashgate.

Don S. Browning, 1991, *A Fundamental Practical Theology: Descriptive and Strategic Proposals*, Minneapolis: Fortress Press.

Avery Dulles SJ, 1974/1987, *Models of the Church*, expanded edn, New York: Doubleday/Image Books.

Edward Farley, 2003, *Practicing Gospel: Unconventional Thoughts on the Church's Ministry*, Louisville: Westminster John Knox.

Arthur Farnsley, 2004,'The Rise of Congregational Studies in the USA', in M. Guest, K. Tusting and L. Woodhead (eds), *Congregational Studies in the UK: Christianity in a Post-Christian Context*, Aldershot: Ashgate.

M. Guest, K. Tusting and L. Woodhead (eds), 2004, *Congregational Studies in* the UK: *Christianity in a Post-Christian Context*, Aldershot: Ashgate.

Roger Haight SJ, 2004–8, *Christian Community in History*, 3 vols, New York/London: Continuum.

Stanley Hauerwas, 2007, *The State of the University: Academic Knowledges and the Knowledge of God*, Oxford: Blackwell.

Nicholas M. Healy, 2000, *Church, World and the Christian Life: Practical, Prophetic Ecclesiology*, Cambridge: Cambridge University Press.

Nicholas M. Healy, 2009, 'What is Systematic Theology?', *International Journal of Systematic Theology* 11:1, pp. 24–39.

Timothy Jenkins, 1999, *Religion in English Everyday Life: An Ethnographic Approach*, New York: Berghahn Books.

Joseph A. Komonchak, 1995, *Foundations in Ecclesiology*, Boston: Supplementary Issue of the *Lonergan Workshop Journal*, p. 11.

John T. Noonan, 2005, *A Church that Cannot Change: The Development of Catholic Moral Teaching*, Notre Dame, IN: University of Notre Dame Press.

David Tracy, 1975, *Blessed Rage for Order: The New Pluralism in Theology*, New York: Seabury.

Frances Ward, 2004, 'The Messiness of Studying Congregations using Ethnographic Methods', in M. Guest, K. Tusting and L. Woodhead (eds), *Congregational Studies in the UK: Christianity in a Post-Christian Context*, Aldershot: Ashgate.

8

The Place of Praxis in the Theology of Edward Schillebeeckx

MARTIN POULSOM SDB

Pursuing the task of theology in the twenty-first century presents a number of challenges, not least that of finding ways to bridge the many gaps that appeared during the previous century. Some of these became so wide that they seemed to become unbridgeable gulfs as the century ended, forcing a choice to be made on the path forward. One such divide has been variously characterized as between 'foundationalism' and 'antifoundationalism', 'correlational' and 'anticorrelational' theology, 'postliberal-ism' and 'revisionism,' 'experiential-expressive' and 'cultural-linguistic' theology, or simply between 'Yale' and 'Chicago', where the major protagonists were to be found, at least at the beginning (Higton 1999, p. 566). Another is the divergence of theory and practice in theology, which have often been treated as if each forms the basis of a completely separate type of theology, with little or no interaction between them. Though far from being an extreme treatment, two of Gerald O'Collins's three styles of theology find their working partner for faith in theory and practice respectively. His first style, the dominant model at Vatican II, is the classic 'faith seeking understanding', a theoretical and systematic mode of theology that finds a ready home in the academy. His second might be thought more appropriate for dialogue between church and society, a 'faith seeking social justice'. This is a style of theology focused on practical and life-giving outcomes, one that has become much more prominent since Vatican II (O'Collins 1993, pp. 9–10).

But is the fragmentation of theology into ever smaller 'communal enclaves' (Lindbeck 1984, pp. 126–7) a way forward, or does it risk colluding in the trivializing of religious traditions into mere 'stylistic preferences' (Williams 2000, p. 327)? Need the various styles of theology on offer at the start of the twenty-first century be thought of as sharply bounded, internally consistent and invariable wholes (Tanner 1997, pp. 53 and 95), self-contained and watertight with respect to each other (Patterson 1999, p. 7)? Or might a more postmodern under-standing of these cultural groupings be helpful, recognizing that there is both variation – and even contradiction – within them (Tanner 1997, p. 57) and also the possibility of real, dynamic and creative dialogue at their boundaries (Tanner 1997, p. 115; Patterson 1999, p. 7)?

Perhaps contemporary calls for non-dualism in theology could bear fruit here, too. Sue Patterson calls for non-dualist forms of theological realism, to find ways of addressing 'the problem with the realist insist-ence on separating language and world' (Patterson 1999, p. 21). In ethics, she avers, it is no longer possible to 'separate being and doing, intention and action [. . . because] the language-riddenly relational understanding of personhood has removed these divisions' (Patterson 1999, p. 122). If her observations are at all pertinent, both theoretically and practically focused forms of theology could benefit from enter-ing into real dialogue with each other, finding ways to bridge the gulf between theory and practice.

As a contribution towards such a project, this chapter seeks to dis-close an internal variation in what is often called correlational theology that can, at the same time, serve as a way of bringing into dialogue theologies that emphasize theory, on the one hand, or practice, on the other. Following the recommendations of Kathryn Tanner, a 'non-contrastive' (Tanner 1988, p. 45) path forward will be indicated and briefly explored, proposing one way 'to fracture anew the language of the ordinary' (Tanner 1988, p. 169) in order to indicate the possi-bility of a theology for church and society that can draw on the best of theory and practice, bringing them into harmony and mutually enrich-ing interaction.

In 1983 Edward Schillebeeckx gave a paper in Tübingen at an event entitled *Paradigm Change in Theology: A Symposium for the Future.* This 'international, ecumenical and interdisciplinary symposium' (Kohl 1989, p. ix) brought together a number of scholars, many of whom could reasonably be designated correlational in the type of theology they pursued, to investigate the usefulness, or otherwise, of the Kuhnian notion of paradigm change in science to describe changes in theology (Küng 1989). In particular, according to Hans Küng and David Tracy in their introduction to the collected papers, the issue under discussion was whether, in fact, a consensus was emerging in theology, 'a new, different, basic pattern' (Küng and Tracy 1989, p. xv).

In his response to Schillebeeckx's contribution, Bernard McGinn commented: 'Schillebeeckx has given us not just a paper, but the bare bones of a book, or of a whole theological programme' (McGinn 1989, p. 348). On the basis of this comment, it seems fair to ask whether that theological programme would be the same as the one envisaged by David Tracy, one of the directors of the symposium. After all, Tracy is not only one of the foremost practitioners of correlational theology, at least in the English-speaking world; he is also someone who has sought to defend that type of theology against the criticisms of it levelled by postliberals such as George Lindbeck and Hans Frei.

Tracy and Schillebeeckx

In offering 'Some Concluding Reflections on the Conference', Tracy proposes a definition of what he takes to be the common project of its participants: 'Theology as hermeneutical can be described as the attempt to develop mutually critical correlations (Tillich, Schillebeeckx, Ricœur, and so on) in theory and praxis between an interpretation of the Christian tradition and an interpretation of the contemporary situation' (Tracy 1989b, p. 462). In a later article, he maintains that the mutually critical character of the correlations involved means that this process does not always involve a drift towards, or inbuilt prejudice in favour of, 'harmony, convergence or sameness' (Tracy 1989c, p. 562). Such a drift or prejudice, which he calls 'the return of the same', also forms part of his critique of Gadamer. He says that Gadamer's portrayal of the dialogue between experience and tradition 'is one tempted by too easy notions of similarity or even sameness, and too sanguine a notion of the complementarity of all differences' (Tracy 1989c, pp. 561–2; cf. 1989a, p. 43). He also admits that there are 'real problems within the tradition from Schleiermacher to Tillich, Eliade, Rahner, Lonergan, et al.' (Tracy 1985, pp. 462–3) in this regard, which need to be addressed. To that extent, the critique of the postliberal theologians is applicable to some correlational theologies, but not all of them. Tracy proposes that his own work has developed in ways that begin to deal with some of these matters (Tracy 1985, p. 464). In the more hermeneutically sensitive form that is the result of these developments:

> Correlation logically entails only the notion that *some* relationship is involved. That relationship may (rarely) be one of identity . . . That relationship may also be one of non-identity (existentially, confrontation) . . . The relationship may also be one of similarity-

in-difference – as in analogical theologies; or identity-in-difference – as in dialectical theologies. The point of correlation is the need to relate critically interpretations of both tradition and situation. (Tracy 1989c, pp. 562–3)

What Tracy is enunciating is a way of differentiating between herme-neutical and dialectical theologies in such a way that they are not necessarily opposed to each other. The dialectical theologians to whom he is reaching out would probably object to their type of theology being subsumed under the general banner of correlation, but it seems fair to grant to Tracy that he is genuinely seeking dialogue. As he points out in his critique of Lindbeck, 'The fact is that a fruitful and critical discussion between Lindbeck's "cultural-linguistic" model and a "her-meneutical-political" model has not yet been posed sharply by anyone' (Tracy 1985, p. 467).

However, it is worth asking *how* different these correlational and postliberal approaches are and whether, perhaps surprisingly, they actually share a common linguistic framework. If so, then according to Tanner's compelling argument in *Theories of Culture*, the two types of theology might be 'functional complements' (Tanner 1988, p. 33). Might the use of the term 'difference' in both of Tracy's descriptions indicate that he has simply flown to the opposite pole with respect to his predecessors, that of difference? He has, indeed, been said to submit 'that the biggest challenge confronting us today is that of facing our differences, of accepting, truly accepting, otherness' (Rolheiser 2004, para. 1 of 11). But is difference the best term to use alongside relation-ship, or will it inevitably perpetuate the return to sameness, if only as a correlative term?

An investigation of the theological programme proposed by Schille-beeckx in his paper at the conference can help form a response to these questions. In the first place, he sounds somewhat wary of using the term 'correlation' to describe what he is doing (Schillebeeckx 1989, p. 312; cf. Schillebeeckx 1990, pp. 33–45), even though he does use it elsewhere in his writings (Schillebeeckx 1980b, p. 51; cf. Schillebeeckx 1984, p. 83). Second, he does not do his theology in a transcendental mode, as Tracy and others do (Portier 2002, p. 21; Kennedy 1993a, p. 105). Schillebeeckx's method is distinctive, too, in that, rather than using a 'correspondence of terms', it uses a 'correspondence of relation-ships' (Abdul-Masih 2001, pp. 92–3; cf. Schillebeeckx 1990, p. 42). Another way of putting this is to say that 'Schillebeeckx's hermeneu-tics is not strictly linear but rather proportional' (Abdul-Masih 2001,

p. 94). It does not involve correlating twin poles by moving back and forth between them in order to balance them against each other (cf. Tracy 1989c, pp. 550 n. 6 and 562 n. 56). Schillebeeckx's method is non-contrastive, to use Tanner's terminology: his reluctance to use polar thinking is reflected in a structure of discourse that is dependent on neither difference nor sameness.

Though Schillebeeckx is, therefore, a sympathetic fellow-traveller alongside Tracy, he may not be treading quite the same path. Tracy's description of 'theology as a community of inquiry grounded in a community of commitment' draws Schillebeeckx into the common endeavour very well. As Tracy himself also recognizes, though, in 'any authentic community of inquiry, pluralism is not merely tolerated but encouraged' (Tracy 1989a, p. 61). In his concluding reflections, he goes further still, asserting that the 'groping, tentative, often conflictual and interruptive character of any of our individual interpretations of tradition and situation . . . is not, therefore, a weakness but a strength. It is, moreover, the only strength available to us' (Tracy 1989b, p. 463).

One way of illustrating these general points – and thereby of contributing both to the strength of correlational theology and to its development into a more hermeneutical and postmodern form – is to consider Schillebeeckx's presentation of praxis and the role it plays in his theology. Tracy's position is instructive here, too, both as starting-point and foil. In the definition offered earlier, which drew on the work of Schillebeeckx among others, Tracy held that hermeneutical theology attempts 'to develop mutually critical correlations . . . in theory and praxis' (Tracy 1989b, p. 462). This suggests that, for him, the terms 'praxis' and 'practice' are somewhat interchangeable, an impression strengthened by his later explanation as to why he insists that the correlations are 'in theory and in praxis'. Stating this explicitly, he says, is 'intended to remind concretely-situated interpreters that every act of theological interpretation is situated in a particular practical situation, and that every correlation in theory is also a correlation in praxis with practical intent' (Tracy 1989b, p. 467).

There are those who read Schillebeeckx in a similar fashion (Goergen 2002, p. 122; Abdul-Masih 2001, p. 95), but doing so results in one of two problems. On the one hand, it can lead to a polarization of Schillebeeckx's thinking, resulting in a dialectical interplay filled with tension (just like Tracy's position) (Thompson 2002, pp. 40–1). On the other hand, it can lead to paradox, as Philip Kennedy points out. Schillebeeckx, says Kennedy, holds to all three of the following statements: theory precedes praxis; however, praxis is primary with respect to theory; third, theory has both a pre- and a post-practical function (Kennedy 1993a, p. 283). If praxis and practice are interchangeable, then these three statements do generate a paradox. But, what if Schillebeeckx's correlation uses not two terms, but three? What if praxis is not, straightforwardly at least, the same as practice?

Theory and Practice

In order to get a clearer picture of what Schillebeeckx is proposing, it is helpful to understand, in the first instance, the way that he relates theory and practice to one another. William Hill points out that, for Schillebeeckx, 'Christian life practice cannot exist in isolation from theory, and without it would lack all criteria for truth' (Hill 2002, p. 3). For Schillebeeckx, theory and practice are inwardly directed towards each other. Thus, good theory leads to the realization of better practice; equally, good practice impels the practitioner towards the realization of better theory.[1] As Schillebeeckx puts it, 'religion is not an interpretation of the world which remains alien to practice, any more than it is a practice without any reference to a particular interpretation of man and the world' (Schillebeeckx 1980a, p. 774). He is not thinking of theory and practice as realities that, in and of themselves, pull in opposite directions and that must be brought together in a tension that is – hopefully at any rate – creative.[2] Rather, each possesses an inner drive towards the other, such that theory and practice can be called mutually co-constitutive.

This interrelation between theory and practice in the lives of Christians is one way in which they follow in the footsteps of Jesus. 'As exegete of God and as practitioner of a way of life in accordance with the reign of God, Jesus acted on the basis neither of a blueprint nor of a well-defined concept of eschatological and definitive salvation.'[3] Schillebeeckx is, first of all, saying that Jesus was one who interpreted God for and with those to whom he was sent, both in a theoretical way (as an exegete of God) and in a practical way (as a practitioner of a way of life in accordance with God's reign). In doing so, he did not use a pre-existing blueprint for action, such that what he did would all have been decided beforehand, with only the theory remaining to be worked out. Neither did he use a perfect conceptual framework formed in advance, which simply had to be put into action. A problem seems to arise here, however: once the points that Schillebeeckx is making here are clarified, it can begin to look as if Jesus either didn't know what he was

doing or didn't know where he was trying to get to by doing it. Schillebeeckx handles this by speaking of the primacy of praxis.

The Primacy of Praxis

In his *Interim Report on the Books Jesus and Christ*, Schillebeeckx pens
a chapter entitled 'Kingdom of God: Creation and Salvation'. At its
beginning, he notes that some people have accused him of paying 'too
much attention to social and political liberation and not enough to
the mystical liberation of mankind' (Schillebeeckx 1980b, p. 105). He
interprets this, in part, as an accusation that his theology focuses too
much on the practical. In response, he says: 'God must, after all, always
be so thought of that he is never merely thought of; talk of God stands
under the primacy of praxis. It stands under the question: "Where are
we headed?"'[4] The beginning and end of this quote can be understood
as expressing the mutual co-constitution of theory and practice that
would be one way of responding to his critics. God presents a challenge
to humanity that is more than a theoretical challenge. 'Where are we
headed?' is a question that calls for *both* kinds of realization – of better
theory *and* of better practice. In that case, what does Schillebeeckx
mean by the primacy of praxis?

A first clue can be gleaned from his contact with liberation theology.
According to Denis Carroll, in their accounts of creation, 'theologies
of liberation' have a 'dialectical notion of praxis as critical interplay of
theory/practice' (Carroll 2003, p. 25). The interaction, however, may
well have been mutual, rather than simply one-way. Gustavo Gutiérrez's first major work, *A Theology of Liberation*, for example, cites
Schillebeeckx twice on the topic of praxis (Gutiérrez 1988, pp. 8 and
10; also see p. 181 nn. 35 and 46). It is worth noting that at around the
same time, Schillebeeckx published several articles on critical theory
that spoke of praxis and orthopraxis. Thus, it is possible that both he
and the liberation theologians with whom he is connected use praxis as a
theoretical term to indicate the interrelation, or mutual co-constitution,
of theory and practice.

This claim can be substantiated by considering an argument that
Schillebeeckx presents towards the end of his *Paradigm Change* paper.
He begins by saying, in a way that noticeably draws on the mutual
enrichment between him and liberation theology, that, today, 'an
authentic faith in God only seems to be possible in the context of a
praxis of liberation and of solidarity with the needy' (Schillebeeckx

1989, p. 318). This might at first seem vulnerable to the very criticism against which he is reacting, that his theology is just too practically focused. This is not, however, what he means by praxis, as the rest of the argument shows. 'It is in that praxis', he continues, 'that the idea develops that God reveals himself as the mystery and the very heart of humanity's striving for liberation, wholeness and soundness' (Schillebeeckx 1989, p. 318). Thus, as Christians strive practically towards the liberation, wholeness and soundness of humanity, their theory – that God is to be found at the heart of that very striving – develops. Praxis must be more than practice if this is to be possible.

Schillebeeckx goes on to say that the 'concept of that mystery, which is at first concealed in the praxis of liberation and making whole, is only made explicit in the naming of that concept in the statement made in faith that God is the liberator, the promoter of what is good and the opponent of what is evil' (Schillebeeckx 1989, p. 318). The opening of this part of his argument does not mean to imply that, when Christians begin practically to strive towards liberation and wholeness, they have no idea where they are headed. They have *some* idea, but it may not yet be fully worked out in a systematic way. As they engage in the task of humanization (Schillebeeckx 1969, p. 227; 1983, p. 100) their original – possibly quite hazy – idea of where they are headed is realized conceptually, coming eventually to the point where they can name the mystery at the heart of their striving as God. Insofar as they are able to do this, that very mystery itself impels them towards practical action for the realization of the kingdom of God. Praxis, therefore, is the dynamic interrelation of theory and practice, within which both develop and are brought to ever deeper realization. In the final analysis, then, what is central is neither the ability adequately to theorize about God, nor adequately to act on behalf of God's kingdom. It is the ability to interrelate both in life-giving praxis. As Schillebeeckx puts it himself: 'Not "Lord, Lord, Alleluia" but praxis is decisive' (Schillebeeckx 1987, p. 274).

Implications for Theology

Schillebeeckx's theory – and his analysis of the practice – of theology can serve as a resource for church and society in many ways. One outcome of his theological programme, to use McGinn's expression, is the way in which, having conceptualized praxis as the mutual interrelation of theory and practice, he also uses that same term to speak of the mutual interrelation of mysticism and politics (Schillebeeckx 1980b, pp. 105 and 122; 1987, pp. 70–5; 1989, pp. 317–19). This not only makes clear why, for him, praxis is not simply interchangeable with practice. It also shows why it is decisive – praxis offers a way of inter-relating theory and practice, mysticism and politics and, by extension, the ecclesial and cultural vocations of the theologian (Borgman 2005, p. 55).

His way of dealing with these complex and important matters shows that he does not fit into Tracy's correlational scheme: his method uses neither 'similarity-in-difference', as Tracy says analogical theologies like his own do, nor 'identity-in-difference', as used in the dialectical theologies of the postliberals (Tracy 1989c, pp. 562–3). Schillebeeckx is a relational theologian – as Kennedy points out, his ontology of rela-tion can serve as a hermeneutical key for the whole of his theology (Kennedy 1993a, pp. 19, 363–4; cf. 1993b, p. 89). It reveals his method as one that uses relation as one of its key terms. The correlative term for relation is not difference – one that is held in common by Tracy and Lindbeck – but distinction. If distinction and difference are not inter-changeable in Schillebeeckx's theological project, neither are relation and relationship. The structure of difference and sameness, as Tracy recognizes, is not sufficiently complex to deal with the middle ground between identity and confrontation (Tracy 1989c, pp. 562–3). Schille-beeckx's proposal takes another step forward, suggesting that it is the contrastive character of the pairing itself that needs to be replaced – the middle ground is to be found *between* difference and sameness, in the subtler, and at the same time more fruitful, realms of distinction and relation.

Schillebeeckx's programme can also provide a way of navigating the often treacherous waters between systematic theology, on the one hand, and pastoral and practical theology, on the other. His first con-tribution to this dilemma arises with the application of his terminology to it. Theoretical and practical theology are neither the same as each other, nor are they fundamentally different from each other. They are distinct and related forms of theology, which can exist in a mutually critical dialogue that seeks to realize each one more perfectly. Better systematic theology can and should impel those engaged in it towards practical outcomes, which are the material of pastoral and practical theology. Better Christian practice can and should impel those engaged in it towards better ideas both of what they are doing and of why they are doing it, the material of systematic theology.

His proposal of praxis as decisive for Christian living might, indeed, suggest the desirability of a praxical theology, in which the theoretical emphases of systematic theology could enter into mutually fruitful interrelation with the practical priorities of pastoral and practical theology, for the benefit of all the sub-disciplines, as outlined above. A vision of a praxical theology like this may underlie Schillebeeckx's description of where he thinks theologians are headed: 'whatever one thinks of contemporary theologians,' he says towards the end of his *Paradigm Change* paper, 'one thing should be granted them: by means of a historical praxis of commitment to mysticism and politics they are trying to discover the human face of God, starting from there in order to revive hope in a society, a humanity, with a more human face' (Schillebeeckx 1989, p. 317).

Notes

1 This use of the metaphorical term 'realization' is deliberate, since it can have twin senses. Thus, it can be used to refer both to the development of theory ('Ah, now I realize!') and also to practical progress (turning something from an idea into a reality). Schillebeeckx's use of it can be found in 1980b, p. 117; 1983, p. 95; and 1990, p. 231.

2 This would be one way of expressing a Lonerganian dialectic, something that would find a home more naturally in Tracy's schema than Schillebeeckx's. For an analysis of the role and character of dialectic in Lonergan's theology, see Lonergan 1972, chapters 5 and 7 respectively, and also Lonergan 1974.

3 Translation by the author (Martin Poulsom) (cf. Schillebeeckx 1980b, p. 124). Dutch text: 'Als exegeet van God en practicus van een handelen overeenkomstig het rijk Gods, heft Jezus evenmin gehandeld vanuit een blauwdruk of vastomlijnd begrip van eschatologisch en definitief heil' (Schillebeeckx 1978, p. 140).

4 Author's translation (cf. Schillebeeckx 1980b, p. 120; 1983, p. 99). Dutch text: 'God moet immers steeds zo gedacht worden dat Hij nooit sléchts gedacht wordt; spreken over God staat onder het primaat van de praxis. Het staat onder de vraag: Waar gaan we naartoe?' (Schillebeeckx 1978, p. 136).

Bibliography

Marguerite Thabit Abdul-Masih, 2001, *Hans Frei and Edward Schillebeeckx: A Conversation on Method and Christology*, Waterloo, Ont.: Wilfred Laurier University Press.

Clodovis Boff, 1987, *Theology and Praxis: Epistemological Foundations*, trans. Robert R. Barr, Maryknoll, NY: Orbis.

Erik Borgman, 2005, 'Gaudium et Spes: The Forgotten Future of a Revolutionary Document', trans. Natalie K. Watson, *Concilium* no. 4, pp. 48–56.

Denis Carroll, 2003, 'An Essay in the Theology of Creation: Gabriel Daly and the Challenge of Modernity', in Andrew Pierce and Geraldine Smyth (eds), *The Critical Spirit: Theology at the Crossroads of Faith and Culture*, Dublin: Columba Press, pp. 15–26.

Donald J. Goergen, 2002, 'Spirituality', in Mary Catherine Hilkert and Robert J. Schreiter (eds), *The Praxis of the Reign of God: An Introduction to the Theology of Edward Schillebeeckx*, 2nd edn, New York: Fordham University Press, pp. 117–31.

Gustavo Gutiérrez, 1988, *A Theology of Liberation*, trans. Caridad Inda and John Eagleson, rev. edn, London: SCM Press.

M. A. Higton, 1999, 'Hans Frei and David Tracy on the Ordinary and the Extraordinary in Christianity', *Journal of Religion* 79, pp. 566–91.

William J. Hill, 2002, 'A Theology in Transition', in Mary Catherine Hilkert and Robert J. Schreiter (eds), *The Praxis of the Reign of God: An Introduction to the Theology of Edward Schillebeeckx*, 2nd edn, New York: Fordham University Press, pp. 1–18.

Philip Kennedy, 1993a, *Deus Humanissimus: The Knowability of God in the Theology of Edward Schillebeeckx*, Fribourg: Fribourg University Press.

Philip Kennedy, 1993b, *Schillebeeckx*, London: Geoffrey Chapman.

Margaret Kohl, 1989, 'Translator's Preface', in Hans Küng and David Tracy (eds), *Paradigm Change in Theology: A Symposium for the Future*, Edinburgh: T&T Clark, p. x.

Hans Küng, 1989, 'Paradigm Change in Theology: A Proposal for Discussion', in Hans Küng and David Tracy (eds), *Paradigm Change in Theology: A Symposium for the Future*, Edinburgh: T&T Clark, pp. 3–33.

Hans Küng and David Tracy, 1989, 'Introduction', in Hans Küng and David Tracy (eds), *Paradigm Change in Theology: A Symposium for the Future*, Edinburgh: T&T Clark, pp. xv–xvi.

George A. Lindbeck, 1984, *The Nature of Doctrine: Religion and Theology in a Postliberal Age*, London: SPCK.

Bernard J. F. Lonergan, 1972, *Method in Theology*, London: Darton, Longman & Todd.

B. F. Lonergan, 1974, 'The Subject', in William F. J. Ryan and Bernard J. Tyrell (eds), *A Second Collection: Papers by Bernard J. F. Lonergan*, London: Darton, Longman & Todd, pp. 69–86.

Bernard McGinn, 1989, 'Response to Edward Schillebeeckx and Jürgen Moltmann', in Hans Küng and David Tracy (eds), *Paradigm Change in Theology: A Symposium for the Future*, Edinburgh: T&T Clark, pp. 346–51.

Gerald O'Collins, 1993, *Retrieving Fundamental Theology: The Three Styles of Contemporary Theology*, London: Geoffrey Chapman.

Sue Patterson, 1999, *Realist Christian Theology in a Postmodern Age*, Cambridge: Cambridge University Press.

William L. Portier, 2002, 'Interpretation and Method', in Mary Catherine Hilkert and Robert J. Schreiter (eds), *The Praxis of the Reign of God: An Introduction to the Theology of Edward Schillebeeckx*, 2nd edn, New York: Fordham University Press, pp. 19–36.

Ronald Rolheiser, 2004, 'Facing Otherness and Differences', http://www.ronrolheiser.com/columnarchive/archive/arco10404.html.

Edward Schillebeeckx, 1969, *God and Man (Theological Soundings II)*, trans. Edward Fitzgerald and Peter Tomlinson, London: Sheed & Ward.

Edward Schillebeeckx, 1978, *Tussentijds verhaal over twee Jesus boeken*, Bloemendaal: Nelissen.

Edward Schillebeeckx, 1980a, *Christ: The Christian Experience in the Modern World*, trans. John Bowden, London: SCM Press.

Edward Schillebeeckx, 1980b, *Interim Report on the Books Jesus and Christ*, trans. John Bowden, London: SCM Press.

Edward Schillebeeckx, 1983, *God Among Us: The Gospel Proclaimed*, trans. John Bowden, London: SCM Press.

Edward Schillebeeckx, 1984, 'The Structure of Belief Experiences', trans. Robert J. Schreiter, in Robert J. Schreiter (ed.) *The Schillebeeckx Reader*, Edinburgh: T&T Clark.

Edward Schillebeeckx, 1987, *Jesus in Our Western Culture: Mysticism, Ethics and Politics*, trans. John Bowden, London: SCM Press.

Edward Schillebeeckx, 1989, 'The Role of History in What is Called the New Paradigm', trans. Margaret Kohl, in Hans Küng and David Tracy (eds), *Paradigm Change in Theology: A Symposium for the Future*, Edinburgh: T&T Clark, pp. 307–19.

Edward Schillebeeckx, 1990, *Church: The Human Story of God*, trans. John Bowden, London: SCM Press and New York: Crossroad.

Stephen L. Stell, 1993, 'Hermeneutics in Theology and the Theology of Hermeneutics: Beyond Lindbeck and Tracy', *Journal of the American Academy of Religion* 61, pp. 679–703.

Kathryn E. Tanner, 1988, *God and Creation in Christian Theology: Tyranny or Empowerment?*, Oxford: Blackwell.

Kathryn Tanner, 1997, *Theories of Culture: A New Agenda for Theology*, Minneapolis, MN: Fortress Press.

Daniel Speed Thompson, 2003, *The Language of Dissent: Edward Schillebeeckx on the Crisis of Authority in the Catholic Church*, Notre Dame, IN: University of Notre Dame Press.

David Tracy, 1985, 'Lindbeck's New Program for Theology: A Reflection', *The Thomist* 49, pp. 460–72.

David Tracy, 1989a, 'Hermeneutical Reflections in the New Paradigm', in Hans Küng and David Tracy (eds), *Paradigm Change in Theology: A Symposium for the Future*, Edinburgh: T&T Clark, pp. 34–62.

David Tracy, 1989b, 'Some Concluding Reflections on the Conference: Unity Amidst Diversity and Conflict?', in Hans Küng and David Tracy (eds), *Paradigm Change in Theology: A Symposium for the Future*, Edinburgh: T&T Clark, pp. 461–71.

David Tracy, 1989c, 'The Uneasy Alliance Reconceived: Catholic Theological Method, Modernity and Postmodernity', *Theological Studies* 50, pp. 548–70.

Rowan Williams, 2000, 'Postmodern Theology and the Judgment of the World', in John Webster and George P. Schner (eds), *Theology After Liberalism: A Reader*, Oxford: Blackwell, pp. 321–34.

PART THREE

Catholic Theology in Practice

Introduction to Part Three

The question, what difference does pastoral and practical theology make, is a basic one. What and whom does it serve? How does it help Catholics (and perhaps others) to believe and to act well in their lives? We have seen in Part Three that a defining characteristic of Catholic pastoral theology is its emphasis on the inherent practical and pastoral import of the great theological doctrines and their roots in the scriptural teachings. In this understanding, the Scriptures cannot be adequately taught nor theology developed without reference to the realities of human life and the challenges of Christian discipleship.

There are two levels at which the issue of practice has to be tackled: the immediate level of Christian life and witness – liturgy and prayer, ethical and social action, ministry and mission; and the level of theological articulation undergirding and inspiring this pastoral living and acting. How are practice and the empirical taken into account within theology? And how is the practical bent worked out in the specific fields of pastoral theology?

These are the concerns in the chapters of Part Three. They show the range of disciplines and methodologies that pastoral theology calls upon – anthropology, sociology, psychology, ritual studies, textual critique, philosophical ethics, law, the arts, qualitative and action research. And they give an account of some of the many fields of pastoral action as seen through the lens of practical theology.

Empirical Enquiry

The exigencies of empirical investigation require pastoral theology to adopt an interdisciplinary methodology, working alongside the human and social sciences. This highlights one of the great challenges: theological enquiry has to find its way among the different discourses, the many methodologies, and the varied modes of human knowledge. Theology is constrained to move beyond the 'household of the faith', as it were, and to engage with the complexity of the world as it is. Such an involvement with society is, of course, a primary aim of theology as well as a matter of method.

There is nothing new here. Theology with its roots in the lived religious tradition – *fides* – needs the human disciplines, traditionally philosophy and history, to accomplish its tasks – *quaerens intellectum*. Aim and method are intertwined. The theological use of Greek philosophy in the early centuries to articulate the gospel message was both heuristic and an engagement with the world and culture of the time. The contemporary alliance of pastoral theology with the social sciences has the same two characteristics.

Contents

There is a risk of merely blundering around here! As Louis-Marie Chauvet demonstrates, anthropological concepts, if they are to be used, have to be well understood; the theologian, blinded by her default assumptions, might spot convergence between a theological notion and an anthropological reality where there is none. On the other hand, the unity of human knowing, beyond disciplinary boundaries, is to be defended; all is not incommensurable discourse. Clare Watkins's critique relates to this point: practical theology has been mesmerized by a supposed radical dissociation ('dis-integrity' is Watkins's word) of contemporary lived reality from the sources and resources of the religious tradition; whereas, at least in some respects, the contemporary is the tradition in another moment of development. This becomes clear within an overarching ecclesiological vision of tradition.

The religious tradition is embodied not in some set of inert practices and texts, but in those realities as they are lived in history. Liturgical practices shape and are shaped by ecclesial communities across time, and the texts of Christian mysticism are received and interpreted experientially by succeeding generations of believers. Andrew Cameron-Mowat in his chapter on the liturgical renewal – perhaps the most contentious area of Catholic practice today – and Peter Tyler on the mystical teaching of the *Corpus Dionysiacum*, both approach their subjects with scholarly textual precision; but they set themselves to interpret the texts in terms of the culture and pastoral challenges of the present time. These rich Christian resources retain the capacity to respond to the challenges of meaning and identity that trouble so many people today, and to do so in real depth. The theological interplay here of serious scholarship and mutual illumination of text and context does much to cut through sterile ideological battles over worship and spirituality.

Bernard Hoose and Brendan Killeen introduce two classical theological disciplines as practical theologies – moral theology and canon law – revealing again the interplay of received tradition and contemporary experience. Moral theology, concerned with the personal dispositions, values and attitudes at the heart of Christian living, draws wisdom inductively from human experience, while bringing to this experience the light of the gospel and drawing norms of behaviour. Christian practices are deeply personal but also socially structured and practised, so the governing function of law both brings order to communal life and protects individuals. But law must always be understood as serving something beyond itself – the life and mission of the Church and the Christian believer. Theology comes first; canon law follows.

Focusing on the practical means giving attention to specific issues such as poverty, ethnicity, ecology and gender, and the human and spiritual challenges these pose to faith. Theology in this key has an added urgency, a yearning for the liberation of the Exodus, for the newness of life that is glimpsed in the Risen Christ – and also a tinge of utopianism. The title of Lilian Dube's chapter on the theological challenges that emerge from the frequently devastating experiences of African women captures it – 'An African Woman's Dream'.

The human practices that are of concern to pastoral theology should not be narrowed to the ecclesial and avowedly Christian. There is a range of practices that sustain human living and creativity; these also are a *locus theologicus*. Wherever true human creativity is expressed, be it ever so non-religious, it is of theological significance. This is in line with Rahner's theology of graced creation, and it is illuminated in David Lonsdale's chapter on the arts and artistic endeavour, poetry and literature.

The usefulness of pastoral theology will only be evident from the work it produces, from its fruits, from solid research that is helpful to practitioners and the Church at large, and the final chapter examines these challenges. It takes up the 'how to' question, and outlines a methodology that has been developed for a concrete research project. The ARCS project at Heythrop College uses a theological action research methodology – a collaborative exercise that examines the evangelizing mission and social action of local church groups, and develops a genuine research partnership with them with the aim of building their capacity for ongoing theological reflection on their practice.

9

When the Theologian Turns
Anthropologist

LOUIS-MARIE CHAUVET

I have been asked to contribute a chapter explaining the point of view of the type of teacher that I am. I am a theologian, who comes at the human/social sciences from the perspective of two types of course: one is a course in sacramental theology, which led me to a specific interest in rituals, and the other is a course in anthropology of religions entitled *Symbols, Myths and Rituals in Religions.*

I will limit myself to suggesting some elements for reflection on the subject of the relationship between theology and anthropology. To start with I will sketch out the aim of my proposal. First of all, it does not focus on the Christian theology of religions, a vast subject that properly belongs to theology, and which for some years now has been the topic of numerous intensive courses, conferences and debates of every kind. Nor does it focus on the epistemology of theology and anthropology: in theory it is quite clear that they are fundamentally different, since Christian theology (to limit myself to this alone) is a discourse that is certainly critical, certainly finds material for consideration in the social sciences, and certainly allows itself to be challenged by them, but is a confessional discourse: a discourse that has as its starting-point what Christians call the 'revelation' of God, and which is at the service of what is understood by this.

As is made clear by my title, my proposal runs the permanent risk, for anyone who is a theologian by trade, of not being sufficiently disconnected from their faith and their concerns, whether objective or subjective, as Christian believers setting out to speak in anthropological terms. Theologians know full well that, in terms of method, they need to suspend their personal religious convictions. And it can be assumed that this is done honestly – hopefully so honestly that listeners belonging to other religious confessions or who are unbelievers could find nothing to complain of in this context. Nevertheless, it may be that theologians are so at home with their own religious convictions that, even with the best of good faith, they are, as it were, secretly on 'automatic pilot', driven, under the appearance of religious neutrality, by what could be described as a 'crypto-theology'. I will illustrate this question with three problems: the sacred, or how to avoid the 'Eliadian' temptation; magic, or how to avoid the 'Barthian' temptation; sacrifice, or how to avoid the 'Girardian' problem. I could undoubtedly have added a good many other examples, notably that of myth, or how to avoid the 'Bultmannian' problem.

Everyone will understand that the fact that I have chosen these authors to characterize each of these temptations in no way disqualifies them in my eyes: all biblicists know what they owe to Bultmann, theologians what they owe to Barth, anthropologists to Eliade or to Girard. Nevertheless there is always the question of the relationship between the writings of Eliade and what his exegetes have made him say. I am intending to pass judgment here not on the author himself, indispensable as he is to religious anthropology, but on the effects often produced by the popularization of his writings.

The Sacred; or How to Avoid the 'Eliadian' Temptation

This idea is very unclear, despite its being so often used. Isambert has referred to it as a 'conceptual funnel' (Isambert 1982). Without going all the way back, as Benvéniste has done, to a common Indo-European language (which has no specific word for what we call the 'sacred'), or even to Greek and Latin, I will content myself with indicating some elements for reflection on this topic (Benvéniste 1969, pp. 179–207).

First of all, the notion of the 'sacred' is in no way universal. Many languages have no notion of it (as, incidentally, they have no notion of 'religion'); or else, if they do know it, as in Greek and Latin, it is not as an absolute noun but as an adjective, which can certainly sometimes be made into a noun, but in the plural, to designate 'sacred things' (*sacra*).

The noun 'sacred' is a relatively recent creation in Western languages. Now for their part words give life to things. To name something is to distinguish, limit and differentiate it. It is at the same time to give rise in the semantic field of a language and of a culture to something that, strictly speaking, did not previously exist as such. Was there an 'unconscious' before Freud? We could reply both yes and no. What we can be sure of is that the creation of this concept gave new life to the reality in question, in a way that modified the manner in which humanity understood and lived the human condition. The same goes for the notion of the 'sacred'; it institutes something new within the relationship with the 'divine'; so much so that this relationship is no longer thought of, lived and carried out in the same fashion afterwards as before the notion emerged.

Therefore, since we are primarily heirs to the Latin language, we are equally heirs to the fact that 'it is in Latin that the division between the sacred and the profane expresses itself most clearly' (Benvéniste 1969, pp. 187–8). This has probably given rise to a double tendency: in our relationship to archaic societies on the one hand, an ethnocentric tendency to project this couplet onto groups that have no sense of such an opposition; in our own society, on the other hand, a tendency to reinforce with considerable frequency the ideological separation between the 'temporal' and the 'spiritual' or between 'laity' and 'priests'. This is as much in the political sphere (cf. for example, the Investiture Controversy in the eleventh century and, in France, at the beginning of the twentieth century, the separation of church and state), as in the cultural (cf. for example, the way in which the sciences have become increasingly autonomous, since the beginning of the modern era, and the phenomenon known as 'secularization'). As an absolute noun, 'the sacred' is a modern creation the characteristics of whose development I will allow myself to sketch out below.

First of all, with Durkheim's famous work *The Elementary Forms of Religious Life* (1912), the 'sacred' designates (a) the result of (b) a collective process experienced as an anonymous force and as a source of energy higher than that of individuals, which (c) comes to objectify itself in certain elements that come to be treated as if invested with a mysterious power. We therefore see that in Durkheim, the adjective 'sacred', which up until then used to qualify objects, places, persons, etc., became a noun designating a reality of a social or collective nature, namely, as he writes, 'a sort of anonymous and impersonal power'. But this noun up until then only had a sociological significance.

It acquired a quite other status in the equally famous work of Rudolf Otto, *Das Heilige* (1926): first of all, at the axiological level, the sacred appeared from then on as ultimate value, next to which all others, including the 'profane', were reckoned as non-values; thus, at the anthropological level, it constituted the primordial condition of all religious experience and was regarded as a disposition originating from the human mind; finally and above all, at the metaphysical level, the sacred was the very essence of the 'Other', therefore of an ontological reality. Thus, for Otto, 'the numinous springs forth from a source hidden in the depths of the human soul. Instead of Durkheim's theory of the *conscience collective*, he posited the theory of an interior revelation, namely the sacred as primordially a category of the mind' (Ries 1985, p. 44).

Within this tradition of Otto's we inevitably find Mircea Eliade. We know that his aim was one of integration, because for him it was a matter of understanding *homo religiosus*, and that this was marked out by a fairly complex process, a process which, with Ries, we can situate at three levels (Ries 1985, pp. 55–60). There is: a historical process, which made him much more attentive than his predecessors, Otto and Van der Leeuw, to the complexity and diversity of religious phenomena, and which prevented him from enclosing his problem within the framework of the individual consciousness (which is what Van der Leeuw in particular had done); a phenomenological process, which aimed to understand religious facts at a deeper level than that of the social and cultural explanation which was dominant among sociologists and ethnographers: every religious phenomenon is a 'hierophany', that is to say the expression of 'the presence of the transcendent within human experience'; finally there was a hermeneutical process, which, going beyond the particular meaning of each religious phenomenon within its culture, allowed us to 'discover the trans-historical content within religious facts in order to render them intelligible and accessible to people today' (Ries 1985, p. 59). It ultimately seemed good that Eliade should be aiming to restore to the West this further aspect of a soul, which secularization was trying to make it lose. Nevertheless, he saw the sacred as the unique and ultimate significance to which multiple cosmic hierophanies refer when it manifests itself within them. This Sacred, Otto's 'Wholly Other', was absolute reality: 'the ultimate reality is the sacred, since only the sacred *is* in an absolute manner, acts effectively and makes things endure' (Eliade 1949, p. 29). The diversity of manifestations of this ontological sacred according to cultures and religions did not prevent it from always being a matter of the same meta-historical and trans-cultural invariable, since it was apprehended by *homo religiosus* according to a universal code linked to 'archetypes' present in all cultures. Hence, there is the convergence in Eliade between a pan-sacralist conception of the cosmos and a theology of 'natural religion', itself perceived as a stepping-stone to Christian revelation. This makes Isambert say, quite justifiably, that 'there is clearly an underlying theology within Eliade's work' (Isambert 1982, p. 264). It anyhow appears explicitly here and there, for example when he writes, in an almost Hegelian manner, that in manifesting itself, 'the sacred . . . limits itself' and that 'God himself accepts self-limitation and historicisation by becoming incarnate in Jesus Christ. This is . . . the great mystery, the *mysterium tremendum*: the fact that the sacred allows itself to be limited' (Eliade 1961/1960, p. 168).

With this notion of the 'sacred' we are therefore witnessing a double semantic elision. We first of all pass from an adjective to a noun, then from the noun to the substance; or, more precisely, from the linguistic constancy of the noun to the ontological consistency of the substance. The fact is, at any rate, that the absolute noun 'the Sacred' belongs from now on, as much as the adjective, to our language and therefore to our representations of the world.[1] We have to make of it what we can.

Now, is it not the case that theologians who turn themselves into anthropologists, especially if they are just starting out, run the risk of finding themselves only too happy to 'make of it what they can'? Indeed a certain number of vested interests will manifest themselves: beyond the so-called 'Sacred' they will willingly allow themselves to be pushed, if they are not careful, into levelling out the diversity of religious systems, into eventually exalting 'popular religion', which they will present as the blessed expression of the riches that proliferate from a natural sacredness stemming from a transcendent source. Above all, finally, they will call upon the whole body of religions to dethrone themselves in favour of Christianity, an act that would lend respectability to what everyone is confusedly searching for, animated as they are by a 'certain sense of the sacred'. Eliade's work, or at least the effects historically produced by his work, as well as the Jungian theory of 'archetypes' with which, as we know, it is not without links, can end up reinforcing its own tendency. In short, for the lack of a sufficient understanding of the ethnocentric relativity of a notion such as that of 'the Sacred', and through lack of a sufficiently critical vigilance, theologians who turn themselves into anthropologists run the serious risk, under an apparent neutrality, of being animated by what I have called a 'crypto-theology'.

Magic; or How to Avoid the Barthian Temptation

The question here is above all an academic one within the sphere of anthropology, namely that of distinguishing between 'magic' and 'religion'. Once again, on this point I take the liberty of rapidly sketching the evolution among anthropological thinkers.

A first criterion of distinction ('manipulation' v. 'propitiation') comes to us from J. G. Frazer. We know that, in his famous work *The Golden Bough*, he set in opposition magic, as the *manipulation* of occult powers, and religion, as the *propitiation* or conciliation of a divinity, while recognizing that religion can become magic as soon as it seeks to constrain the divinity and that magic can become religious as soon as it seeks the favour of spirits in order to succeed (Frazer 1922).

A second criterion of distinction ('private' versus 'public') came to us from Henri Hubert and Marcel Mauss, in their *Esquisse d'une théorie générale de la magie*. First of all, they took up Frazer's idea: magical rituals 'constrain, whereas religious rituals conciliate; the first have an immediate mechanical action, the second act indirectly and by means of a sort of respectful persuasion' (*L'année sociologique*, 1904, p. 13). But in the face of the frequent transformation of the said magician into a religious person who appeals to the good will of spirits, Hubert and Mauss suggested another criterion of differentiation: magic belongs in the *private* or illegitimate sphere, insofar as it never enjoys the official recognition from which religion benefits, whereas religion belongs in the *public*, therefore the legitimate sphere. 'A magician has a clientele, not a church', Durkheim wrote with reference to this (Durkheim 1912, p. 62). This does not prevent them both having the same object, the *mana*, or mysterious power that lies at the root of things; it is just that magic seeks to make use of it for private ends.

Nevertheless this second criterion does not seem to be enough. Indeed, the shaman who practises a rainmaking ritual performs a public act, which therefore becomes religious; whereas when a healing ritual is performed, the private act turns into magic. G. Gurvitch also claimed to have found a more relevant differentiating characteristic by distinguishing a *mana* that is strictly speaking non-sacred, a power that is immanent with regard to beings and things, and a sacred *mana* that implies transcendence (Gurvitch 1950, ch. 7). Magic has to do with the first, thus with a power that is immanent with regard to things, a power that people seek to master; religion corresponds to the human attitude of humility and subordination before the transcendent sacred. In this view we find something of Frazer's opposition between magical manipulation and religious propitiation.

Finally, 'we can suggest seeing between magic and religion a polarity rather than a frontier. The accumulation of the three criteria yields facts which are unmistakably magical and unmistakably religious – at least in our view', writes Isambert, who offers the following pattern (Isambert 1979, p. 44):

Magic	*Religion*
Immanence	Transcendence
Manipulation	Propitiation
Private	Public

For example, the case most often quoted by the three preceding authors, that of sympathetic magic, 'is characteristic in this regard: use of immanent powers, manipulation, private act' (Isambert 1979, pp. 44–5). In the logical coherence of the preceding table, there is an 'ideal type' in Weber's sense, 'a type whose reality is more or less close to one or more criteria which is lacking' (Isambert 1979, p. 45).

Indeed, as M. Mauss had already observed in his statement saying that, in order to understand systems of symbolic exchange among the Melanesians we have simultaneously to use terms that are opposed in our Western languages ('obligatory gifts', 'necessary generosities'), here we hit up against the barrier of language (Mauss 1924 (1973 edn), p. 267). Or again, as R. Bastide writes, 'Western linguistic categories (religion, magic, sorcery) do not necessarily carry the same meaning as among other peoples.'[2] We finally end up asking ourselves if it is not our opposition that 'is not significant' with regard to traditional societies, and if it is not our Western mental universe 'in which public and private interests are opposed' that we are projecting onto them. Might it not be *we*, asks Isambert finally, who, since the dawn of 'modern Christianity', need to oppose magic to religion, thus proceeding to 'an unprecedented clash between theological thought and scientific thought'? The success of such an opposition, in which he detects an ideological ulterior motive, is probably not without its links to 'a series of oppositions that have been put forward for some time now: popular religion/informed religion; tradition/innovation; ritualism/activism; faith/religion (Isambert 1979, pp. 58–9).

Of course none of this annuls the distinction between magic and religion, insofar as (a) it is used in a flexible manner, that is to say not as a fixed frontier existing in the very nature of social realities, but as an ideal-typical polarity, and (b) we recognize in the three criteria we have retained assumptions emanating from our own anxieties concerning the religious sphere. That there should be assumptions there does not disqualify them on scientific grounds: it is impossible to do otherwise in the social sciences; the important thing is not to confuse scientific discourse with reality. On these two conditions, the proposed distinction is of methodological value: it therefore tries to give an account of the fact that, for example, a private technique of sympathetic magic cannot be considered in the same way as a thanksgiving sacrifice.

Here again, theologians who turn into anthropologists are running the serious risk, if they are not careful, of using in a simplistic manner the opposition between magic and religion. We can certainly assume that today they avoid denoting as 'magical' the practices of traditional religion (as missionaries so often did up until the 1950s, and even afterwards), in opposition to the Christianity that they always placed entirely in the category of religion (Auge 1982). It is rather within Christianity itself that they risk too easily using the opposition: are they not indeed tempted to qualify as 'magic' the popular practices of a certain number of Christians that seem of doubtful theological taste, at the same time situating themselves, as well as 'informed' Christians, on the side of 'true' religion and defending the institution of which it is a tributary? The polemics of the 1970s, as Isambert has well analysed, were carved out by this sort of ideological *a priori*, where the 'magician' is always the other, those assumptions being furthermore strengthened by an opposition still in operation, and equally highly ideological, between real 'faith' and 'religion'.

But then, theologians forget to ask themselves why they see no difference between the two situations shown by the Italian director Olmi in his film *The Tree of Wooden Clogs*: on the one hand, an old man is preparing a mixture made up of different ingredients in order to cure someone at death's door; while doing so, he is rattling off Our Fathers and invoking a multitude of angels and saints in a speech that rumbles along and is manifestly not addressed to these supernatural beings but to other interlocutors whom he begs to grant him their favour. He shows the true behaviour of the magician, whom L. de Heusch says has a message 'with no hearer'; rather it is a 'mechanical discourse' or 'a technique turned into a language and a language into a technique', given that he is not communicating with supernatural powers but simply seeking, through the power of his words, to strike the material elements he is manipulating so as to make a hidden energy emerge from them (de Heusch 1974, p. 701). On the other hand, in the same film, Olmi shows us a woman who has no other resources for staying alive than her one cow, which is seriously ill; driven to desperation, the woman goes down to the river to draw water and she places her bucket of water on the altar of a little chapel, begging God or the Blessed Virgin to come to her help. It is clear that what this woman does can be read in the same light as the behaviour of the 'magician': so why should she not also be put into the class of 'magic'? But if we concede that the woman's spontaneous prayer for her cow arises from religious behaviour, in the same way as pious pilgrims in Lourdes make their spontaneous prayers to the Virgin visible through a candle in front of the grotto, why should we necessarily judge her to be fundamentally different from the 'good Christian' who asks God: 'give us this day our daily bread'? Besides, what is the difference between a statue venerated by a traditional pagan, an icon kissed by an orthodox Christian and the Eucharist adored by a Catholic (and we could add a Bible used by a Protestant)? There certainly is one, if only because the system of meanings and references in which each of these religious objects is situated is different. But before we outline this or that difference, would it not be better to recognize what they might have in common? Like the magician, the 'idolater' is always 'the Other'.

In short, theologians, when they become anthropologists, have to remain critical of the reflexes that they have acquired in theology if, as is only right, they want on the one hand to avoid making value judgements on the religious facts that constitute their object of study, and on the other hand, not to be intellectual victims of their own implicit paradigm. According to this paradigm it is inevitably always Christianity, that is to say their own religion, that is in the right and, within Christianity, the 'scholars' who are never wrong about the difference (a pertinent one, it is true, in certain cases) between 'faith' and 'religion'. Their problem, therefore, is to avoid the 'Barthian' temptation of a 'Word of God' that always towers over concrete history and a reception of this Word in the existential decision of faith that tends to iron out the relative opacity of cultural and social mediations in which it takes place.

Sacrifice; or How to Avoid the 'Girardian' Temptation

This is an important subject for Christian theologians, by reason of the sacrificial interpretation of the death of Christ and of the Eucharist that is celebrated in memory of it. It happens that some years ago my colleagues in the Institut de Sciences et de Théologie des Religions gave me the task of undertaking in synthesis a rereading of their respective works concerning sacrifice in their given special subject areas: from African traditional religions to Taoism, passing through Judaism, Christianity, Islam, Hinduism, Buddhism and ancient China.[3] When I read their texts, I was struck by the fact that, in cultural areas that were nevertheless so different, three things could be seen.

First, sacrifices, in their extreme diversity, seem to be structured by a link between four agents: a sacrificer, who is in charge of the operation; the person on whose behalf the sacrifice is made, who is its beneficiary (and who is sometimes, as an agent, the same person as the sacrificer); a sacrificed object, which is alive, or something that symbolically represents life; and finally a recipient, who always belongs to a category of beings superior to humans (even if the Hindu ascetic is himself the person on whose behalf the sacrifice of his own self is made, since the Self or '*atman*' to whom he makes the sacrifice is identified with the Supreme Brahma).

Second, sacrifices consequently can be interpreted as a symbolic exchange structured by a series of opposed couples of which the most all-embracing is without doubt that of conjunction/disjunction, a couplet that itself mixes with fundamental oppositions like death/life, debt/repayment, sacred/sacrilegious, without mentioning elsewhere their links with social structures (like the opposition man/woman), cultural paradigms (like the one that exists between nature and culture) or economic conditions (like that between prodigality and penury, or between the excessive and the derisory), which come symbolically into play in this global negotiation. It seems that the notion of the 'debt of existence', given such strong prominence by Luc de Heusch in his work *Le Sacrifice dans les religions africaines*, is the key to quite an interesting general reading on the subject (de Heusch 1986).

Finally, and above all for what concerns us here, a tension exists everywhere, although to different degrees, between sacrificial rites and ethics. Now, Christian theologians have to lay stronger emphasis on the discontinuities between different religious systems than the continuities in this context. Here again, they have to submit their *assumptions* to critical consideration. This is because the difference is so great between: the Mossis of Burkina who, in an attitude that we have to call one of humility and trust, for want of any other word, offer their lamb to a God whom they believe to be a protector and guide (Pasquier 1994); Taoists for whom 'true sacrifice' consists above all in 'the kenotic pouring forth of their vital energies for the sake of others' (Lagerwey 1994); Hindus who extend the notion of sacrifice to hospitality offered to another or to the mental recitation of a mantra; the *Bhagavad-Gita*, which aims, as A. Cahn writes, at offering as a sacrifice 'any act achieved without egoism, without attachment, for the love of God' (Cahn 1994); Greek philosophers who, like Socrates, and without mentioning the Stoics, declare that 'the most beautiful sacrifice "consists of living like" the most noble and just of human beings'; Jews who, according to Philo of Alexandria, consider that sacrifices offered in the Temple of Jerusalem are only pleasing to God if they are the expression of an offering by the faithful of their good interior dispositions ('it is a good thing to scrutinize one's own motives for thanksgiving and to choose the best of them, because it is better to give thanks for the love of God rather than for the purposes of self-interest');[4] Muslims for whom sacrifice aims at expressing a 'total . . . identification with the attitude of submission of Abraham to God and should be an opportunity, as the Koran dictates, for nourishing "the poor and the wretched"'.[5]

It goes without saying that there are differences between all these cases. But they do not lie where Christian theologians might tend to place them, that is to say in the degree of 'spiritualization' of the sacrifice or of the ethical implications of the subject in itself, which appears spontaneously higher to them within Christianity, whereas, as has just been shown, this degree can also be high within Hinduism or Judaism. The differences lie in the symbolic system of significance at the heart of which sacrifice finds its place and its meaning. The difference within a Christian sacrifice, for example, appears to be linked to the inversion that it makes of the gift and the counter-gift, since Christians can only respond to the initial and gratuitous gift of God's self in Christ, in the same way that the 'spiritual' interpretation of God's sacrifice is justified, in this belief system, not at the level of morality but at that of theology: it is the gift of the Holy Spirit and not the refining of a person's moral conscience that forms the basis of this interpretation (Neusch 1994, p. 134).

Furthermore, the success twenty or so years ago within Christian circles of the non-sacrificial reading of Jesus' death by René Girard should also be noted. It was indeed tempting to make use of the author's general theory in order to denounce a theological interpretation of Christ's death and the Eucharist that laid excessive stress on sacrifice and expiation, notably since the Middle Ages, but particularly in the aftermath of the Council of Trent. Theologians indeed had good biblical and patristic reasons for relativizing such emphases and even for correcting the errors of which they were sometimes the expression: theological errors regarding the figure of a judgemental God onto whom humankind's most primitive vindictive reactions were projected; moral errors regarding a Christianity fixated on pain that laid excessive guilt on itself. But there are also good reasons to beware of Girardian theory: first of all, is he not in the process of burning the sacrifice that the Church so much 'adored' in the past? Then, 'how can one not be a Christian' if one follows Girard to the letter; that is to say, in saying that the heart of Jesus' message is to denounce the victimizing sacrificial process in the way that he understands it? Finally, if theologians turn anthropologist, it is a truism to say that they run the serious risk of levelling out the cultural and religious particularities of sacrifices in a general theory that may be seductive but is dangerous in its very generality. This does not mean that such a theory might not give pause for thought, as much for theologians as for anthropologists. But, by reason of the mental structure (what the Scholastics would have called the *habitus*) that theology has given them and that persuades them to place in dialogue with the one and only God a generic and only human being, i.e. a being whose universality is conceptually established at the price of crushing its characteristic socio-historic mediations, they must remain particularly vigilant in order not to adopt over-hastily a general theory that follows their reflexes and their Christian self-interest. On the question of sacrifice, as with those of the sacred and of magic, theologians must critique their crypto-metaphysical and crypto-theological reflexes.

I will finish by making three points.

First of all it is clear, after what I have just said, that 'scientific' anthropology, as I have perceived it in my examples, can be of considerable service to theologians. First of all, it can be of *critical* service, because it flushes out their prejudices and even forces them to review their paradigms. We know that this is true for all scientists and is difficult for all of them. But it may be that it is particularly so for theologians, by reason of the confessional, and thus implicating nature of their discipline. Then it can be of *epistemological* service, because insofar as anyone advances in the mastery of whatever touches on anthropology it becomes clearer that the object of theology, that is to say God revealed in Jesus Christ, can never be the end of any anthropological behaviour whatsoever; which is not to say that theologians might not entertain some formal connivance or other with it. Lastly, it can properly speaking be of *theological* service, insofar as practising or frequenting anthropology requires them to rethink from scratch a certain number of classical questions within theology. In short, theologians cannot emerge from such frequentations scot-free; as Bouillard used to recognize, it brings with it 'a new way of practising theological reflection'.[6]

I would like to add that the fact of being a theologian 'by profession', or more simply again, the fact of being a believer when one is doing anthropology, is not only a source of inconvenience. It is possibly also an opportunity when one takes religions as one's object of study. I will rapidly explain what I mean. Religious expression constitutes a particular form of 'language game', in the sense given to this concept by its creator Ludwig Wittgenstein. This means particularly that, no more than any other, can this language game be reduced to its purely verbal form: it is intrinsically linked to a specific 'life form'. Now, as J. Greisch has written, 'religious language games, notwithstanding their empirical diversity, have a strong resemblance in common and in this sense they form a "system" '. That they form a system means that their 'consequences and premises offer one another mutual support' and that, through them, a 'totality of judgments becomes plausible for us'. Such a system cannot be assimilated to an axiomatic point of departure: Greisch remembers, in quoting Wittgenstein, that 'systems are not so much the starting point for arguments as their vital context', which means that 'any verification of what we accept to be true, any confirmation or contradiction already takes place within a system . . . What is fixed is not so by virtue of its intrinsic quality of clarity or of evidence, but solidly maintained by all that surrounds it' (Greisch 1991, pp. 321–80; p. 369). We therefore understand the justness of Wittgenstein's observation, according to which when believers ask 'where does the world come from?' they 'are not asking for a causal explanation; the cleverness of their question is that it is nevertheless the expression of such a desire. They are in fact expressing an attitude with regard to all explanations' (Greisch 1991, p. 372 n. 6). We also understand the failure of logical positivism with regard to religious language, which in no way, of course, allows us to fall into 'fideism' (Greisch 1991, pp. 347–56). If therefore the 'reasons' for believing are inseparable from a certain 'way of life', would not the fact of being a believer, and therefore of sharing in this way of life, beyond all the empirical differences that make religions specific, obviously with a reinforced critical vigilance, constitute an opportunity rather than an obstacle in the domain of the science of religion?

It remains for us to ask the question, which will be my third and last point: might not Christian theology, doubtless less in its content than its manner, have some service to render to anthropology, since it is constantly battling not only with interpretation but also and above all with the question of the implication of the confessing subject in an object that s/he is nevertheless seeking to treat with all the resources of critical reasoning? I leave this question open.

This article appeared as '*Quand le théologien se fait anthropologue. . .*' in Jean Joncheray (ed.), 1997, *Approches scientifiques des faits religieux*, Paris: Beauchesne, pp. 29–46; English translation by Gemma Simmonds, CJ.

Notes

1 As was demonstrated by a research project of A. Vergote, it is a semanteme that, in our culture, tends to symbolize itself spontaneously on a vertical axis, but with a dominance of depth or from a more or less mysterious source within human existence, where for 'God', the dominance, on the same axis, is that of height, of power, of majesty. See A. Vergote 1983, pp. 150–1.

2 E. Evans-Pritchard, 1937, had already used two English words where we only use one: 'witchcraft', which denotes substance that is often inherited, which can be found in certain people's stomach, and which therefore refers to a power working in a mechanical way on people, whereas 'sorcery' designates the use of supernatural powers that allow one to work on nature, powers acquired through a particular initiation. C. Kluckhohn, 1944, goes even further, since he adds a third term, 'wizardry', while emphasizing that the different terms used are anyway not the semantic equivalent of those used by the Navaho.

3 These contributions became part of a book: M. Neusch 1994.

4 Philo, *De specialibus legibus* 1.283. Cf. J. Laporte 1972.

5 Sura 22.28. E. Platti 1994.

6 H. Bouillard, 1978, 'Naissance et développement de l'Institut de Sciences et de Théologie des Religions', *Nouvelles de l'Institut Catholique de Paris*, p. 45.

Bibliography

M. Auge, 1982, *Génie du paganisme*, Paris: Gallimard.

E. Benvéniste, 1969, *Le Vocabulaire des institutions indo-européennes*, vol. II, Paris: Minuit.

A. Cahn, 1994, 'Le sacrifice dans l'hindouisme', in M. Neusch (ed.), *Le Sacrifice dans les religions*, Paris: Beauchesnes, ch. 8.

E. Durkheim, 2008 [1912], *The Elementary Forms of Religious Life*, trans. Carol Cosman, ed. Mark S. Cladis, Oxford: Oxford University Press.

M. Eliade, 1989 [1949], *Le Mythe de l'éternel retour*, Paris: Gallimard.

M. Eliade, 1961, *Mythes, rêves et mystères*, 2nd edn, Paris: Gallimard; trans. from the French by Philip Mairet, 1960, as *Myths, Dreams, and Mysteries*, London: Harvill Press.

E. Evans-Pritchard, 1937, *Witchcraft, Oracles and Magic among the Azande*, Oxford: Clarendon Press.

J. G. Frazer, 1922 [1890], *The Golden Bough*, London: Macmillan.

J. Greisch, 1991, 'La religion à l'intérieur des limites du simple langage', in Collectif, *Penser la religion*, Paris: Beauchesne.

G. Gurvitch, 1950, *La Vocation actuelle de la sociologie*, Paris: Presses Universitaires de France.

L. de Heusch, 1974, 'Introduction à une ritologie générale', in Centre de Royaumont, *L'Unité de l'Homme*, Paris: Seuil.

L. de Heusch, 1986, *Le Sacrifice dans les religions Africaines*, Paris: Gallimard.

F. A. Isambert, 1979, *Rite efficacité symbolique*, Paris: Cerf.

F. A. Isambert, 1982, *Le Sens du sacré. Fête et religion populaire*, Paris: Minuit.

C. Kluckhohn, 1944, *Navaho Witchcraft*, Cambridge, MA: Peabody Museum of American Archaeology and Ethnology.

J. Lagerwey, 1994, 'Le sacrifice taoïste', in M. Neusch (ed.), *Le Sacrifice dans les religions*, Paris: Beauchesne, ch. 11.

J. Laporte, 1972, *La Doctrine eucharistique chez Philon d'Alexandrie*, Paris: Beauchesne.

M. Mauss, 1924, 'Essai sur le don', in M. Mauss, 1973, *Sociologie et anthropologie*, Paris: Presses Universitaires de France, 1973.

M. Neusch (ed.), 1994, *Le sacrifice dans les religions*, Paris: Beauchesne.

E. Platti, 1994, 'Le sacrifice en Islam', in M. Neusch (ed.), *Le Sacrifice dans les religions*, Paris: Beauchesne, ch. 7.

A. Pasquier, 1994, 'Le sacrifice aux ancêtres dans le devenir du « Moaaga »', in M. Neusch (ed.), *Le Sacrifice dans les religions*, Paris: Beauchesne, ch.2

J. Ries, 1985, *Les Chemins du sacré dans l'histoire*, Paris: Aubier-Montaigne.

A. Vergote, 1983, *Religion, foi, incroyance*, Brussels: Mardaga, 1983.

Texts and Practices: An Ecclesiology of *Traditio* For Pastoral Theology

CLARE WATKINS

The concern of this chapter emerges from the difficulties experienced in much contemporary practical/pastoral theology with 'the Christian theological tradition'. The concept itself, by its very nature, is not clearly defined, adding to the difficulties. This essay develops an understanding that, rooted in Scripture and the subsequent texts and practices of the Christian community, sees pastoral/practical theology as, above all, ecclesiologically centred. It is in the Church that texts and practices are discerned, lived and critically struggled with, in ways that embody and disclose *traditio* – that faith and wisdom that is handed on.

The basic thesis here is twofold. First, it is argued that in much pastoral theology[1] the difficulty of engaging with Christian tradition is marked by an unhelpful dichotomizing – between past and present; texts and practices; faith and action; and so on. These dichotomies have not only undermined practical theology's theological maturity, but they also limit its reading of practice. There is an assumption of dis-integration, alongside a constant struggle for integration. Second, it is suggested that another, more helpful, context for practical/pastoral theology can be provided by ecclesiology. In particular, an ecclesiology that understands 'church' from the fundamental perspective of divine revelation, allows many of the dichotomies of pastoral theology and tradition to be overcome, as an integrated approach to tradition and contemporary practice comes to light as proper to church life and faith. In what follows, this revelation-centred ecclesiology is articulated from the Second Vatican Council's *Dei Verbum*, and is described as an ecclesiology of *traditio*.

The 'Disconnections' of Tradition: The Question Raised by the Late Modern Development of Pastoral Theology

One way of understanding our first point is through the word *integrity*. I choose this word because it draws attention to our habit of assuming disintegration, even while we teach, write and develop systems for ensuring integration. We suffer, then, from a certain fragmentation and separation of aspects of the Christian tradition and life, which is damaging to our sense of the theological vocation and impairs its fruitfulness.

David Cornick, in an essay on the history of Christian pastoral care, writes:

> The severest dislocation in the history of pastoral care in the West came not at the Reformation but at the Enlightenment. The focus of care in medieval Christendom and in early modern Europe was on reconciliation. The penitential system and Reformed discipline shared a single aim – reconciliation with God. The gradual decline of discipline was indicative of a massive shift in intellectual history – the establishment of the primacy of reason, the autonomy of the human self, and the slow shrinking of the realm of the supernatural. (Cornick 2000, p. 362)

This makes it clear that we are dealing not so much with the Reformed or Catholic flavour of pastoral theology but its nature as a theological response to the effects of the Enlightenment. Theology in our time has had to work with a worldview that forms theologians and society as a whole in a culture of the rational, the materially demonstrable. Pastoral theology, as that form of theology that seeks especially to be in the places of Christian practice, is implicated in this post-Enlightenment development in profound and complex ways. In particular, Cornick's 'severest dislocation' has brought about a situation in which we are constantly struggling with disconnections, or 'gaps', and consequently with the need to connect things that for much of the Christian tradition have been accepted as integrated into a whole. As pastoral theologians we work with fragmented realities that seem to need joining up – 'theology' and 'practice', 'tradition' and 'experience', past and present.[2]

This dislocation has had manifold effects on theology. Our concern here is with the difficulty we have as late modern Christians, after generations of that 'slow shrinking of the realm of the supernatural' of which Cornick speaks, in relating our present experience and life as disciples to the Christian theological tradition as it has been developed and handed on through the history of the Church.

This does not identify a new question. Writers in this field have for some time recognized the difficulty.[3] In its earlier forms, modern pastoral theology, perhaps taking a level of theological education for granted, tended to concentrate on how pastoral care was to be carried out.[4] Late modern pastoral theology, reacting to the 'academic' (that is, non-practical) nature of much university theology, has emerged as a discipline characterized by interdisciplinarity and a privileged hearing of contemporary experience and practice. What is rarely developed, however, is a sense of real – or 'living' – continuity with the longer Christian tradition, even including Scripture itself.

That this fracturing within pastoral theology is now receiving more attention is welcome. It is now more than twenty years since Thomas Oden highlighted the problem as he moved to a radical critique of his own work in pastoral care, to reflect on the traditions of pastoral care in early medieval times.[5] Edward Farley and Ellen Charry, in different ways, have shown the importance of classic theological Christian texts for contemporary growth in Christian discipleship.[6] More recently in the British context, Elaine Graham, Heather Walton and Frances Ward produced a two-volume work that explicitly responds to the difficulty we are treating. They recognize that theological reflection – a major pastoral theological method – 'is often weak in its use of traditional Christian sources', and quote research showing that in teaching there is 'a "paucity or complete absence of guidelines on how the Bible and Christian tradition are to be used in theological reflection"'.[7] Notably, these authors root this weakness in the ways theological formation and training has been broken up into discrete subject areas, in which 'pastoral theology' has come to be the subject that deals with the practical, contextual and ministerial questions. This suggests that the dis-integration of theology into Scripture, history, doctrine and the pastoral – a fruit of post-Enlightenment pedagogy – goes right to the heart of our teaching and learning of theology. It is in part to remedy this situation that Graham, Walton and Ward put together texts and sources and an introduction to a variety of methods:

so that those undertaking theological reflection today may gain confidence and insight from a realization that what they do is a perennial and indispensable part of the history of Christian doctrine. It is our contention that 'theological reflection' is not a novel or exceptional activity. Rather, it has constituted Christian 'talk about God' since the very beginning.[8]

This assertion is broadly in line with the thesis of this chapter. However, I feel that these authors have only gone part of the way towards resolving the difficulty they identify. In fact, the late modern concern with 'making connections' is not characteristic of theology through the ages; it is dependent on a worldview that already gives credence to a fragmentation of knowledge and wisdom. Our very struggle as pastoral theologians to find ways of 'making connections' is dependent on the culture of dis-integration, and so carries into its own methodologies the very dichotomies it seeks to overcome. As ever, the tackling of the established pattern of thought will necessarily be marked by the very assumptions it seeks to leave behind.

The fundamental question might be put thus: how are late modern theological concerns with Christian living to be worked out in integrity with the Christian tradition as a whole? This question lies behind the 'need for connection' in the contemporary pastoral theological enterprise, and the various approaches that have been developed in response. This essay suggests that what we need is not a series of new methodologies, but a reorientation of thought through a specifically ecclesiological turn in our thinking. This is where the ecclesiology of *traditio* provides a helpful way for our thinking.

Effects of the 'Breach' in Tradition

Before giving an account of this ecclesiological approach, it will be as well to illustrate more clearly what I mean by 'dis-integrity' (which is absolutely not anything to do with a 'lack of integrity' in the usual sense!). I shall outline, with illustrations from the literature, certain instances of the effects of dis-integration as a starting-place for pastoral theological thinking.

The Correlative Patterning of Pastoral/Practical Theology

In one of the key texts for teaching pastoral theology, Stephen Pattison and James Woodward helpfully offer students a chapter giving an account of the main features of the field. The authors identify fourteen 'essential characteristics' for pastoral theology (Woodward and Pattison 2000, pp. 13–16), among which is a dialectical form of articulation:

Proceeding by way of a kind of critical conversation, many contemporary practical theologies hold in creative tension a number of polarities such as:

- theory and practice
- the religious tradition emanating from the past and contemporary religious experience
- particular situational realities and general theoretical principles
- what is (reality) and what might be (ideal)
- description (what is) and prescription (what ought to be)
- written texts and other 'texts' of present experience
- theology and other disciplines
- the religious community and society outside the religious community. (pp. 15–16)

As a description of the patterns at work in much pastoral theology this is uncontentious. Indeed the point is underlined in the same text book's presentation of the methodological discussions in pastoral theology, which centre around questions of how these 'creative tensions' are to be worked with. So, Don Browning gives an account of his 'revised correlative method';[9] and Alistair Campbell offers a helpful critical account of the different ways of 'relating' practical theology to 'other theological disciplines' (Campbell 2000, pp. 78–88). According to Campbell, 'concrete situations' and the theological tradition are to be set side by side:

> not in order to correct according to some canon of relevance, nor in order to be corrected according to some canon of orthodoxy. It is more an exercise in creative imagination, the interplay of idea and action, with all the ambiguity and inconclusiveness which this implies. (p. 85)

What is clear in all these discussions of correlation is the assumption that there is a gap to be worked with, to be held together creatively, or to be imaginatively bridged.

The Pervasiveness of Dichotomies/Polarizations and its Effects

Discussion of correlation and making connections runs all the way through pastoral theology.[10] In the growing attention given to theological reflection as a method in pastoral theology the concern is for bringing together experience and the tradition; for example through models of conversation between, as Pattison puts it, '(a) her [the theologian's] own ideas, beliefs, feelings, perceptions and assumptions, (b) the beliefs, assumptions and perceptions provided by the Christian tradition (including the Bible) and (c) the contemporary situation which is being examined' (Pattison 2000, p. 139).

In the literature on theological reflection we find many examples of excellent attempts to bring to students' attention the importance of integrating their own reflections on a particular pastoral experience, with the Bible and the wider theological tradition.[11] What is striking, however, is the prior assumption of separation of experience from tradition or doctrine. In the process of theological reflection both the experience of the reflector, and that bit of the tradition with which she is working, are 'objectified', in order to be set alongside, or brought into conversation with, each other. It is this abstraction, both of the practicality under consideration and of the theological theme employed, that is fundamental to methods of correlation. It is an abstraction or objectification that must surely, and necessarily, de-form both experience and doctrine, and undermine their 'conversation' by a prior assumption of disconnection (dis-integrity) which is then built in to the process as a given. For example, dialogue built on such abstraction suggests that practices are to be considered 'alongside' tradition, implying they are not already part of and bearers of that tradition; furthermore, and at the same time, the objectification of what is taught in and by the tradition reduces it to 'doctrine' in a narrow, formal sense, too-often cut apart from its own historical context and practice-base. Thus violence is done both to Christian practices as theology (instances of faith seeking understanding) and to the texts of the Christian tradition, as themselves fruits of faith practised. In the end, we run the risk of doing violence to the nature of theology itself.

All this is inauthentic to the Christian theological tradition. The patterns of thinking that are thus brought about make an authentic integrative account of present Christian practice and the Christian tradition problematic from the start.

The Ecclesiology of *Traditio*: Looking at Things Another Way?

This all too brief account of the dis-integrity of much of our pastoral theological approach stands as an introduction to an alternative theological approach drawn from an ecclesiological understanding of the pastoral theological task as discernment and articulation of God's presence to us – his self-revelation in time and space. My contention is that such an ecclesiology of *traditio* provides a different way of looking at pastoral theology, one that begins with an assumption of connection. As we shall see, this ecclesiological emphasis does not do away with controversy, tensions, fractures and conflicts of understanding, but relocates them to the living context of theological tradition as embodied in the life, practice, current conflicts, and intellectual and worshipping memory of the Church.

This ecclesiology is characterized by an understanding of ecclesial life in which the Church is understood as the place of divine revelation. The Church of *traditio* is the place of the hearing and handing on of God's Word, his self-revelation. In order to explore what this might mean I offer an account of ecclesiology drawn explicitly from the Second Vatican Council's Dogmatic Constitution on Divine Revelation, *Dei Verbum*, whose profound ecclesiological implications are reflected in the other constitutions of that Council.[12]

Beginning with God: Divine Revelation and God as Father, Son and Spirit

Our approach begins with the central Christian fact of divine revelation. The reason we have anything to say at all theologically lies in the fact of God having 'spoken' to the world, in history, addressing men and women with his own Word. Within the Catholic tradition attention is paid here both to that 'natural revelation' of the gracedness of creation, with the potential of the human person made in the image of God, and to the particular revelation of God through the salvation history attested to by the scriptural texts. God wills to reveal himself, so that all people 'should have access to the Father, through Christ, the Word made flesh, in the Holy Spirit, and thus become sharers in the divine nature'. God goes out from himself, as Word and Spirit, so as to move among men and women, addressing them as friends 'in order to invite and receive them into his own company' (*Dei Verbum*, 2).

Much of the struggle with making connections in pastoral theology has to do with the questions of what kind of reality we are 'reading' and what theological 'authority' such readings might have. Indeed, all theology has to work with that fundamental question of what it is that it is working to articulate. The ecclesiological approach I am suggesting takes as a working premise that God has revealed himself, and continues to be present to us in his Word and Spirit; and that the theological vocation – within which 'professional theologians' have a particular role, but not a monopoly – is one of discerning that revelation in our own time and space. The key question then becomes not what sort of solution to a practical problem we might come up with, but rather what God is already working out ahead of us, and what his Spirit is opening up by way of a path into a closer 'keeping company' with God. The pastoral theologian is no longer asked simply to tackle pastoral situations and come up with responses, but is asked fundamentally to attend to the call that is being made to the Church from beyond itself, from the Trinity.

This position runs the risk of sounding like the kind of piety that actually closes the door on pastoral theology as an endeavour of intellectual and practical discipleship. This is not the intention. Rather, this starting position, while radically altering the sense of our task as pastoral theologians, also opens up a new set of questions as to how we are to be attentive to divine revelation in the way suggested. This orientation of approach, characterized by discernment, leads us not (only) to quiet contemplation, but also to new critical and practical questions: Where, then, are we to look for this leading of the Spirit? How are we to learn this attentiveness to God's presence in the world? Responding to such questions as these we begin to see more clearly the shape of the pastoral theological vocation.

The Church as Characterized by the 'Handling' and Handing On of Divine Revelation

The primacy of revelation in this approach to pastoral theology provides a particular perspective for understanding Church. It recognizes the essential nature of the Church as to do with its handing on of that which has been and is revealed in Christ. This giving away of what is received through the abiding presence of the Spirit describes that evangelizing 'single end' of the Church to which John Paul II draws our attention (*Redemptor hominis*, 13).

The Church as defined by *traditio* looks constantly at what it has received through time and space, and seeks to serve that tradition, whether written or oral, or embodied in practices, by reflecting on contemporary articulations/practices. It is through gazing at what has been received that we come to glimpse something of what God is. So:

This sacred tradition, then, and the sacred scripture of both Testaments are like a mirror, in which the Church, during its pilgrim journey here on earth, contemplates God, from who she receives everything, until such time as she is brought to see him face to face as he really is (1 Jn. 3:2). (*Dei Verbum*, 7)

At the same time, the doctrine of revelation presupposes an abiding presence of God in the world, which summons the Church to a reading of the signs of the times:

> With the help of the Holy Spirit, it is the task of the whole People of God, particularly of its pastors and theologians, to listen to and distinguish the many voices of our times and interpret them in the light of the divine Word, in order that the revealed truth may be more deeply penetrated, better understood, and more suitably presented. (*Gaudium et spes*, 44)

In all this the community of the faithful, with its variety of tasks, is caught up in a complexity of voices, which it is called to approach in a spirit of discernment or listening-in. This attentiveness leads to response; but this response is not about making of the voices objectified abstractions that we can work with or analyse. Rather, the response is to be one of discerning the single voice of the God who reveals himself, and moving in relation to that call into the next step. The struggle is to hear the underlying harmony of a cacophony of simultaneous voices – Scripture, tradition, magisterium, devotional practices (past and present), worldly wisdoms – in the faith that there is an underlying symphony, because the one God wills to reveal himself to us. Our history as well as present experience make it clear that such ecclesial discernment is rarely peaceful or easy; indeed, both theologically and sociologically levels of conflict, struggle and controversy are a proper part of this handling of the mystery of divine revelation.[13] What is important for our present purposes is the recognition of this controversial ecclesial process as distinctly different from systematic attempts at making connections; here, in the ecclesial living of revelation, the assumption of connection can be more clearly felt and nurtured.

Revelation as Words, Deeds and Person (Word)

Another aspect of this ecclesiology concerns the understanding of divine revelation as a coherent whole in which words, deeds (practices) and persons are thoroughly implicated, in ways that cannot be cut apart one from the other. We see this explicitly set out at the start of *Dei Verbum*:

Revelation is realised by deeds, and words, which are intrinsically bound up with each other. As a result, the works performed by God in the history of salvation show forth and bear out the doctrine and realities signified by the words; the words, for their part, proclaim the works, and bring to light the mystery they contain. The most intimate truth that this revelation gives us about God and the salvation of man, shines forth in Christ who is himself both the mediator and the sum total of Revelation. (*Dei Verbum*, 2)

Such an appreciation of the holistic way in which God reveals himself militates against any polarization of text and practice, proclamation and witness of life. When God speaks he speaks by means of practices-and-speech together. This is ultimately a communication of person. When God chooses to reveal himself most perfectly, not even words-and-deeds will suffice: God's Word is most fully expressed as a person – Jesus.

This suggests to me that we may need to think again about our rational[14] approach to theological analysis of words, texts, practices, traditions, experiences. While much of the established pastoral theological approach sees its preliminary task as, in part, distinguishing, abstracting and objectifying these sources or authorities, this theology-ecclesiology of revelation suggests a more personal way of encountering and knowing the truth God is willing to reveal to us; it cannot split apart aspects of personal knowing into distinct categories, without losing something of the essential nature of that Truth which is a Person.

Revelation as Eternally Present and the Abiding Presence of God (Holy Spirit)

It has been important to stress within this revelation-based ecclesiology the abiding presence of the God who wills to reveal himself. This suggests strongly that, whether we are reflecting on Scripture or some other aspect of the Christian tradition, we are not simply working with texts or analysing practices, but are also being invited into living fellowship with God through the presence of the Holy Spirit in these texts and practices. Spiritual life is thus clearly seen as the root of theology, in all its forms. Revelation is not seen as a static deposit, an objectified source; but rather something alive and present, which 'makes progress' in the ordinary life of faith:

The Tradition that comes from the apostles makes progress in the Church, with the help of the Holy Spirit. There is a growth in insight into the realities and words that are being passed on. This comes about in various ways. It comes through the contemplation and study of believers who ponder these things in their hearts (Luke 2:19, 51). It comes from the intimate sense of spiritual realities which they experience. And it comes from the preaching of those who have received, along with their right of succession in the episcopate, the sure charism of truth. (*Dei Verbum*, 8)

The Christian community that lives an ecclesiology of *traditio* is that community which actively participates in this ongoing dynamic of God's self-revelation, through the repeated and living meeting with the Lord in prayer, Scripture, liturgy and the everyday experiences of discipleship. What is handed on in such a Church is not a record of the story so far, but a living witness to God's continuing presence to his people – a historical witness that by its very nature is always fresh and new by virtue of the Spirit who always speaks afresh. This is a context for which polarities and correlations seem inappropriate ways of understanding.

Tradition as a Living Historical Embodiment of Revelation (Communion of Saints)

The ecclesiology I am outlining articulates not only the abiding presence and reality of God's self-revelation but also the manifold loci where we might reasonably expect to see or hear something of that revelation. This revelation is not a simple, static deposit, but an ongoing, multifaceted dynamic within which the life of the Church is thoroughly implicated. A fuller account of this ecclesiological perspective would examine the variety of voices to which we must attend in discerning God's 'practices' of revelation: a closer account of Scripture, of the baptismal and eucharistic nature of the Church, of the charismatic giftedness of God's people, and of the theology of conscience – all these, and others, are themes through which to understand more clearly what this ecclesiological approach has to offer a pastoral theology in the Catholic tradition. Above all, being attentive to the complexity-in-unity that is implied draws us away from methodologies of abstraction, objectification, polarities and correlation, towards a discipline of discerning the integrity of God's Word and Spirit.

One theme seems important to highlight, because it is too easily forgotten in our engagement with the tradition: the communion of saints. This particularly Catholic theme emphasizes the way the Church here present – historically and culturally contextualized – is none the less surely in living communion with those many Christian brothers and sisters who have gone before and now enjoy the fullness of life with Christ:

> Therefore the union of the wayfarers with the brethren who have gone to sleep in the peace of Christ is not in the least weakened or interrupted, but on the contrary, according to the perpetual faith of the Church, is strengthened by communication of spiritual goods. For by reason of the fact that those in heaven are more closely united with Christ, they establish the whole Church more firmly in holiness, lend nobility to the worship which the Church offers to God here on earth and in many ways contribute to its greater edification. (*Lumen gentium* 49)

Believing this about the Church makes a real difference in how we approach the question of engaging with tradition. Faith in the communion of saints suggests that we are drawn into the writings and life practices of those saints by way of invitation into a living relationship. In particular, this relational approach to our 'past' (the communion of saints as a doctrine does much to trouble our sense of the linear nature of past–present–future) is expressed in the ways in which, traditionally, the lives and writings of the saints have been celebrated as living realities through devotions, feasts and the liturgy. This suggests afresh some 'old' ways in which 'tradition' and 'texts' become living and truthful sources to us – through the practices of prayer, liturgical worship and devotion.[15] There are rich implications here for the formation of pastoral theologians, and for the nurture of pastoral theology as a vocation.

By Way of Conclusion

I have very briefly indicated what an ecclesiology of *traditio* might look like, and what sort of effects it might have on pastoral theology. Fundamentally, it provides pastoral theology with a framework within which the primary reality to be discerned and described is what God is doing within a particular situation, practice or experience. This suggests an assumption of coherence between our various sources for reflection, whether texts or practices, whether from the thirteenth century or the present day. Such coherence does not imply an easy similarity; the discipline of careful hermeneutics remains necessary. What a conviction about such coherence does, however, is fundamentally shift the hermeneutical task from a simply critical one, towards one orientated to connection and continuity. Above all, the Trinitarian emphasis calls for a thorough appropriation of an effective pneumatology that gives a firm theological authority for a prior sense of connection. The thoughtfulness then required is less likely to take a correlative or conversational form, in which text and practice, tradition and the contemporary are set up as mutually critical partners. It is, rather, the language of attentiveness and discernment that best describe the activities of pastoral theology, as the question is consistently asked: Where is God in all this? What is the Spirit prompting here?

The specifically ecclesiological description of this theology of *traditio* ensures that such a pastoral theology does not become simply a matter of individual or small group discernment, still less a kind of theological piety. Rather, it is constantly challenged by what may seem to be the strange and alien discernments of other Christians, close to us, and across time and space. The communion of saints sets us in an ever new and alive relationship with the texts of the ages and the practices they describe and which have been handed down. What also becomes clear is the centrality of prayer and sacramental worship (liturgy) for the pastoral theologian seeking to operate within such an ecclesiology of *traditio*; it is in these 'places' that past, present and future are made present, and the texts and practices of the whole communion of saints are discovered as central to the reality of faith.

This is very much a work in progress. I finish, then, not with conclusions but some questions and thoughts for further consideration. This chapter has argued for an ecclesial perspective for pastoral theology. In our post-Enlightenment and university-based contemporary practice of theology, this raises some sharp questions about the location of theology in the life of the Church. The implications of my position here are that theology is (like it or not, intentionally or not) practised in the life of the Church, and that there is a proper place for the pastoral theologian as such in working with this contemporary practice of a living tradition. The question must surely be asked, how can such an ecclesiological vocation to theology be more fully enabled in our current ecclesial and academic contexts?

The person of the theologian within this scheme also requires some attention. Within the ecclesiology of *traditio* and its working out in practice,[16] much depends on the expertise of the theologians involved in discernment of practices, as people formed in the tradition, in prayer and sacramental participation. It is in these persons that the continuity between history and present, text and practice finds embodiment. This, in turn, has significant implications for the appropriate formation of pastoral theologians, and for their continuing formation and discipline of life. Prayer, liturgy, *lectio divina*, active charity, study of the tradition, understanding of the saints as well as scriptural and systematic doctrinal scholarship all suggest themselves as having necessary parts to play in theological education and continuing scholarship in such a perspective.

Another question concerns the relationship of this kind of theological activity with those other vocations in the Church that engage with the same dynamic – ordained and lay ministers. Are there structural tasks required to ensure an ecclesial dynamic communion for this kind of ecclesiology of *traditio* to be properly effective?

These few questions – and the many others that may be suggested – imply that in an ecclesiology of *traditio* there is the possibility of a call to some radically renewed ways of going about our theological business. Above all I believe it can offer hopeful ways forward for contemporary Christian living and thinking that are rooted in the integrity and reality of God's divine presence.

Notes

1 The term 'pastoral theology' will be used throughout this chapter to refer to the field variously described by both terms: 'practical' and 'pastoral' theology.

2 See below.

3 For example, Stephen Pattison in his preface to the third edition of his *Critique of Pastoral Care*, 2000; Thomas Oden 1984, pp. 26–42, devotes a chapter to this concern; and the observations in Graham, Walton and Ward 2005, pp. 6–7.

4 See Schleiermacher's influential scheme, as discussed by Lartey 2000.

5 Oden 1984. The resulting 'school' of 'palaeo-orthodoxy' can be seen reflected in the volume of essays edited by Tanner and Hall 2002.

6 Edward Farley (1989) has especially contributed to thinking about appropriate formation/education for those preparing for pastoral ministry, developing an influential *habitus* approach to pastoral theological learning. Ellen Charry's (1997) work develops 'sapiential theology', and employs study of texts from the long Christian theological tradition, as a way of pedagogy into Christian wisdom.

7 Graham, Walton and Ward 2005, p. 7, quoting a report, Walton 2003.

8 Graham, Walton and Ward 2005, p. 1. See this volume, and its companion volume *Theological Reflection: Sources*, 2007.

9 Thoroughly worked out in D. Browning 1991. His account of the revised correlative method, in Woodward and Pattison 1999, can be found in 'Pastoral Theology in a Pluralistic Age', pp. 89–102.

10 See also Paul Ballard's discussion of the work of the Catholic theologian Matthew Lamb in Ballard's essay of 1992, 'Can Theology be Practical?', in which Lamb's presentation of the relation of theory and praxis forms a focus for the argument. D. Willows and J. Swinton (eds) 2000, pp. 29ff. It is striking that both Ballard here, and Browning in his use of David Tracy, work with Catholic accounts of the connection between things. It is interesting to ask whether the much spoken of 'sacramental' instinct of Catholic Christianity carries with it just this sensitivity to the significance of connectivity.

11 For example, Robert L. Kinast 2000; and O'Connell Killen and de Beer 1994, 2006.

12 Dogmatic Constitution on the Church, *Lumen gentium*; the Constitution on the Sacred Liturgy, *Sacrosanctum Concilium*; and the Pastoral Constitution on the Church in the Modern World, *Gaudium et spes*. Translations are taken from the texts edited by Austin Flannery.

13 Something of the intrinsically 'conflictual' aspect of this kind of ecclesiology can be seen in Watkins 1993, pp. 369–84.

14 My use of the word 'rational' here is dependent on the kind of reading of *ratio* and *intellectus* given by Josef Pieper 1952, pp. 33ff.

15 For some helpful observations from Lubac's work, see Henri de Lubac 2006, p. vii.

16 Something of this understanding of practical theology can be illustrated in the research of ARCS (Action Research Church and Society) described in Chapter 17 of the present volume.

Bibliography

Don Browning, 1991, *A Fundamental Practical Theology: Descriptive and Strategic Proposals*, Minneapolis: Fortress Press.

Alistair Campbell, 2000, 'The Nature of Practical Theology', in James Woodward and Stephen Pattison (eds), *The Blackwell Reader in Pastoral and Practical Theology*, Oxford: Blackwell.

Ellen Charry, 1997, *By the Renewing of Your Minds: The Pastoral Function of Christian Doctrine*, Oxford: Oxford University Press.

David Cornick, 2000, 'Post-Enlightenment Pastoral Care: Into the Twentieth Century', in Gillian Evans (ed.), *A History of Pastoral Care*, London: Cassell.

E. Farley, 1989, *Theologia: The Fragmentation and Unity of Theological Education*, Minneapolis: Fortress Press.

Elaine Graham, Heather Walton and Frances Ward, 2005, *Theological Reflection: Methods*, London: SCM Press.

Elaine Graham, Heather Walton and Frances Ward, 2007, *Theological Reflection: Sources*, London: SCM Press.

John Paul II, Pope, 1979, *Redemptor Hominis* (encyclical letter, available at Vatican website).

Robert L. Kinast, 2000, *What are They Saying about Theological Reflection?* New York: Paulist Press.

E. Lartey, 2000, 'Practical Theology as a Theological Form', in J. Woodward and S. Pattison (eds), *The Blackwell Reader in Pastoral and Practical Theology*, Oxford: Blackwell, pp. 128–34.

Henri de Lubac, 2006, *Corpus Mysticum: The Eucharist and the Church in the Middle Ages*, trans. Gemma Simmonds CJ with Richard Price, London: SCM Press.

Patricia O'Connell Killen and John de Beer, 1994, 2006, *The Art of Theological Reflection*, New York: Crossroad.

Thomas Oden, 1984, *Care of Souls in the Classic Tradition*, Minneapolis: Fortress Press.

Stephen Pattison, 2000, *Critique of Pastoral Care*, 3rd edn, London: SCM Press.

Josef Pieper, 1952, *Leisure: The Basis of Culture*, London: Faber & Faber.

Kenneth Tanner and Christopher A. Hall (eds), 2002, *Ancient and Postmodern Christianity: Paleo-Orthodoxy in the 21st Century – Essays In Honor of Thomas C. Oden*, Downers Grove: Intervarsity Press.

Vatican II, 1965, *Gaudium et spes*, Pastoral Constitution on the Church in the Modern World (available at Vatican website).

Vatican II, 1965, *Dei Verbum*, Dogmatic Constitution on Divine Revelation (available at Vatican website).

R. Walton, 2003, 'The Bible and Tradition in Theological Reflection', *British Journal of Theological Education* 13.2, pp. 133–51.

Clare Watkins, 1993, 'The Church as a Special Case: Comments from Ecclesiology concerning the Management of the Church', *Modern Theology* 9.4, pp. 369–84.

D. Willows and J. Swinton (eds), 2000, *Spiritual Dimensions of Pastoral Care: Practical Theology in a Multidisciplinary Context*, London: Jessica Kingsley.

J. Woodward and S. Pattison, 2000, *The Blackwell Reader in Pastoral and Practical Theology*, Oxford: Blackwell.

Liturgical Theology: Experiencing the Presence of Christ

ANDREW CAMERON-MOWAT SJ

This exploration of contemporary liturgical theology takes place in the context of Catholic theological debate in general, with a particular focus on the celebration of rites, on the renewal of those rites, and on how theology speaks of the experience of the faith we celebrate in our rituals. After setting out the map of post-Vatican II liturgical theology, I will explore issues raised by the document *On the Way to Life*,[1] and will then offer an illustration of a recent development in liturgical theology.

There has been a great deal of debate about the renewal of the liturgy after the Second Vatican Council. In 2007, in the document *Sacramentum Caritatis*, Pope Benedict XVI drew attention to the view of the bishops at the Synod on the Eucharist (2005), during which there were 'many expressions of appreciation' for what had so far been achieved, and pointed to 'the benefits and the validity of the liturgical renewal'.[2] At the same time, the Pope noted that there was still much that needed to be done to achieve the necessary richness and growth in appreciation for and effectiveness of the renewed liturgy, and he called for a far-reaching appropriation of the *ars celebrandi* (*Sacrosanctum Concilium*, 38–43, 64, hereinafter *SC*). The development of the liturgy around the time of the Council and in the decade that followed indicated that a radical transformation took place in the experience of the Church as a whole in the public celebration of its sacraments. Emphasis was placed on the promotion of full, conscious and active participation by all of the people (*SC* 14), on the inculturation of certain aspects of the liturgy, particularly through the use of the vernacular (*SC* 36), and on a desire to simplify what had become overly stylized or complicated, whether in the prayers, in the liturgical styles, or in the symbols (*SC* 21, 50). Emphasis was also to be given to the communal celebration of the rites, as a preference over their private use (*SC* 26, 27). These changes were signs of the transformation, or even the discovery of the celebration of the liturgy as a central component of church life, from which a rich source of theology could be derived. The Church is made up of many parts, and the one body is to be found in both the head and the members. Christ is present in the Eucharist, in the mode of the transubstantiated bread and wine, but is also present in the mode of the presider, the proclamation and preaching of the word, and in the assembly. On the wider plane, the Church opened its doors to the world to learn from and be enriched by the discoveries of the social, philosophical and other sciences. The exploration of historical texts, both liturgical and biblical, as well as developments in architecture, music and art, would all play some role in the renewal of the liturgy, as would a deeper appreciation of psychological, anthropological and developmental sciences, in addition to what was learned from pastoral experience and experimentation. One common recent element has been the assumption that the *lex orandi* and the *lex credendi* intertwine and influence each other. Several writers place the emphasis on the authority of the *lex orandi*. Yet they do not make clear what this *lex orandi* is, or how it should be understood in the wider context. Recently, some are questioning whether the phrase *lex orandi lex credendi* is still useful, since its application has become so diffuse, and its original meaning (within the context of early baptismal rites) is so far removed from how it is understood today; they advocate that it should be reformulated, reinterpreted or allowed to die out altogether.[3]

Of particular interest has been the development in the grammar of theological language, together with the ways in which the pre-conciliar evolution of theology and the influence of the Liturgical Movement came together at the Council and thereafter led to further debate and development. This development was not simply a product of liturgical theologians in the West, but was also to be found in the writings of influential theologians of a more Orthodox orientation, such as the Melkite Catholic Jean Corbon, the Russian Orthodox scholar Alexander Schmemann (d. 1983) and John Zizioulas of the Greek Orthodox Church.

Scholars now look at new ways of understanding *symbol* (Louis-Marie Chauvet, in particular) and of considering sacraments as *events*.[4] They explore how the proclamation of the word in the liturgy is a mode of the presence of Christ and therefore, in some way, *sacrament* (Otto Semmelroth, and Paul Janowiak in particular). They argue about the radical significance of the call for 'full, conscious and active participation by all of the assembly' and about its consequences for the liturgy, particularly in the area of inculturation and the use of vernacular languages (Anscar Chupungco has been particularly influential in this area). They look at Karl Rahner's insights into the 'Liturgy of the World' and how the official liturgical rites relate to it. They reconsider the nature of *presence*, particularly eucharistic presence, and seek to update the notion of *transubstantiation*, with varied degrees of success (David Power and Nathan Mitchell have both published books and articles on the nature of sacraments and sacramental presence). They consider the radical consequences of understanding the necessary interactions between *sacramental* and *liturgical* theology, and the need to develop these in pastoral liturgical theology (Mark Searle made a significant contribution in this area, building on and reconsidering the approach of Romano Guardini and others). Sacraments are now seen as effective signs of grace, as encounters with Christ (Edward Schillebeeckx). They are symbolic actions of the Church, in the fullest meaning of the terms symbol, action and Church. They are symbols of human meaning at its very depth, and both bring about and are signs of the transformation of reality (Bernard Cooke).

Much of this shift in theological grammar has brought suspicion and defensiveness from those who would seek to maintain the theological hegemony that they assume was present before the Council. Groups both within and without the Church maintain that the theological bases for the reforms of the Council and afterwards were fundamentally flawed, and so the resulting changes to the liturgy were based on false preconceptions. These groups have refused to acknowledge that Paul VI's approval of the 1970 Rite replaced all prior Roman Rites, and they continue to be critical of the renewed rites. There have been repeated calls for (a) the full restoration of the pre-conciliar rite (that of 1962) or at least for (b) a 'reform of the reform'. More extreme groups reject Vatican II *in toto*. Several writers have developed an approach known as 'radical orthodoxy' to bring intellectual weight to what is, in essence, a somewhat elitist harking back to former ritualism.

The conversation now takes place in the context of a landscape of pluralistic languages, in which different meanings can be, and are, placed on once universal concepts, structures and vocabularies; however, the stakes are still high because not all approaches have equal value. Simply to allow whatever Roman Rite a particular person or group wants means that tradition is no longer regarded as an important aspect of the Church's self-understanding. The significance of the reforms of Paul VI rested on the assumption that new versions of the rite replaced previous ones, just as the 1550 Rite of Pius V did in his time, and the rite of 1962 in the time of John XXIII.[5] The truth of the matter is that tradition and creativity must go together for the life of the Church to be sustainable. Developments in sacramental theology respond to the challenge of postmodernity by showing that the Church continues to learn from its experience of God at work in the world. Creativity and genius are not enemies of tradition (Kenan Osborne is perhaps the most widely read scholar in this area).

Given this exploration of the shifts in theological grammar, begun before the Council and very much prevalent after it, the document *On the Way to Life* provides a significant example of how a more positive and less pessimistic (but no less realistic) account of the theological, cultural and philosophical landscape in Britain today can lead to beneficial insights about the nature of our liturgical and sacramental life and to proposals for future development and reform.

On the Way to Life was originally intended to provide an analysis of the landscape of contemporary culture, in order to assist in the provision of religious education and catechesis in Britain today. For the purposes of this present exploration of liturgy it provides in addition a useful means of opening up reflection on liturgical and sacramental praxis and theology today. I will treat these in the order that they occur in the document, commenting on the appropriateness of the insights of the document's authors for a reconsideration of contemporary Catholic liturgical theology.

Part 1: Significant Elements in Contemporary Culture

The first section, on contemporary culture, contributes to our understanding of what it means to be 'the Church' gathered into one, whose purpose is to celebrate liturgically and sacramentally.

Thus as well as the doctrines mentioned in the document, liturgical practice and its tradition offer one of the classic 'grammars' (p. 11) that serve to underpin believers' understanding of their presence in their world (and in the Church). For Yves Congar, liturgy is one of his 'monuments of tradition', and so is an essential part of the self-expression and continued presence of the Church.[6] From this perspective, the renewal of the various liturgical rites around 1970 may be understood as a powerful disruption of just such a deep grammar. On the other hand, we can also perceive, in the area of liturgy as in other areas, the destructive effects of nostalgia (p. 23) and its false memories, which continue to affect so many, including those born long after 1970.

The notions of equality and mutuality that are outlined in this first section can be related to post-conciliar movements that seek to reject liturgical and sacramental theological development. The question 'Whose truth is it?' (p. 15) can be applied directly to the present situation, with respect not only to those who maintain what they call 'traditional' liturgy, but more widely to those who reject the reform of the liturgy wholesale, in part through quasi-gnostic reasoning.[7]

In addition, the 'turn to the self' in contemporary culture has important consequences for a liturgy and a liturgical theology that seeks to build an awareness of the reality of the gathered community. Pastoral issues arise frequently: 'my child should have a right to express himself by kicking and screaming throughout Mass'; 'I have a right to have my children confirmed in the 1962 Rite'; 'we phone in advance to see if Fr X is saying Mass because he takes too long'; 'the Sign of Peace is an unnecessary disruption'. These are but a few examples of the sort of attitude that arises from too much authority being given to the needs of the individual.

Section 5 of Part 1, entitled 'A Spiritual Revolution?' invites the Church to re-examine what it is doing through teaching and proclamation in a society whose ways of perceiving reality and of engaging in its own *aggiornamento* have changed.[8] As the liturgy is itself (through its symbols, its gestures, its proclamation and its word) an experience of the Church's life, theology and tradition, it needs to be examined as one of the primary modes of the *ecclesia docens* as well as *discens*, the teaching Church as well as the learning Church. The question arises: how effectively does the liturgical celebration of sacraments proclaim the wisdom of tradition and the ever-present saving power of Christ?

Section 6 in Part 1 of *On the Way to Life*, entitled 'Frenetic Longueurs', contributes a number of themes that are directly applicable to consideration of the liturgy. The seeming addiction to instant communication, in a remote-control society with a short attention span, can play a significant part in how people understand, experience and evaluate liturgical ceremonies: are they seen to be ineffective, or do they open people up to true mystical experience of the divine and an awareness of the presence of the Body of Christ in the community of faith?

Professionalization, with its 'high expectation of performance and delivery' (p. 24) is a less thoroughly explored problem, although it is an important issue for presiders coping with the *versus populum* orientation, where the presider faces the assembly across the altar. For those presiding at the liturgy, there can be a tendency to 'move on to the next bit' rather than to reflect and wait, with our minds and senses open to the voice of the Spirit. The practice of recent Popes to celebrate gigantic 'event liturgies' has the unfortunate consequence, particularly for the young, of a raising of expectations or a misdirecting of priorities in liturgical preparation and evaluation. The demand for the 'wow' factor leads quickly to the perception that Mass elsewhere is 'boring', and a solution is attempted that corresponds with the perceived needs of the remote-control push-button generation: easy songs with banal lyrics, little or no silence, constant movement. Here the attraction of the 1962 'usage' may be that it is different, strange, mysterious, and so it is, but it had serious problems that should not be ignored: unnecessary repetition, a theologically flawed structure, inappropriate emphases and so on. By making the liturgical signs much more perceptible to the senses, the reforms of the Second Vatican Council provided a significant opportunity to present the liturgical and ecclesial narrative in a new way: more direct, more immediate, more clear. The current rites are all of these things, but we should also continue to encourage beauty, prayerfulness and a real sense of the mystery at their heart. We need to rediscover the genius of the 'ordinary' in the liturgy: that which is day-to-day, that with which we become accustomed or comfortable, and thereby more open to the challenge or prompting of the Spirit. Our common narrative does not then simply go from liturgical event to liturgical event, but forms us as part of a worshipping community on a continuing journey of faith.

The liturgy then offers us the way to counteract the search for 'this-worldly transcendence' (p. 25) that is so much part of the Christian's response to the demands of late modernity and its 'turn to the subject'. Much of liturgical experience consists of the *kenosis* of one's own self-interest in the offering up to God of Christ's body, head and members. We become one with our brothers and sisters in the sacral *koinonia* of our giving thanks and praise. And in the celebration of the sacraments, those who experience adult baptism are offered a profound experience of dying to self and rising with Christ into new life.

Section 7 of Part 1 explores the new 'religious subject', the pilgrim and the convert, as studied by Danièle Hervieu-Léger (p. 26). For her, liturgical participants are either 'communicants', who are members of the Church in some ratified and institutional way (normally through baptism and the other sacraments) or 'pilgrims' who go from one place to another in the search for truth or some other form of validating identity. Those who are 'converts' have found what they are seeking; they abandon one form of religious faith and its expression to find authenticity in another (such as Anglicans who are received into the Roman Catholic Church); they reject the glamour of secularism for the narrow way of counter-cultural religious faith; they rediscover the faith and practice within themselves but from which they had lapsed (pp. 26–7). Liturgy is at the front line here, in offering the possibility of three modes of conversion. While continuing its primary function in offering praise and worship to God, it also opens the Church's arms to welcome those who are searching, those who are lost and those who have gone astray. The Church does this through the attitude of the community to newcomers, through the rendering present of Christ's salvific will in the proclamation of the word and the preaching, in the radical relevance of its prayers and texts, particularly in the vernacular, in the experience of Christ's presence in Eucharist. All this happens as a work of grace through which Christ enters into relationship with the person. The free will to change is 'an obedience to a call or a charge rather than an act of self-stylisation' (p. 27) and is given as a gift. This gift can be particularly evident in effective celebrations of the Church's sacraments. Liturgy again presents the key narratives of the interaction between God and humanity in the moments of profound transformation through which Christ, by the mysteries of his incarnation, his transfiguration, his passion, and his resurrection, not only takes our nature on himself but transforms it forever, making possible our own continued transformation into parts of his glorious Body. The liturgy waits to hear our response to these mysteries and to these transformations. Far from being an individual transformation only, the one becomes part of the many, and the community of faith receives the converted pilgrim as a great blessing. So liturgy is not seen as a commodity to which we look for some kind of aesthetic satisfaction, but the celebration of the community transformed by Christ, in which each person responds to the question, 'What gift can ever repay God's gift to me? I raise the cup of freedom as I call on God's name! I fulfil my vows to you, Lord, standing before your assembly' (Ps. 116, ICEL text). The experience of a community giving thanks and praise is the experience of faith offered to pilgrims as the place to which their journey is beckoning them. The Church, principally, but not exclusively, through its liturgical life, provides a sure road for these pilgrims on their journey. 'At the heart of this is the presence of Christ in whom all things "live and move and have their being"' (p. 29).

Part 2: The Theological Context

This part of *On the Way to Life* explores in greater depth the achievements of the Second Vatican Council, incorporating its retrieval of 'tradition' and its support for a Catholic theological modernity, recognizing Christ at the centre of the Church and his place in human history. Particular liturgical emphases are offered, such as the rediscovery of the Church's history and tradition, which was a key part of the work and significance of the Liturgical Movement. The ability to understand the movements and changes in liturgical and sacramental theology through history, and in particular the reasons behind those changes, has situated the history of theology in a radically different context from what had been regarded as normative in previous centuries. There has been a significant development in the understanding of tradition, which opened up the way towards liturgical change and renewal, not as a challenge to tradition, but as a continuation of it. Yves Congar saw in these developments a correcting of mistaken notions about tradition, law and rubric:

> The problem is that the norms should not become a sort of ready-made straightjacket, sufficient to itself and imposed on people without truly coming to life within them. This would be making man for the Sabbath . . . The Church is not just an establishment where past forms are preserved. It is Tradition [*author's capital letter*], and true Tradition is criticism and creativity as well as the handing-down and preservation of identical realities. (Congar 1986, p. 55)

On the Way to Life speaks of the unique 'profound adaptive movement within the community' that the Second Vatican Council inaugurated (p. 36); this would be one lens through which to read the progress of inculturation as a serious aspect of the development of the liturgy. Developments such as the priest turning to face the people across the altar, the introduction of the use of the vernacular, the adaptation of contemporary musical forms, the use of styles of movement, vesture, sacred objects, and the design of churches are just some of the many elements through which communities around the world have responded to the tiny seed of adaptation and inculturation that the Council sowed.

Within this discussion of the Council, *On the Way to Life* explores the 'Retrieval of "Tradition"' (pp. 36–7) of which the liturgy is one of the essential 'marks'. Section 1.3 dwells at length on the contemporary understanding of revelation and of the continuing presence of Christ.

The application of this insight to the proclamation and preaching of the word seems particularly appropriate. For preachers, 'Revelation becomes an experience not just a proposition: it is the Person of Christ' (p. 38) and so the proclamation and preaching of the word is a sacramental encounter with the living Christ. Because preaching rises out of the preacher's own personal encounter with Christ and draws on the inspiration of the living Christ in his proclaimed word, preaching as well as faith 'must be a movement of the heart and will as well as the intellect' (p. 38). We not only teach what we believe but practise what we teach: the living word has become part of us.

Therefore those who take the liturgy seriously cannot avoid the consequences of the Church's deliberate 'engagement with modernity' (p. 39). Our liturgy, whatever it may have been in the past, can no longer be regarded *simply* as a refuge, a resting place, a chance for peace and quiet, a vision of the eternal mystery beyond and above our everyday concerns and troubles. Christ is already here among us; we celebrate his presence and encounter him in our daily living, within which there is made possible a universal call to holiness. And so 'every member of the Church – not just the ordained priesthood and hierarchy – becomes a minister of grace and has the possibility of mediating it in and through their lives' (p. 41). Consideration of this point contributes to our understanding of how Christ is present in the assembly at the celebration of the Church's liturgy. Through their transformation by word and sacrament, the members of the assembly are then given the mission from the Church to carry out their own priesthood in the community by acts of service and witness. For Benedict XVI, this is the true meaning of *actuosa participatio* (active participation). True participation is found in the engagement of people in the life of the Church, particularly in proclaiming its message to the world and in showing the love of God to others.[9]

Part 3: Resources and Responses

Central to Catholic liturgical and sacramental theology is the understanding that Christ is at the heart of the Church and that through the sacramental life he is both in relationship with us and the one who acts. Christ is free to be in relation with us in many ways, but the claim of Catholic theology is that the sacraments, particularly in their fullest liturgical celebration, provide specific, unique and profound experiences of the presence and action of Christ that are not available to us in any other way. The celebration of sacraments continues and deepens the 'personal relationship between God and God's people' (p. 58), leading to a true *communio* with others within the body of Christ.[10] Within the scope of this developing relationship, the liturgy not only acts as the voice of the Church and its people, but is also the primary and most effective means of communication whereby the Church discloses itself to others and to itself. Liturgical language, and the controversies that surround the appropriateness and 'correctness' of translations into the vernacular, are the neuralgic meeting point where 'a process in which expression is also a self-becoming and self-disclosure' (p. 61) takes place. Effective participation in the celebration of the Church's liturgy involves an encounter with Christ through which 'we become that which we confess' (p. 61). The liturgy therefore is seen as the opportunity to experience the *communio* of the Church in all its fullness. Paul VI's emphasis that the renewed liturgical rites were faithful to the tradition of the Church through the ages may be seen as his attempt to maintain the unity of the Church as a communion at a time of considerable change. Benedict XVI's re-categorization of the *Novus Ordo* as one 'usage' of equal status with the pre-conciliar form is his solution to the considerable problems presented by the polarization of liturgical groups that have until now acted against true liturgical communion.

Liturgical theology will continue to explore serious questions about participation, communication and meaning. It will explore how Christ is present in ritual and in the life of the Christian community. It will consider aspects of the present age, drawing fruit where appropriate from developments in anthropology and other social sciences, to explore how the context of liturgy and its practice brings further insights. The connection between ethics and liturgy will continue to develop, as will the exploration of postcolonial liturgy, drawing on the genius of local cultures.

Eucharist as Gift-Exchange

As a concluding illustration of liturgical theology in practice, let us consider one aspect of the theology of Eucharist that has recently come to light thanks to an examination of its liturgical celebration. Recent scholars, particularly Louis-Marie Chauvet, have explored the common human ritual of gift-exchange as a meaningful symbolic act that helps us to understand the symbolic nature of Eucharist as we celebrate it in the Church of our age. In his article 'O Marvelous Exchange: A

Consideration for Eucharistic Catechesis', Scott O'Brien, OP, further develops this insight, whereby gift-exchange can be read as a metaphor to deepen our understanding of Eucharist, to be added to such well-known images as sacrifice and banquet. This provides a contemporary way to round out scholastic catechism definitions, and builds on Catherine LaCugna's important work on the Trinity, with her emphasis on God's desire to enter into personal relationship with humanity:

> God is no less mystery on account of God's radical immanence in Christ. Indeed, the God who is absolutely other, absolutely transcendent but also absolutely near to us – this God is absolute mystery. The God of Jesus Christ does not withdraw into seclusion or isolation so that we are forced to speculate on a hidden God. Rather, the personal self-expression of God in Christ points to God's ineffable personhood. The Spirit of God incorporates all creatures into the mystery of this divine life. (LaCugna 1994, pp. 323–4)

O'Brien posits the conclusion that the relationship into which God enters by becoming human in Christ is the relationship that God seeks to have with all humans:

> The gift that lies at the heart of the mystery of God incarnate is exactly this: Jesus Christ was born into the world so that the world may live in communion with God and with one another. This gift is mediated in the Eucharist by the personal presence of the crucified and risen Christ. (O'Brien 2001, p. 25)

Gifts of peace, forgiveness, communion with God and others, are all made available through this presence of Christ in the Eucharist.

Chauvet's work on gift-exchange, principally in his major work *Symbol and Sacrament*,[11] provides the anthropological and theological underpinning of O'Brien's pastoral reflections. The gift given and received carries with it the expectation that the gift will be reciprocated, in one form or another. Indeed, the understanding that the giving of the gift represents the opening of some form of relationship, and that the acceptance of the gift signifies that some form of further exchange will take place, seems to be part of the nature of the meaning of the word 'gift', as commonly understood in most societies. For O'Brien:

> The notion of the Eucharist as gift-exchange broadens and clarifies the often-used concept of sacrifice in approaching the death of Christ,

the Lord's Supper, and the Christian life. In fact, the use of metaphor of gift-exchange inverts the meaning and the literal application of the concept of sacrifice to the Eucharist by describing, first and foremost, the humble posture of a God who 'descended' into creation in order to offer us the way of peace. (2001, p. 26)

In the face of the overwhelming act of God in Christ, becoming human and offering himself in sacrifice to free us from our sins, our response is praise and thanksgiving, certainly, but also humble acceptance that without this we remain in our sin and in the death of sin. Christ's self-emptying act of love is the gift of freedom to us, and carries with it the expectation that we will respond in freedom and generosity of spirit. Benedict XVI's Apostolic Exhortation *Sacramentum Caritatis* shows us that liturgical sacramental theology along these lines is right at the heart of a true understanding of what Eucharist is about. Benedict reminds us that our full, conscious and active participation in the eucharistic liturgy must be seen in how we respond to the extraordinary gift of Christ in giving himself to us in the Eucharist. Communion is 'communion with God and communion with our brothers and sisters . . . And wherever we do not live communion among ourselves, communion with the Triune God is not alive and true either' (p. 76). Further, 'a Eucharist which does not pass over into the concrete practice of love is intrinsically fragmented' (p. 82). In the same vein, our relationship to the Eucharist brings certain expectations about the quality of our life in general, particularly with regard to our promotion of the common good and 'a service of charity towards neighbour' (p. 88).

It seems clear, therefore, that Catholic liturgical theology includes this metaphor of gift-exchange as a way to understand what Eucharist is about, and also that the celebration of liturgy, whether it is Eucharist or some other rite, contains within it the possibility of transformation into the people Christ wants us to be.

The language of the liturgy, allied to the rituals that prayer speaks and enacts, has real power, in that it brings about the sacramental presence of Christ, and brings us into the realm of God's love. For O'Brien, 'in the Christian use of linguistic activity there is the hope then that narrative, symbol, and ritual truly position us to receive that presence that draws us into communion with the divine' (2001, p. 28).

The language, however, is not the totality, and neither is the gift. This is the emphasis of Chauvet, who reminds us that in this process, there is always the stage at which God is radically *other*. In Rahner's terms, God maintains incomprehensibility in order that we may continue to seek out the one who has loved us into life, and, yet more crucially, to remind us that we cannot own God or restrict God's own freedom. While it is Catholic faith that the symbols contain within them the reality that they express, this further development of theology reminds us that at the *eschaton* the fullness of grace and life will be ours, and that these elements of Eucharist are but a partial experience of the total reality of Christ in God. The liturgy reminds us too that Christ is present in his word, in the presider, and in the assembly, as well as in the sacramental symbols. The liturgical celebration of the sacraments within a community gathered faithfully together, therefore, is an opening to the full life of grace that God offers to us in Christ, and also an invitation to find Christ in one another.

Notes

1 The Heythrop Institute for Religion, Ethics and Public Life, 2005, *On the Way to Life: Contemporary Culture and Theological Development as a Framework for Catholic Education, Catechesis and Formation*, London: Catholic Education Service, 2005.

2 Post-Synodal Apostolic Exhortation, *Sacramentum Caritatis*, 2007, 3. Hereinafter *Sac. Car.*

3 Paul De Clerk warned about inappropriate use of this phrase in '*Lex orandi, lex credendi*: The Original Sense and Historical Avatars of an Equivocal Adage', *Studia Liturgica* 24 (1994), pp. 178–200. See also Paul V. Marshall, 1995, 'Reconsidering "Liturgical Theology": Is there a Lex Orandi for All Christians?' *Studia Liturgica* 25, pp. 129–35; Paul Bradshaw, 1998, 'Difficulties in Doing Liturgical Theology', *Pacifica* 11/ 2, pp. 118–94; Michael Aune, 2007, 'Liturgy and Theology: Rethinking the Relationship, Part I – Setting the Stage', *Worship* 81/1, pp. 46–68; and 2007, 'Liturgy and Theology: Rethinking the Relationship, Part II – A Different Starting Place', *Worship* 81/2, pp. 141–69.

4 Louis-Marie Chauvet, *Symbol and Sacrament*, also *The Sacraments: Word of God at the Mercy of the Body*. A thorough exploration of Chauvet's thinking and importance for liturgical theology is to be found in Philippe Bordeyne and Bruce T. Morrill (eds), *Sacraments, Revelation of the Humanity of God; Engaging the Fundamental Theology of Louis-Marie Chauvet*.

5 See John F. Baldovin, *Reforming the Liturgy: A Response to the Critics* for a recent examination of the history of the renewal of the liturgy and on the *Motu Proprio* 'Summorum Pontificum' of Benedict XVI.

6 See Congar, 1997, pp. 434–5: 'The liturgy acts according to the general manner of Tradition, and since it is endowed with the genius of Tradition, it fills Tradition's role in a superlative way. Speaking about the liturgy, and describing its activity, I have felt myself to be speaking of Tradition itself and describing *its* work.'

7 The arguments of groups opposed to the renewal of the liturgy after the

Second Vatican Council take up much of the first part of John Baldovin's recent volume, *Reforming the Liturgy: A Response to the Critics*.

8 Pope John XXIII introduced this hermeneutic of 'bringing up to date' along with *ressourcement* – the return to the sources – during the preparation for Vatican II.

9 *Sacramentum Caritatis*, 55: 'The faithful need to be reminded that there can be no *actuosa participatio* in the sacred mysteries without an accompanying effort to participate actively in the life of the Church as a whole, including a missionary commitment to bring Christ's love into the life of society.'

10 Considerable attention is given in the document to the importance of *communio* as a constitutive part of the retrieval of the Catholic sacramental imagination (pp. 62–4).

11 See Chauvet, 1995, pp. 99–105; and also 2001, pp. 117–27.

Bibliography

John F. Baldovin, 2009, *Reforming the Liturgy: A Response to the Critics*, Collegeville: Liturgical Press.

Benedict XVI, Pope, 2007, Post-Synodal Apostolic Exhortation, *Sacramentum caritatis* (available at Vatican website).

Philippe Bordeyne and Bruce T. Morrill (eds), 2008, *Sacraments, Revelation of the Humanity of God: Engaging the Fundamental Theology of Louis-Marie Chauvet*, Collegeville: Liturgical Press.

Louis-Marie Chauvet, 1995, *Symbol and Sacrament: A Sacramental Reinterpretation of Christian Experience*, Collegeville: Liturgical Press.

Louis-Marie Chauvet, 2001, *The Sacraments: Word of God at the Mercy of the Body*, Collegeville: Liturgical Press.

Anscar Chupungco, 1995, *Worship: Beyond Inculturation*, Beltsville: Pastoral Press.

Yves Congar, 1986, *The Word and the Spirit*, London: Geoffrey Chapman.

Yves Congar, 1997 edition, *Tradition and Traditions*, Irving, TX: Basilica Press.

Bernard Cooke, 2005, *Christian Symbol and Ritual: An Introduction*, Oxford: Oxford University Press.

Jean Corbon, 2005, *Wellspring of Worship*, 2nd edn, San Francisco: Ignatius Press.

Romano Guardini, 1998 edition, *The Spirit of the Liturgy*, New York: Crossroad.

Heythrop Institute for Religion, Ethics and Public Life, 2005, *On the Way to Life: Contemporary Culture and Theological Development as a Framework for Catholic Education, Catechesis and Formation*, London: Catholic Education Service.

Paul Janowiak, 2000, *The Holy Preaching: The Sacramentality of the Word in the Liturgical Assembly*, Collegeville: Liturgical Press.

Anne Koester and Barbara Searle (eds), 2004, *Vision: The Scholarly Contributions of Mark Searle to Liturgical Renewal*, Collegeville: Liturgical Press.

Catherine LaCugna, 1994, *God for Us: The Trinity and Christian Life*, San Francisco: Harper.

Paul McPartlan, 1993, *The Eucharist Makes the Church: Henri de Lubac and John Zizioulas in Dialogue*, Edinburgh: T&T Clark.

Nathan Mitchell, 1998, *Real Presence: The Work of Eucharist*, Chicago: Liturgy Training Publications.

Scott O'Brien, 2001, 'O Marvelous Exchange: A Consideration for Eucharistic Catechesis', *Liturgical Ministry* 10 (Winter), pp. 23–30.

Kenan B. Osborne, 2000, *Christian Sacraments in a Postmodern World: A Theology for the Third Millennium*, Mahwah, NJ: Paulist Press.

Catherine Pickstock, 1997, *After Writing: On the Liturgical Consummation of Philosophy*, Oxford: Blackwell.

David Power, 1984, *Unsearchable Riches: The Symbolic Nature of Liturgy*, New York: Pueblo.

Edward Schillebeeckx, 1963, *Christ the Sacrament of the Encounter with God*, London: Sheed & Ward.

Alexander Schmemann, 1990, *Liturgy and Tradition: Theological Reflections of Alexander Schmemann*, ed. Thomas Fisch, Crestwood, NY: St Vladimir's Seminary Press.

Mark Searle, 2006, *Called to Participate: Theological, Ritual, and Social Perspectives*, ed. Barbara Searle and Anne Koester, Collegeville: Liturgical Press.

Otto Semmelroth, 1965, *The Preaching Word: On the Theology of Proclamation*, New York: Herder & Herder.

Michael Skelley, 1991, *Liturgy of the World: Karl Rahner's Theology of Worship*, Collegeville: Pueblo Books.

Vatican II, 1963, Dogmatic Constitution on the Liturgy, *Sacrosanctum Concilium* (available at Vatican website).

12

The Catholic Mystical Tradition as a Guide to Contemporary Pastoral Care

PETER TYLER

Introduction

I will suggest in this chapter that at present we see two broad trends in society: a resurgent interest in 'spirituality' in a general unfocused way and 'fundamentalisms' of various hues in all the world faiths, not least Christianity. I will further argue that what has been called the Catholic mystical tradition offers a middle way between the Scylla of spirituality and the Charybdis of fundamentalism. Accepting that the term 'Catholic mystical tradition' is almost too vague to be usable I will concentrate in particular on the medieval stance of 'Affective Dionysianism', in particular its strategies of unknowing and embodiment, and show, through one key example, how study of this tradition can inform pastoral care of adults today. My own methodology draws upon my training in psychology and theology to present a mode of pastoral theology that incorporates both in response to questions concerning the nature of Christian spirituality.

The Spirituality Revolution and Fundamentalism

The Australian academic David Tacey suggests that we are in the midst of what he terms a 'spirituality revolution'. He describes it as 'the emergence of the sacred as a leading force in contemporary society', which is not to be confused with 'the rising tide of religious fundamentalism'.

> Spirituality and fundamentalism are at opposite ends of the cultural spectrum. Spirituality seeks a sensitive, contemplative relationship with the sacred and is able to sustain levels of uncertainty in its quest because respect for mystery is paramount. Fundamentalism seeks

certainty, fixed answers and absolutism, as a fearful response to the complexity of the world and to our vulnerability as creatures in a mysterious universe. (Tacey 2003, p. 11)

At various times in history, he suggests, the stream or hidden river of spirituality rises and falls according to its own mysterious rhythms. We live in one such time when a rising tide of spirituality is emerging on all sides. This affects all of us in society – the churches, politicians, education and the realm of pastoral care – 'cure of souls' as it has been called. There are numerous responses to this rising tide of spirituality. One such has already been mentioned – fundamentalism – the grasping after illusory (usually religious) certainties as a bulwark against the uncertainities of a faith or 'higher power' that challenges all our strongly held habitual beliefs. Tacey characterizes the choice between fundamentalism and authentic spirituality as that between 'conscious intimacy and unconscious possession' (2003, p. 12). It will be my argument in this chapter that what I term the 'Catholic mystical tradition' offers a middle way between these two extremes and that reflection upon it can be of immediate help in contemporary Christian pastoral action.

The Catholic Mystical Tradition

The first question to be asked is: 'What do we mean by the Catholic mystical tradition?' This is best answered by specifying what we *don't* mean by the term. By the term we are not suggesting a monolithic, experientialist, cross-credal entity called 'mysticism'. Such an entity, as has been pointed out by Lash (1988), Katz (1978) and others seems to be largely a late nineteenth-century/early twentieth-century creation, crafted very much in the writings of Vaughan (1856), Inge (1899) and Underhill (1910). Rather, I would prefer to see 'the mystical' in terms specified by Bernard McGinn in his monumental four-volume study of the subject, *The Presence of God* (McGinn 1991, 1994, 1998, 2005). Here, following von Hügel (1908), McGinn sees the mystical element of Christianity as 'that part of its belief and practices that concerns the preparation for, the consciousness of and the reaction to what can be described as the immediate or direct presence of God' (McGinn 1991, p. xvii).

The term, then, signifies that element of religion that is concerned with the immediate and lived-out aspect of faith rather than the theoretical or theological speculation upon it. Bouyer (1981, p. 46) traces the term as used by the Church fathers and mothers as a metaphor for the experience of the risen Christ in his Church to its origins in the *mus* or *mustikos* of the Greek mystery religions. By the time we reach the twelfth and thirteenth centuries and the growth of the university in western Europe, it is inextricably bound up with the enigmatic texts of the pseudonymous Dionysius the Areopagite. Consequently, for the rest of this chapter I shall concentrate on the effect these texts had on the subsequent development of medieval *theologia mistica* and draw out some key strategies from these texts that may inform our pastoral work today.

The Dionysian Corpus

The four works and epistles of the *Corpus Dionysiacum*, the *Mystical Theology* (MT), *Celestial Hierarchy* (CH), *Ecclesiastical Hierarchy* (EH) and *Divine Names* (DN), make their first entry in western intellectual life through the Greek manuscipt presented to Louis the Pious, the Frankish king, by the eastern emperor, Michael the Stammerer, in 827.[1] Attributed to the Areopagite who appears in Acts 17.34, the works retained semi-canonical status throughout most of the Middle Ages until Erasmus and Lorenzo Valla began to question the attribution in the early sixteenth century. Despite this, the apostolic authority of Dionysius continued to be defended into modern times. However, scholarly work in the nineteenth century by Stiglmayr and Koch (published 1895) demonstrated conclusively the link between Dionysius and the Neoplatonic circle around Proclus, one of the last heads of Plato's Academy in Athens, the Academy itself being closed in 529 by the Emperor Justinian. Accordingly, it looks as though the author could not have been writing before the middle of the fifth century and most likely dates from the turn of the fifth and sixth centuries. In the words of Andrew Louth: 'Denys the Areopagite, the Athenian convert, stands at the point where Christ and Plato meet. The pseudonym expressed the author's belief that the truths that Plato grasped belong to Christ, and are not abandoned by embracing faith in Christ' (Louth 1989, p. 11).[2] Whoever the real author was, and perhaps we shall never know, the texts represent a fascinating insight into the world of late paganism and emerging Christianity, suggesting, as Louth indicates, an interplay between the two forces.

Over the next seven centuries the manuscripts were subject to a process of annotation and correction, usually in the addition of marginalia, so that by the time the Latin West re-engaged with the documents in the 'twelfth-century Renaissance' they were already heavily annotated from 700 years of commentary. In Harrington's words: 'The thirteenth-century reader came to the text of the *Mystical Theology* with much of the interpretative work already done for him, finding difficult metaphors and foreign concepts set within a more familiar Latin framework' (Harrington 2004, p. 27).

Central to the twelfth-century revival of interest in Dionysius was Paris, especially its emerging university and the still influential Abbey of Saint-Denis (see Leclercq 1987, p. 27). In addition, the group of writers and commentators associated with the Abbey of St Victor in Paris took particular interest in the Dionysian *corpus*. Following the *Rule of St Augustine*, the community was at the forefront of clerical renewal through prayer, study and liturgy and grew with the schools of Paris being open to the new theological developments that were arising there. From its inception it was concerned with questions on the relationship between the *intellectus* and *affectus*. The distinctive Victorine tradition that was established combined 'a vigorous program of Bible study, serious and creative theological investigation and disciplined pursuit of contemplation all set in the context of a community orientated towards liturgical regularity and shared experience' (Zinn 1979, p. 3). The abbey continued to flourish throughout the twelfth and thirteenth centuries, surviving until the French revolution, when it was destroyed.

Recent scholarship has highlighted the complexity of the nature of the *corpus Dionysiacum* as it was taught at the University and disseminated throughout Europe.[3] The Victorines were at the forefront of the reintroduction and re-examination of the corpus, introducing innovations that have been referred to as the interpretation of 'affective Dionysianism' (see Rorem 1993, p. 16; McGinn 1998, p. 84). For the purpose of this paper, then, when I refer to the 'Catholic mystical tradition' I am particularly making reference to the affective Dionysianism that arises from the twelfth- and thirteenth-century Parisian/Victorine schools.

Having thus established what I understand by this tradition it is now necessary to delineate how it relates to pastoral practice today. To do this I will concentrate on two particular 'strategies' adopted in the Dionysian texts and consequently found in the tradition of *theologia mistica* – that of what I term 'the unknowing' and the 'erotic/embodiment'.

The Strategy of Unknowing

The centre and heart of the Catholic mystical element since its beginning is *contemplatio*, that is, the contemplation of the soul on the presence of God through the inspiration of the Scriptures. This relates to the *intellectus*, but it is primarily through the famous Dionysian 'unknowing' of the *affectus* (as interpreted by the Victorine schools) that this occurs. Dionysius begins the *Divine Names* by stating that what he is about to set down, must, by necessity, transcend the 'realm of discourse or of intellect' (DN1.1). The 'hidden divinity' cannot be set down by means of 'words or conceptions'. The heart of this revelation lies in the 'sacred oracles' or 'scripture' (DN 1.4). He talks of a 'divine enlightenment . . . into which we have been initiated by the hidden tradition of our inspired teachers . . . a tradition at one with scripture'.

If such 'divine names' transcend all conception and words, how can we speak of them? For, 'the union of divinised minds with the Light beyond all deity occurs in the cessation of all intelligent activity' (DN 1.5). Drawing from Scripture, the names are primarily *praised*. The Trinity, for Dionysius, cannot be expressed, only the 'aporias of unknowing' (see Sells 1994) can contain it. Thus Dionysius introduces his *hyper*-terms in DN 2.4 ('supra-essential subsistence, supra-divine divinity, supra-excellent goodness, supremely individual identity'), which will be reproduced at the beginning of the *Mystical Theology*. For God, for Dionysius, is 'beyond every assertion and denial'. Dionysius will often resort to the strategy of aporia through his ὑπερ- words to make this point: 'mind beyond mind, word beyond speech, it is gathered up by no discourse, by no intuition, by no name, it exists as no other being' (S: *et intellectus non intelligibilis et verbum non dicible et irrationabilitas et non-intelligibilitas* (R: *unintelligibilitas*) *et innominabilitas, secundum nihil existentium existens*).[4] For in the following chapters of the *Divine Names*, Dionysius does not try to *describe* the divine reality but rather plays with various models and pictures of the divine.

For Dionysius, then, when we 'say anything about God . . . we set down the truth not in the plausible words of human wisdom but in the demonstration of the power guided by the Spirit (1 Cor. 2.4)' (DN 1.1). For there is a 'power by which, in a manner surpassing speech and knowledge, we reach a union superior to anything available to us by way of our own abilities or activities in the realm of discourse or of intellect' (S: *secundum quam ineffabilibus et ignotis* (R: *incognitis*) *ineffabiliter et ignote* (R: *incognite*) *conjungimur secundum meliorem nostrae rationabilis et intellectualis virtutis et operationis unitonem*)

(DN 1.1). Which is why 'we must not resort to words or conceptions concerning that hidden divinity (S: *occulta Deitate*) which transcends being, apart from what sacred scriptures (S: *ex sacris eloquiis*) have divinely revealed' (DN1.1).

Dionysius deliberately dances around the nature of the mystical 'initiation' or 'knowledge'. It *cannot* be disclosed in the text, by its very nature: it is not to be learnt from theological disputation in the faculty of reason and intellect. How then is it communicated? Dionysius states that his own teacher, Hierotheus, has been initiated, and in his description of this Dionysius points in the direction we must look:

> Whatever he learned directly from the sacred writers, whatever his own perspicacious and laborious research of the scriptures uncovered for him, or whatever was made known to him through that most mysterious inspiration, not only learning but also experiencing the divine things (S: *non solum discens sed et patiens divina*; E: *non solum discens sed et affectus divina*; R: *verum etiam iis animo affectus et permotus*; Gk: χαί παθών τά θεϊα). For he had 'sympathy' (S: *compassione*; E: *coaffectione*; Gk: συμπαθείας) with such matters, if I may express it that way, and he was perfected in a mysterious union with them and in a faith in them which was independent of any education. (DN 2.9)

In contemporary language, we would say that the Catholic mystical tradition is essentially heart-centred or experiential. Although it is not anti-intellectual the goal of the tradition is succinctly put by the late Dominican scholar Herbert McCabe:

> Prayer is really a waste of time. The incarnate form of our prayer may be concerned with getting something done, forwarding our plans, and the generosity of God is such that he will let himself be incarnate even in these ways. But the very heart of prayer is not getting anything done. It is a waste of time, an even greater waste of time than play . . . For a real absolute waste of time you have to go to prayer. (McCabe 2002, p. 75)

Any form of prayer and meditation is, in many ways, an affront not only to reason but to our mortality. In the sacred space of contemplation we stand outside time and challenge not only the rush of time but our mortality and the busy-ness of the technologically advanced world within which we dwell at this moment. Thomas Merton makes the same point slightly differently in one of his last books, *On Contemplative Prayer*, published posthumously:

> We should not look for a 'method' or 'system', but cultivate an 'attitude', an 'outlook': faith, openness, attention, reverence, expectation, supplication, trust, joy. All these finally permeate our being with love in so far as our living faith tells us we are in the presence of God, that we live in Christ, that in the Spirit of God we 'see' God our Father without 'seeing'. We know him in 'unknowing'. (Merton 1973, p. 39)

This 'divine unknowing', what was called by Dionysius and his successors the *stulta sapientia* (literally: 'foolish wisdom', cf. 1 Cor. 1) is the beginning of all wisdom and the heart of Christian contemplation. Teresa of Avila's 'master', Francisco de Osuna, for example, writes in his *Tercer Abecedario Espiritual*: 'Even though the understanding may discover and analyse numerous sublime matters there is good reason for you to believe that complete, fulfilling repose is not to be found through functions of the intellect (*por la operación intelectiva*) and that ultimately the least part of what we do not know exceeds everything we do know' (Osuna 1998, ch. 12.1).

Adopting a phrase of the nineteenth-century English poet John Keats, some recent commentators in the tradition of psychotherapy and counselling talk of this attribute as the need for 'negative capability' in our pastoral interactions with others. Keats used the term to specify a key attribute of the poet, which makes a person 'capable of being in uncertainties, Mysteries, doubts, without any irritable reaching after fact and reason' (Keats 1970, p. 43). Robert French, a contemporary commentator, writes:

> Thus, Keats's poet is 'related' to the therapist, and indeed to many other 'family members': mother, teacher, priest, consultant, manager – anyone, perhaps, whose role involves responsibility for others. What links them is this 'disposition of indifference', which Pines called 'aeolian' after the aeolian harp: 'to show how the therapist's mind can be stirred by the communication of the patient, and how, unselfconsciously, the therapist finds himself responding in depth to the patient's hidden meanings'. (French 2000, p. 3)

This attitude of 'unknowing' opens up new possibilities in our engagements with the people we care for. The British Object Relations analyst

Wilfred Bion was aware of Keats's dictum and tried to put it into practice in his interactions with clients: 'Discard your memory; discard the future tense of our desire; forget them both, both what you knew and what you want, to leave space for a new idea' (Bion 1980, p. 11).

He suggested we must have the courage and humility to step into this 'space of unknowing' when we engage with others. A place that requires us to put aside our memories, our need to control, our need to define – all the whirring chatter of the 'monkey mind' – and allow ourselves to be present for the other before us:

> When we are in the office with a patient we have to dare to rest. It is difficult to see what is at all frightening about that, but it is. It is difficult to remain quiet and let the patient have a chance to say whatever he or she has to say. It is frightening for the patient – and the patient hates it. We are under constant pressure to say something, to admit that we are doctors or psychoanalysts or social workers to supply some box into which we can be put complete with a label. (Bion 1980, p. 11)

Especially when Christians in today's world take on the role of 'professional carers' there is a pressure to be 'the expert' or the 'wise one' whereas often what is required is for us to have the humility to divest ourselves of our power position. To do this may challenge our very selves as well as our roles and make us question again why we do the work we do:

> It is indeed, difficult to say how to denude one's mind of preconceptions, memories and desires which make such a noise that one cannot hear the patient speak – at least not the one that we need to hear speak. In my experience the noise of my past has so many echoes and reverberations that it is difficult to know whether I am really listening to the patient or being distracted by one of these ghosts of the past. (Bion 1989, p. 65)

So then, if we take the position of *stulta sapientia* seriously, Christians engaged in pastoral care need to be open to the unknowing of their position. The 'foolish wisdom' of the medieval writers is not about 'second guessing' the person we are engaged with but about having the humility to let them tell us what they want from us.

Embodiment: *Eros*

It may seem surprising when talking about the Christian tradition to talk about *eros* and embodiment. But the mystical element of Christianity has always maintained a healthy balance between *eros* and *agape*. In the *Divine Names* Dionysius stresses the importance of a healthy balance between the two forms of love in the Christian life:

> Indeed some of our writers on sacred matters have thought the title *eros* to be more divine than *agape* . . . So let us not fear this title of *eros* nor be upset by what anyone has to say about these two names, for, in my opinion, the sacred writers regard *eros* and *agape* as having one and the same meaning. (DN 4.12)

In DN 4 Dionysius introduces his discussion of *eros* and the erotic and how *eros* connects us with the deity. In McGinn's words: 'The Dionysian program is a cosmic one in which the divine Eros refracts itself into the multiple theophanies of the universe, which in turn erotically strive to pass beyond their multiplicity back into simple unity' (1991, p. 161).

All movement in the hierarchy of creation, for Dionysius, comes from above and is 'fundamentally erotic'. Not only do all things strive erotically for the Beautiful and the Good (DN 4), but the Deity itself is *Eros*: 'Divine *Eros* is the Good of the Good for the sake of the Good' (DN 4.10, McGinn's translation). Using the Proclean procession of *monē* (remaining), *proodos* (proceeding) and *epistrophē* (reverting), God in God's being as *eros* is able to proceed out to all creation and remain in the Godhead at the same time:

> It must be said that the very cause of the universe in the beautiful, good superabundance of his benign *eros* for all is carried outside of himself in the loving care he has for everything. He is, as it were, beguiled by goodness, by *agape* and by *eros* and is enticed away from his dwelling place and comes to abide within all things, and he does so by virtue of his supernatural and ecstatic capacity to remain, nevertheless, within himself. (DN 4.13, McGinn)

Thus, the 'sympathetic' initiation described by Dionysius above is also an *erotic* initiation. *Eros* is the occasion for the 'special experience of knowing' (*pathein*) in contrast to the 'knowing by mental effort' (*mathein*).[5] It is the arena of Hierothus' initiation 'by some more divine inspiration, not only learning the things of God but experiencing them, and through this sympathy with them, if we may say this, having been consummated in initiation into mystical union and faith in them which cannot be taught' (DN 2.9, McGinn). Or to put it in our terms above, it is a knowing which involves the libidinal or *affectus* as much as the *intellectus*. Within Dionysius' mystical game the strategy of deconstruction/unknowing is complemented by the strategy of the libidinal/erotic/affective.

'What cannot be demonstrated' by the Church, McGinn suggests, is according to Dionysius 'made present both on the material level of symbols used by scripture and in liturgy and also by extension, on the conceptual or intellectual level, where the negation of names and eventually the removal of both affirmation and negation bring the soul to union with the divine mystery' (1991, p. 173). This union, I suggest, being the *erotic union* engendered by *eros* through the *affectus* and the libido. This is the ex-stasis, the ecstasy: 'Through ecstasy we pass beyond the human condition and become divinized' (1991, p. 179).

Letter 9 of Dionysius describes God as a drunken lover 'standing outside all good things, being the suprafullness of all these things' (Ep. 9.5). The model here being St Paul, Dionysius' ecstatic teacher and erotic initiator:

> This is why the great Paul, swept along by his yearning for God and seized of its ecstatic power, had this inspired word to say: 'It is no longer I who live, but Christ who lives in me' (Gal 2:20). Paul was truly a lover and, as he says, he was beside himself for God (2 Cor 5:13), possessing not his own life but the life of the One for whom he yearned (in eros), as exceptionally beloved. (DN 4.13)

Following Roques (*DS* 2.1908–10) McGinn sees Dionysius' concept of union as based on the transcendentalization of knowing into unknowing and yearning *eros* into ecstatic possession. The two processes we have identified as key to the 'mystical strategy of elucidation' are intimately connected. I argue here that Dionysius' exposition of the unknowing-erotic strategy allows later Christian writers to mine the erotic side, especially through the medium of the exposition of the *Song of Songs*. As McGinn points out, Dionysius here is standing in already established Christian tradition of equating the *agape* of the New Testament with the *eros* of the Platonic tradition, beginning, he suggests, with Origen's *Commentary on the Song of Songs* (McGinn 1991, p. 120): 'The power of love is none other than that which leads the soul from earth to the lofty heights of heaven, and . . . the high-

est beatitude can only be attained under the stimulus of love's desire'
(prol., ed. 63.9–11).

McGinn's expositon of this topic is of a special clarity. However,
his device of dividing *eros* into what he calls EROS I, when referred
to the Deity and eros ii when referring to the creature seems to defuse
the potentially subversive nature of the erotic language, which, as we
suggest here, is one of the key reasons for adopting it in the mystical
strategy. As with Origen, so with Dionysius, the talk of the erotic is
accompanied by the libidinal and embodied, thus the use of the erotic
is subversive from its first entry into Christian discourse.

The rediscovery of *eros* within the spiritual has been one of the excit-
ing developments of the past century. Starting with Freud (1930), the
relationship has proved a fruitful mine for many twentieth- and twenty-
first-century thinkers as diverse as Herbert Marcuse (1956), William
McNamara (1977) and even Pope Benedict XVI in his first encyclical
Deus Caritas Est (2005). As McNamara, a contemporary Carmelite
priest, puts it:

> Eros pertains essentially to the art of making love (coming into union
> – communion). Sex is limited to the manipulation of organs. Eros
> attracts and lures us into union with everything. Eros is wakeful, vigi-
> lant, remembering whatever is true and beautiful, whatever is good.
> Sex is need; eros is desire. The sex act, is, indeed, the most symbolic
> and specific celebration of relatedness imaginable. But eros is related-
> ness. Excitement accompanies sex. Tenderness dominates the erotic
> quest. (McNamara 1977, p. 118)

The Christian tradition has always emphasized the integration of all
aspects of the human being: body, mind, heart and soul. When faced
with the people we care for we cannot afford to split off one from the
other. Sexual and relational problems may present a spiritual wound
that needs healing and vice versa. The phenomenon of 'erotic transfer-
ence' is well known to therapists and one that is worth remembering by
all care-givers. As well as the integration of the sexual and the spiritual
we need too to remember the integration of the feminine and masculine
in our approaches, following the example of Jung.

The school of Catholic mystical theology – what I call here the *theologia mistica* – is not just a school of the head but a school of the heart
and intuition that gives as much importance to the arts, liturgy and
embodied expression as it does to scholastic theology. As Merton puts
it in *Zen and the Birds of Appetite*:

In our need for whole and integral experience of our own self on all its levels, bodily as well as imaginative, emotional, intellectual, spiritual, there is not place for the cultivation of one part of human consciousness, one aspect of human experience, at the expense of others, even on the pretext that what is cultivated is sacred and all the rest profane. A false and divisive 'sacredness' or 'supernatural-ism' can only cripple us. (Merton 1968, p. 30)

Therefore, when we engage with the spiritual dimension in our care-giving it is important that we do not divorce it from the other dimensions of our being. A disembodied spirituality is not only unhealthy but also ultimately destructive. Our spiritual care-giving must be rooted in the body of the here and now.

The Dionysian Strategies of Affectivity and Unknowing

As we have seen above, this *sympatheia* is the *erotic* initiation of Dio-nysius (DN 4.10). The *eros* as 'Good seeking Good for the sake of the Good' (S: *est divinus amor bonus boni propter bonum*). And, following the essential understanding of the human person as *persona ecstatica*, *eros* brings us to our essential ecstatic being: 'Eros brings ecstasy so that the lover belongs not to self but to the beloved' (S: *Est autem faciens exstasim divinus amor*). For Dionysius, God himself is enticed by *eros* 'from his transcendent dwelling place and comes to abide within all things, and he does so by virtue of his supernatural and ecstatic capac-ity to remain, nevertheless, within himself' (DN 4.13).

From the above we can see that Dionysius presents a synthesis of two textual strategies: deconstruction and erotic, in one overarch-ing survey of the *erotic-ecstatic* nature of the human person. As von Balthasar points out, his text beguiles and plays with us as he stretches us beyond our intellectual and rational limits to make connection with the divine through the play of *pathé* – emotions and affect (Eriugena's *affectus*).

My argument here is that this vision of the ecstatic union and return of the self to God, this erotico-deconstructive strategy, is a key aspect of the medieval tradition of *theologia mystica*. This erotico-deconstructive strategy (Dionysius' *stulta sapientia*: DN 7.1; Gk: μωράν σοφία – which is '*alogos*' and '*anous*') seems to be fundamental to the tradition of *theologia mistica* and it is this that winds its way through the 'mysti-cal discourse' of the late Middle Ages. Further, we can now usefully participate in it as a helpful articulation of Christian pastoral care, in particular through the lenses of *unknowing* and *affectivity*.

Conclusions: Consequences of the Unknowing-Affective Dionysian Strategy for Pastoral Care Today

I will conclude this short chapter by illustrating in one practical area where the medieval Latin writings of the *theologia mistica* based on Dionysius can have practical implication today. That is, in the process and formation of adults, especially in mid-life transition points.

The Priority of Adult Formation was produced by the Committee for Catechetics and Adult Christian Education of the Catholic Bishops' Conference of England and Wales in 2000 (hereafter PAF). It begins by reiterating one of the stated aims of the 1997 *General Directory for Catechesis* that one of the key functions of catechesis is the 'formation of mature, responsible adult Christians'. On p. 5 of PAF it is stated that the mature adult should be:

> aware of his or her journey through life with God. His or her potential and God-given gifts and talents will be developed, she or he will be enabled by the community, within the community to contribute to the life of the community.

All of which leads finally to:

> This call to maturity may lead individuals into distinct roles, vocations and ministries at various times – and the call is for all.

Thus we have a vision of adult catechesis or formation that begins with reflection on our 'journey through life with God' leading to an awareness of our potential, 'God-given gifts and talent'. This in turn is fed by reflection on our place in the *ecclesia* and the call to expression of these gifts through 'distinct roles, vocations and ministries'. The stated aim is nothing if not practical and functional. As someone involved in adult formation from a psycho-spiritual perspective, I find it noteworthy that the document nowhere states what it means by an 'adult' and how the 'special needs' of adults are to be distinguished from those of children.

Accordingly, feeling the need to make this distinction I will rely broadly on the notion of 'Faith Development Theory' as developed by James Fowler (see Fowler 1996). In doing this I am well aware of the critiques of Fowler, in particular in Slee (2004) and Astley (1992); however, be that as it may, Fowler's theories are granted broad acceptance today, and even a trenchant critic like Slee recognizes the importance of Fowler's contribution and the light it can throw on an investigation of adult faith development.

From the perspective developed in this paper I would suggest that the Dionysian affective-unknowing strategy provides a means to access the needs of adults in what Fowler terms the period of *Midlife Transition and Middle Adulthood*.

The onset of the transition from early adulthood to middle adulthood is marked by emotional burnout, neurosis, exhaustion and collapse of values. It is the time for the contra-psychological to emerge: the executive ego must begin to surrender control to the unconscious and suppressed. In Jungian terms, it is the time of integration of the shadow, the contrasexual and the archetype of the Self. Fowler (1996) stresses that this phase requires 'nurturing methods of meditation, contemplation and therapy that nurture a safe permeability of the defensive membrane that separates conscious from unconscious'. In other words, we need to be given a safe space where we can explore what has been suppressed during our earlier developmental phases. Interestingly enough Jung sees the churches as the ideal container for this transition, and in his essay 'The Stages of Life' suggests that the churches have held the wisdom of containing this transition for centuries:

> Wholly unprepared, we embark upon the second half of life. Or are there perhaps colleges for forty-year-olds which prepare them for their coming life and its demands as ordinary colleges introduce our young people to a knowledge of the world? . . . Our religions were always such schools in the past, but how many people regard them like that today? How many of us older ones have been brought up in such a school and really prepared for the second half of life, for old age, death and eternity? (Jung 1953, p. 398)

A key dimension of this phase, and this holds for people of faith as well as those engaged in secular therapies, is the acknowledgement of the spiritual dimension of the person. For Fowler (1996), the therapies of middle age 'cannot do their work without acknowledging the spiritual nature of the task, and without reliance upon a spirit of love and acceptance, of healing and forgiveness beyond the power of humans alone'.

In contrast to the certainties of early adulthood the onset of middle adulthood is often characterized by collapse, crisis, breakdown and breakthrough. It is a time when we are required to develop what Fowler calls an 'epistemological humility'. In Jung's words, 'what was great in the morning will be little in the evening, and what in the morning was true will at evening have become a lie' (Jung 1953, p. 399). This is a period in a person's life that calls for the appreciation of paradox, mystery and what de Cusa calls the 'coincidence of opposites'. Precisely the movement into 'unknowing' that we have characterized as peculiar to the Catholic tradition of Affective Dionysianism/*theologia mystica*. From the point of view of this present chapter the importance of this tradition is the importance it places on paradox and the use of 'holding of opposites' in the evolution of right relationship with the Living God. Ever since Cyprian Smith's classic work *The Way of Paradox* (Smith 1987), commentators have begun to see how the seemingly abstruse ideas of a dense writer such as Eckhart can have real, practical pastoral application. My own work in this area, especially in recent years with the writings of Teresa of Avila and John of the Cross (see especially Tyler 1997, 2010) has shown how quick adults are to respond to the paradoxical challenges of such writers. These lovers of paradox and mystery appeal to the battered and bruised souls who have weathered the collapse of the young adult ego in their mid-life crisis. Coupled with the 'epistemological unknowing' of this transition, there is, as I have said above, the need to become aware of embodiment, affectivity and the contra-sexual – here again our Dionysian 'mystical strategies' can be of help, as we have seen, in articulating a course or method whereby these elements of the self can be integrated into our spiritual being. Loss, illness, unemployment, disillusionment beset us all in one shape or another, and if the Church needs to find help in the catechetical formation of adults at this time then it will do worse than turn to its own 'best kept secret' of the mystical tradition.

Notes

1 The most recent scholarly edition of the original Greek texts is the *Corpus Dionysiacum* edited by Suchla, Heil and Ritter (Berlin 1990). In this chapter we shall largely be concerned with the twelfth-century interpretations of the text that formed the tradition of *theologia mystica* in the West. Accordingly we shall concentrate on the Latin versions of the text found in *Dionysiaca* (Paris, 1937–50), *Patrologia Latina* (Paris, 1844), *Strassbourg 1502* and Harrington (Paris, 2004) and McEvoy (Paris, 2003). For English translations we shall draw on *Pseudo-Dionysius: The Complete Works*, trans. Luibheid and Rorem (New York, 1987), *Dionysius the Areopagite on the Divine Names and Mystical Theology*

(London, 1920) and *Denis Hid Divinity*, ed. McCann (London, 1924) and Walsh (New York, 1988).

2 The main works I have drawn upon for this study of Dionysius are as follows: the article in the *Dictionnaire de spiritualité* (DS), 'Denys L'Aréopagite: Doctrine', 3.244–86, by René Roques, and R. Rorem's 1954 work *L'univers dionysien* and *Pseudo-Dionysius: A Commentary on the Texts and an Introduction to their Influence* (Oxford, 1993); Louth 1989; McGinn 1991; and the commentaries and articles found in the texts by Luibheid, Harrington, McEvoy and Walsh mentioned above.

3 See especially Dondaine 1953 and the editions of Harrington (2004) and McEvoy (2003).

4 See also DN 2.3 : over-good, over-divine, over-existent, over-living, over-wise (S: *superbonum, superdeum, supersubstantiale, supervivens, supersapiens*).

5 The *sympatheia*, as McGinn following Rorem (1982) points out, is a key term in late Neoplatonism in making the connection between the different levels of the 'theurgy' possible: '*sympathy* for Dionysius is not so much an ontological bond by which material things are manipulated to acquire an access to the upper world as it is an affinity for "reading" the inner meaning of the hierarchies as manifestations of the Thearchy' (McGinn 1991, p. 172). Hence Dionysius' adoption of the phrase 'so as to speak' to suggest he is adapting a term from the Neoplatonic school.

Bibliography

The Dionysian texts

DN   *On the Divine Names*
MT   *The Mystical Theology*
CH   *The Celestial Hierarchy*
EH   *The Ecclesiastical Hierarchy*
Ep.   The Letters

The most recent scholarly edition of the original Greek texts is:
Corpus Dionysiacum edited by Suchla, Heil and Ritter (Berlin, 1990).
Latin versions of the text can be found in:

Dionysiaca (Paris, 1937–50),
Patrologia Latina (Paris, 1844), and Harrington (Paris, 2004) and McEvoy (Paris, 2003).

When quoting Latin versions I have taken them from *Dionysiacum* and given the translator as follows:

S = Sarracenus
E = Eriugena
R = Robert Grosseteste

For English Translations see:

Pseudo-Dionysius:The Complete Works, trans Luibheid and Rorem, New York, 1987;
Dionysius the Areopagite on the Divine Names and Mystical Theology, London, 1920; and *Denis Hid Divinity*, edited by McCann, London, 1924; and Walsh, New York, 1988.

Church documents

Benedict XVI, Pope, 2005, *Deus Caritas Est*, Rome: Libreria Editrice Vaticana.
Catholic Bishops' Conference of England and Wales, 2000, *The Priority of Adult Formation*, London: Catholic Media Office.

Articles and books

J. Astley (ed.), 1992, *Christian Perspectives on Faith Development*, Leominster: Gracewing.
W. Bion, 1980, *Bion in New York and São Paulo*, Strathtay, Perthshire: Clunie Press.
L. Bouyer, 1981, 'Mysticism: An Essay on the History of the Word', in R. Woods (ed.), *Understanding Mysticism*, London: Athlone.
H. Dondaine, 1953, *Le Corpus dionysien de l'université de Paris au XIIIe siècle*, Rome: Edizioni di Storia et Letteratura.
J. Fowler, 1996, *Faithful Change*, Nashville: Abingdon.
R. French, 2000, '"Negative Capability", "Dispersal" and the "Containment of Emotion"', Unpublished paper.
S. Freud, 1930, *Das Unbehagen in Die Kultur und Andere Kulturtheoretische Schriften*, ed. Lorenzer and Gorlich, 1994, Frankfurt-am-Main: Fischer.
L. Harrington (ed. and trans.), 2004, *A Thirteenth-Century Textbook of Mystical Theology at the University of Paris, The Mystical Theology of Dionysius the Areopagite in Eriugena's Latin Translation with the Scholia translated by Anastasius the Librarian and Excerpts from Eriugena's Periphyseon*, Paris: Peeters.
W. R. Inge, 1899, *Christian Mysticism*, London: Methuen & Co.
C. G. Jung, 1953, 'The Stages of Life', in *Collected Works*, vol VIII: *The Structure and Dynamic of the Psyche*, trans. R. F. C. Hull, London: Routledge.
S. Katz, 1978, *Mysticism and Philosophical Analysis*, London: Sheldon.
J. Keats, 1970, *The Letters of John Keats: A Selection*, ed. R. Gittings, Oxford: Blackwell.
N. Lash, 1988, *Easter in Ordinary: Reflections on Human Experience and the Knowledge of God*, London: University of Notre Dame Press.
A. Louth, 1989, *Denys the Areopagite*, London: Geoffrey Chapman.
H. McCabe, 2002, *God Still Matters*, London: Continuum.
J. McEvoy (ed.), 2003, *Mystical Theology: The Glosses by Thomas Gallus and the Commentary of Robert Grosseteste on 'De Mystica Theologia'*, Paris: Peeters.
B. McGinn, 1991, *The Presence of God: A History of Western Christian Mysticism*, vol. I: *The Foundations of Mysticism*, London SCM Press; 1994,

vol. II: *Gregory the Great through the Twelfth Century*, London: SCM Press; 1998, vol. III: *The Flowering of Mysticism: Men and Women in the New Mysticism, 1200–1350*, London: SCM Press; 2005, vol. IV: *The Harvest of Mysticism in Medieval Germany*, New York: Herder & Herder.

M. McIntosh, 1994, *Mystical Theology*, Oxford: Blackwell.

W. McNamara, 1977, *Mystical Passion: The Art of Christian Loving*, Shaftesbury: Element.

H. Marcuse, 1956, *Eros and Civilisation: A Philosophical Enquiry after Freud*, London: Routledge

T. Merton, 1968, *Zen and the Birds of Appetite* New York: New Directions.

T. Merton, 1973, *Contemplative Prayer*, London: Darton, Longman & Todd.

T. Merton, 1985, *The Hidden Ground of Love: The Letters of Thomas Merton on Religious Experience and Social Concerns*, ed. William H. Shannon, New York: Farrar, Straus & Giroux.

Francisco de Osuna, 1998, *Tercer Abecedario Espiritual*, ed. S. López Santidrián, Madrid: Biblioteca de Autores Cristianos.

R. Roques, 'Denys L'Aréopagite: Doctrine', in *Dictionnaire de spiritualité* (DS), 3: 244–86.

R. Roques, 1993, *Pseudo-Dionysius: A Commentary on the Texts and an Introduction to their Influence*, Oxford: Oxford University Press.

P. Rorem, 1954, *L'Univers Dionysien*, Paris: Aubier.

P. Rorem, 1982, 'Iamblichus and the Anagogical Method in Pseudo-Dionysian Liturgical Theology', in *Studia Patristica*, vol. XVIII, ed. E. A. Livingstone, Oxford: Pergamon.

M. A. Sells, 1994, *Mystical Languages of Unsaying*, Chicago: University of Chicago Press.

N. Slee, 2004, *Women's Faith Development*, Aldershot: Ashgate.

C. Smith, 1987, *The Way of Paradox*, London: Darton, Longman & Todd.

D. Tacey, 2003, 'Rising Waters of the Spirit', *Studies in Spirituality* 13, pp. 11–30.

Teresa of Avila, 1980, *The Interior Castle*, in *The Collected Works of St Teresa of Avila*, vol. II, trans. K. Kavanaugh and O. Rodriguez, Washington: ICS.

P. M. Tyler, 1997, *The Way of Ecstasy: Praying with Teresa of Avila*, Norwich: Canterbury Press.

P. M. Tyler, 2007, 'Divine Unknowing: Lessons from the Christian Mystical Tradition for Healthcare Today', *Spirituality and Health International* 8:2, pp. 64–73.

P. M. Tyler, 2010, *St John of the Cross*, London: Continuum.

E. Underhill, 1910, *Mysticism: The Nature and Development of Spiritual Consciousness*, 12th edn 1930, reprinted 1993, Oxford: Oneworld.

R. A. Vaughan, 1856, *Hours with the Mystics: A Contribution to the History of Religious Opinion*, 3rd edn 1895, London: Gibbings & Co.

H. U. von Balthasar, 1961–9, *Herrlichkeit: Eine theologische Ästhetik*, Einsiedeln: Johannes Verlag, ET *The Glory of the Lord: A Theological Aesthetic*, 1982–6, ed. J. Fessio and J. Riches, trans. O. Davies, A. Louth, J. Sayward, M. Simon, B. McNeil, F. McDonagh, J. Riches, E. Leiva-Merikakis and R. Williams, Edinburgh: T&T Clark.

F. von Hügel, 1908, *The Mystical Element of Religion as Studied in Saint*

Catherine of Genoa and her Friends, London: Dent.

R. Williams, 1979, *The Wound of Knowledge*, London: Darton, Longman & Todd.

G. Zinn, 1979, *Richard of St Victor: The Book of the Patriarchs, The Mystical Ark, Book Three of the Trinity Classics of Western Spirituality*, New York: Paulist Press.

13

Moral Theology as Pastoral Theology

BERNARD HOOSE

The above title suggests two things. The first is that moral theology is rightly termed 'theology'. The second (assuming the correctness of the first) is that it is, in some way, a branch of pastoral theology. Do these suggestions, however, have any basis in fact? In order to answer that question we need to establish just what moral theology is or should be. In doing so we will hopefully uncover something that is far richer than the popular image of that discipline might suggest.

From Rules to Riches

Many people, it seems, think of moral theology as being concerned only with attempts to determine which acts are right and which are wrong. That is, in fact, one of its roles, and such a role does, of course, have a good deal of importance for pastoral theologians. Nevertheless, in view of the fact that a similar role is played by moral philosophy, it could appear that moral theology is not really theology at all. Arguing to the contrary, some might point out that, during recent decades there has been a tendency among many moral theologians to accentuate the development of persons rather than simply the rightness or wrongness of acts performed by persons. Thus, they might note, we have seen a major revival of debate about virtues as qualities of persons. That can be done, however, without any reference to God, Jesus or the gospel, and, indeed, a similar development in regard to virtues has taken place among the ranks of moral philosophers in the same time period. Once again, therefore, one could be forgiven for thinking that there is nothing theological about moral theology.

Writing in 1964, moreover, Sean O'Riordan argued against the second of the suggestions referred to above:

Moral theology is the science of moral principles; pastoral theology is concerned with the *concrete working-out* of these principles in given historical circumstances. The two spheres of operation are quite distinct, though of course closely related. It would be to the advantage of both sciences to adopt this line of demarcation once for all, and to assign the aspect of moral life involving human historicity quite definitely to pastoral theology. (O'Riordan 1998, p. 167)[1]

Given the fact that he was writing as a Roman Catholic moral theologian before the end of the Second Vatican Council, O'Riordan's conclusion is not surprising. Some forty years later, Norbert Rigali spelt out a number of shortcomings in Catholic moral theology before the Second Vatican Council. Among these was 'a tendency to reduce morality to decision-making, and ethics to scientific reflection on decision-making'. Another was a tendency to ignore how narrative, vision, virtue and character are constitutive elements of the moral life. The ways in which moral living is moulded by tradition and community, moreover, were not given sufficient attention, and there was also a lack of historical consciousness (Rigali 2004, p. 5).[2] As for the theological side of things, Rigali observed that no mention of 'Jesus' or 'Christ' is to be found in the index or table of contents of a typical three-volume manual of moral theology used in seminaries in the period immediately preceding the Council. He also noted Timothy O'Connell's comment, made more than a decade after Vatican II, that, far from being theology, what we call moral theology is nothing other than moral philosophy (Rigali 2004, p. 4; see also O'Connell 1978, pp. 39–41). William Spohn, moreover, notes that Catholic moral theology paid little attention to Jesus Christ for centuries (Spohn 2004, p. 24).

Although the roots of these problems can perhaps be traced much further back in the history of the Church, the separation of moral theology from the rest of theology in the sixteenth century does not appear to have been an entirely positive move. As Charles Curran put it:

Dogmatic theology no longer interacted with moral theology. Separation at times might be necessary to achieve particular purposes, but moral theology now became totally isolated from the broader theological enterprise. Moral theology also became separated from scripture with scripture being used only as a proof text to show that certain actions were wrong. (Curran 1997, p. 16)

A major cause of the growing independence of moral theology seems to have been the way in which those in authority reacted to a felt need to ensure that priests were well equipped to administer the Sacrament of Penance (Confession), a sacrament that received a good deal of attention at the Council of Trent. In earlier times priests had often been illiterate and ill-prepared. After the Council, however, diocesan seminaries for the proper training of priests began to spring up all over Europe. Manuals dedicated to moral theology also appeared around this time, and such manuals continued to be written and published well into the twentieth century. Noting the enormous role that the growth and proliferation of oral confession played in the development of moral theology, John Mahoney makes the very positive point that, 'over the centuries the work of confessors and moral theologians has brought God's grace and consolation to countless Christian souls'. He also describes, however, some not so helpful attributes and effects of the moral theology that developed within the Catholic Church:

> The pessimistic anthropology from which it started, and which served inevitably to confirm and reinforce itself, particularly when the subject was pursued in growing isolation from the rest of theology and developed as a spiritual arm of the Church's legal system, drove moral theology increasingly to concern itself almost exclusively with the darker and insubordinate side of human existence. The miasma of sin which emanates from the penitential literature and from the vast majority of manuals of moral theology is not only distasteful, but profoundly disquieting. (Mahoney 1987, p. 28)

Mahoney goes on to note that the tendency of moral theology to concentrate on 'spiritual pathology' led it to leave the consideration of the good in humans almost entirely 'to other branches of theology, notably to what became known as spiritual theology' (1978, p. 29). Spiritual theology was also known as ascetical or mystical theology. While moral theology dealt with the basics of right behaviour and development, or perhaps rather with what is obligatory, this other theological discipline was concerned with seeking after higher things. As Rigali puts it, 'Moral theology, accordingly, was "the theology for salvation" while ascetical theology was "the theology for perfection"' (Rigali 2004, p. 7). Given his own observation, noted above, about the lack of attention to Jesus, one might wonder why Rigali makes any reference at all to a *theology* of salvation here. As he notes, however, the manuals of moral theology were divided into two parts. The first part dealt with general principles, whereas, in the second, the general principles were applied to the Ten

Commandments and to obligations that were seen as arising from the sacraments, as well as from rules developed within Roman Catholicism. These last mentioned were referred to as 'commandments of the Church' (Rigali 2004, pp. 9–10).

There appears to have been an assumption of a two-tier Christianity behind much that was written within Catholicism during the period under review. This can be seen in numerous references in influential literature to higher forms of life – usually meaning the still rather exclusively termed 'religious life' taken up by monks, nuns, friars and religious sisters, although there was also acknowledgement of the fact that, occasionally, ordinary lay people and members of the diocesan clergy managed to rise to extraordinary levels.[3] These special souls were apparently those most likely to be interested in ascetical or spiritual theology. Nowadays, the notion of such a two-tier Christianity seems repulsive to most of us, and, indeed, there were moves away from that way of thinking within Roman Catholicism itself even before Vatican II. Perhaps the most influential author in this respect at that time was Bernard Häring, for whom Christ was at the very centre of moral theology. As Richard Gula puts it:

> After Häring's work, there has been no turning back on his major thesis that morality is the response to the spiritual experience of God's enabling love. His insight, that the dynamics of the spiritual experience contain the moral impulse to pass on what has been experienced, is key to appreciating that morality and spirituality are inseparably intertwined. (Gula 2004, pp. 163–4)[4]

It would be far from the truth, of course, to conclude that changes in direction and emphasis have been necessary only in Roman Catholic circles. Writing in the 1970s, the Anglican scholar Keith Ward noted, on the one hand, in traditional Catholic moral theology a tendency to somehow present the purposes of God for humans as 'impersonal or subpersonal purposes of Nature', with nature itself appearing as an autonomous reality. In some Protestant traditions, on the other hand, he saw a tendency to

> undermine the freedom and creativity of human response by tying morality up in a strict and exhaustive set of rules for living; or they have stressed the sovereignty and absoluteness of the divine imperative to such an extent that any notion of a rational purpose in the created order, to be worked out in society as well as in personal life,

has virtually disappeared. Categorical rules have ousted the notion of a proper end and goal for man from some Protestant accounts of ethics; and so the 'natural man' becomes a fallen, totally depraved creature, and God's commands come, not to show him his possible goal, but solely to convict him of sin and to discipline his unruly will. (Ward 1976, p. 14)

As Ward saw things, 'the divine purpose is being worked out in nature'. It is, however, 'a fully personal purpose'. What is required of humans, then, is a response that is fully personal, and humans have a large measure of freedom when making their response (1976, p. 14).[5]
Further on in the same work, he writes:

If I had to choose one phrase with which to characterize the Christian's moral outlook, that phrase would be: 'creative response'. One must respond to the moral claims of one's situation, but one must do so by the exercise of spontaneous and creative freedom; the moral life largely consists in the skilful balancing of these two factors of freedom and response. (Ward 1976, p. 106)

Many present-day Roman Catholic moral theologians, including the present author, would also be happy to speak and write in terms of creative response. Movement in this direction within Catholic moral theology since Vatican II, however, has been far from speedy, and it has certainly not been universal. Nevertheless, we can say that, in general, the discipline has become much more concerned with Christian living as a response to the call and grace of God, who is Love. Moreover, far from being immersed only in the negative aspects of ethics, moral theology tends nowadays to be much more concerned with the creative aspects of persons and with the encouragement of such creativity.

The Role of Conscience

This can be seen more clearly by examining the role of conscience in our lives, although, as we shall see, it is not as easy as one might expect to get to grips with that topic. Conscience is often described as the human person making decisions. It could be argued, however, that a good deal of what has been taught about right and wrong behaviour over the centuries, in Anglican, Protestant and Roman Catholic circles, has merely helped to reinforce conditioning rather than promote free human decision-making. In recent times it has become common to resort to the Freudian term 'Superego' when describing and analysing such conditioning. Whether or not one agrees with Freudian psychology, it seems fairly obvious that some internalizing of the commands of authority figures occurs in childhood. It also seems obvious that such conditioning can go on being reinforced by one's culture – or perhaps we should say the various cultures that have an impact upon a person in the various spheres in which that person lives and acts – far beyond childhood and adolescence.[6] It is also clear that people often experience feelings of guilt without being able to explain what, if anything, is wrong with the action about which they feel guilty. In a sense, we might say, they have been programmed to feel guilty for not conforming to the expectations of those early authority figures, even if those authority figures have not been around for many years, the people now feeling guilty have been adults for a long time, and they now live in very different cultures from those that were dominant in their formative years.[7]

Although this non-reflected internalization of the commands of authority figures seems to be an unavoidable and perhaps even necessary part of our upbringing, it has to be distinguished from conscience in the proper sense. So what, then, is conscience? We noted above a common tendency among moral theologians nowadays to describe it in terms of the person making decisions. We must beware, however, of interpreting this in any kind of superficial sense. In a number of passages in the writings of Saint Paul we find the Greek word *synderesis*, the Latin equivalent of which is *conscientia*, from which the English word 'conscience' was derived. In those books of the Old Testament that were written in Hebrew, however, and in various other parts of the New Testament, there are, instead, numerous references to the heart of a person. When we use the word 'heart' figuratively in modern English we are usually referring to the centre or source of a person's emotional life. For the Jews at that time, however, the heart was much more. It was the very core of the person. That is how we should understand conscience. 'His conscience is man's most secret core, and his sanctuary. There he is alone with God, whose voice echoes in his depths' (*Gaudium et spes*, 16).

Over the centuries, numerous Christian writers have spoken of more than one aspect to this core of the human person. Thomas Aquinas, for instance, like many others who came after him, wrote about our awareness that we should seek after and do good, and avoid evil. This intuitive grasp of the first moral principles he termed *synderesis*.[8] Some others now refer to it as the first or basic aspect or level of conscience. Alone with the Holy Spirit, who lives in our hearts, and having this innate awareness about good and evil, we are urged to try to find out which acts are good and which are wrong. This searching and enquiring is a second aspect of our inner core, our conscience. As traditionally understood, the first aspect appears not to tell us much about *how* good can be achieved and evil avoided in particular kinds of activity. Hence the need for enquiry and education. This process of enquiry and education is sometimes referred to as formation of the conscience, and is expected to involve learning from Scripture, the Tradition of the Church, those who are more knowledgeable than we are, our own and others' experience, and our reasoning powers. Now, learning about what, in theory, one should or should not do is, of course, quite different from having to make a decision in practice. Thus, Richard Gula (1989, pp. 131–5) and Timothy O'Connell (1978, pp. 88–93) refer to the actual conscientious decision-making as a separate, third aspect of conscience.

The formative process is notoriously fallible. Because of numerous factors, including this fallibility of the formative process, the third aspect of conscience also proves to be fallible. Moreover, it is not only poorly educated individuals who make mistakes about the rightness and wrongness of actions. Over the centuries numerous influential teachers and authority figures in various branches of Christianity have made spectacular errors concerning such matters as slavery, burning heretics at the stake, torture, religious liberty, and the roles that women may play in society. In other words, the information available from so-called 'authoritative sources' is sometimes faulty. Taking this into account, along with our own personal inabilities, we can see that our mistakes are sometimes blameworthy, and occasionally not so. We may make mistakes, for instance, because we have been misled, or simply because of ignorance about something. Clearly such ignorance could conceivably be the fault of the person who is in error. He or she should have made reasonable efforts to acquire the necessary knowledge, and perhaps did not. On other occasions, however, it would be unreasonable to expect the person concerned to have acquired the knowledge needed to avoid the error. It could be the case, for instance, that such knowledge is available to a very few extremely clever people, or perhaps it will become available to no one at all until several generations later, as a result of scientific discovery.

There are, then, different types of ignorance. One of the most puzzling types is that which results from what are sometimes referred to as structures and systems of sin, and attitudes that grow out of such structures and systems. It appears obvious to us that burning someone at the stake because they refuse to consent to certain theological notions is downright wrong. It seems inconceivable that anyone could have thought otherwise, even a few centuries ago. And yet, there is evidence to suggest that many people sincerely did think so at certain stages in history. Their moral vision, it seems, was impaired by a kind of fog that descended during particular situations of sin.[9] In situations like these, however, the moral vision of some people may not be impaired by the fog that renders others morally blind in some respects. This seems to have been the case, for instance, with Erasmus and Sebastien Castellio in regard to the appalling intolerance displayed on both sides during the Reformation period, and with Friedrich von Spee in regard to the burning of witches (Hoose 2006, pp. 619ff.). This, however, changes nothing concerning the dignity of conscience. One always has to strive to do one's best with the knowledge, ability to see, and other gifts that are available.

Conscience and Spirituality

But what does all this tell us about conscience and a creative response to God's love? The key would seem to lie in that observation that conscience is the core of my personality, where I am alone with God. There is, however, also a common enough tendency among Christians to refer to conscience as 'the voice of God'. The above quotation from the Vatican II document *Gaudium et spes* does, of course, talk about the voice of God echoing in the depths of the person. That, however, is not quite the same as the claim that conscience simply *is* the voice of God. James P. Hanigan points out that:

> conscience is human; it is a human capacity, a human process, and the judgment that is conscience is a human judgment. However moved, inspired, instructed or guided by the Holy Spirit, the so-called voice of conscience which I hear is my voice, my judgment for which I must take full and final responsibility. There is simply no basis in faith or in reason to think or to assert otherwise. For the judgment is always I should do X and only I can make such a judgment. (Hanigan 2004, p. 175)

Hanigan goes on to say that appeals to the guidance or inspiration of the Holy Spirit when trying to determine the moral status of particular actions have settled nothing at all. 'Indeed,' he continues, 'such appeals are not only unhelpful and misguided, they are positively harmful, for they too easily turn our attention away from the reality to which we need to attend' (2004, p. 179). What, then, is the role of the Holy Spirit in conscience, and how do we respond creatively to that Spirit? In some branches of Protestantism there are those who would argue that an immensely important role of the Spirit was to inspire the writers of the various books of the Bible, and that our role is simply to obey what is written in Scripture. Those books, however, were written in very different times in very different situations from our own. There are therefore serious problems of translation and interpretation of numerous texts. Certain issues that we have to face nowadays, moreover, such as genetic engineering, insider-dealing and nuclear fission, are not even mentioned in the Bible. Complicating things even further is the fact that there are episodes and apparent teachings in the Bible that we find to be ethically questionable, even morally repulsive. Take, for instance, the attitudes to war and its aftermath found in various sections of the Old Testament. We find them disturbing, and, for most of us, it seems, the same is true of various decrees concerning the execution of wrongdoers also found in books of the Old Testament. Interestingly, rabbinic opposition to capital punishment in the early centuries after the birth of Christ is recorded in the Mishnah.[10] David Novak comments that, although there is certainly a scriptural mandate for capital punishment in the case of premeditated murder, later Jewish sages explained the opinion of the rabbis concerned by suggesting that their interpretation of the rules of evidence would have been so strict that it would have been impossible to sentence anyone to death. 'And, if anyone asked why Scripture would mandate what is in effect a null class, they could answer that the purpose of the law is moral instruction about the gravity of the crime of homicide' (Novak 2004, p. 36). This, of course, raises once more the question of interpretation of Scripture, but here again some Protestants would see a role for the Spirit in helping the reader of the biblical text to see the right meaning. Different people, however, all claiming the assistance of the Holy Spirit, have come to different conclusions concerning the meaning of particular texts. This would appear to be one of the reasons for the numerous splits within Protestantism.

In the 1970s a good deal of attention was given to the kind of situation ethics that holds that, in any situation in which we find ourselves, love will tell us what to do. Examples of apparently loving people who made dreadful mistakes concerning women, slavery, the crusades, torture and the execution of apparent heretics do not fill us with confidence in this regard. The present writer, however, has considered the possibility that love does somehow tell us what to do, but that, given our brokenness and the situations of sin in which we find ourselves, we are unable to hear what Love is saying to us (Hoose 1999, pp. 44–5, 623–4). Even if that is the case, of course, we are still left asking how, given these problems, we can possibly gain from the help of the Holy Spirit in our moral struggles and deliberations. Hanigan addresses the matter thus:

> What, then, does the Holy Spirit do in conscience? It is the work of the Spirit in us when we are willing to face the particular situation in all its difficulty and complexity. It is the work of the Spirit in us when we are moved to seek the truth, the good rather than the convenient, when we are willing in this search to listen to the Spirit as the Spirit speaks through the Church, our fellow believers, and through the natural abilities and talents of our fellow human beings. The Spirit, in short, teaches us how in conscience to search for the truth. (Hanigan 2004, pp. 185–6)

There are reasons for believing that there may be more than this, especially, perhaps, when we come together in the Spirit, searching for insight about a particular problem. The progress that members of the Society of Friends made in regard to slavery is an encouraging case in point. Regardless of this, however, Hanigan would seem to be right in saying that:

> Those who seek to be faithful to Christ can never invoke the Spirit or their experience of the Spirit as evidence that the judgements of their consciences are objectively right; they can only appeal to the Spirit for evidence that those judgments have been conscientious. (Hanigan 2004, p. 186)

This is core, so much so that, when I come to a decision in conscience, I should act in accordance with that decision. Why? Because I firmly believe that this is the right thing to do. To act against my conscience would be to act in a way that I believe to be wrong, in a way that is, therefore, not in accordance with the will of God. It is important to point out that this is very different from acting in accordance with wayward inclinations. To act in conscience means to act in sincerity. Understood thus, conscience reigns supreme.

The *creative* aspect of my conscientious response assumes greater importance when consideration is given to the fact that at least some of my decisions in conscience are not just about what would be right in general for any human being in this kind of situation, but rather about what is right for me in this situation. Should I marry this person? Should I earn my living using this talent rather than that one? Should I join a religious order? Given my particular gifts and training, should I use Buddhist techniques when praying? In examples such as these, the scope for creative response to God's love becomes clearer. This is also the case when we consider that much of our moral life is not just about whether to do this or that. It is about *how* I should do this or that, and how I do it may be quite different from how you would do it because our talents are different. Indeed, although we are equally human, *we* are different. As Martin Buber put it, 'Every person born into this world represents something new, something that never existed before, something original and unique.' The foremost task for each of us, he goes on to add, is the actualization of our 'unique, unprecedented and never recurring potentialities, and not the repetition of something that another, and be it even the greatest, has already achieved'. By way of illustration, he tells us that, a short time before his death, Rabbi Zusya said: 'In the world to come I shall not be asked: "Why were you not Moses?" I shall be asked "Why were you not Zusya?"' (Buber 1966, p. 17).

The Role of the Virtues

Creatively responding in conscience means being authentically me, and moral theology, like all good pastoral theology, should help me to be me. In striving to be authentic and in striving to do what is right, however, we need to acquire the necessary personal qualities. I may know what I should do in a particular situation, for instance, but I may lack the necessary courage to do it. Such personal qualities as courage and patience are what we call moral virtues. The cardinal virtues, on which all other virtues hinge, are usually listed as prudence, justice, fortitude and temperance.[11] These and the other virtues that are linked to them can be acquired by human effort and training. Thomas Aquinas, however, also refers to three theological virtues, which are infused directly by God. These are faith, hope and love. The most important of these for our purposes in this chapter is love. Saint Paul tells us that everything we do should be done in love (1 Cor. 16.14). Clearly, he is not just talking about a weak emotion that is here today, gone tomorrow and reignited by a smile or a 'come hither' look next Wednesday. He could just as well have said 'Let everything you do be done under the influence of the Holy Spirit' because the Holy Spirit *is* love. Alone with God in the core of our being, we are alone with love. The person who is taken over by love is a good person, and personal goodness, rather than the rightness of acts, is the most important aspect of morality. The good person strives, out of love, to do what is right. Perfection, however, is not attained in this life. We all make mistakes, sometimes in good conscience. Moreover, even right action without love is never enough. Even the most hardened criminals do what is right a fair percentage of the time, if for no other reason than the fact that the right thing to do is often the easiest and most convenient thing to do. One can tell the truth, give to the poor and comfort the sick for the basest of motives. Rightness without love is simply not fruitful in any deep sense (1 Cor. 13.3).

The Pastoral Role of Moral Theology

In its renewed state, then, moral theology, like all good pastoral theology, is about love because it is about our relationship with God and with each other in God. It is about a loving, creative response to Love itself. Given the considerable differences between the moral theology that held sway in the Roman Catholic Church in the period between the Council of Trent and the Second Vatican Council and what goes under that name now, Rigali argues in favour of ceasing to apply the term 'moral theology' to the latter, preferring instead to refer to it as 'theology of the Christian life'.[12] Whether we are inclined to embrace that proposal or not, the fact remains that the new discipline that has evolved over the last few decades – whatever we call it – is certainly richer and more dynamic than its predecessor. It is concerned with human development in relationship to God and other people. In contradistinction to the discipline that O'Riordan had in mind in the quotation above, present-day moral theology (or theology of the Christian life, if you prefer) is not clearly distinct from pastoral theology. There is not a clear demarcation line between the two disciplines. As Mark O'Keefe notes:

> The task of Christian moral theology cannot be simply to offer a structure by which Christians live well the 'lesser' life to which they believe themselves to be called. Rather, it is the task of moral theology to challenge, guide, and empower Christians to seek the fullness

of life that a loving God offers to them. Only then will moral theology live up to the challenge given to it by the Second Vatican Council to 'throw light on the exalted vocation of the faithful in Christ and their obligation to bring forth fruit in charity for the life of the world'. (O'Keefe 1999, p. 84)

That sounds like a truly pastoral role for a truly pastoral discipline.

Notes

1 This piece originally appeared as an article in *Studia Moralia* 2 (1964), pp. 255–75.

2 Rigali also lists: 'an exaggerated sense of the individual as autonomous agent and a corresponding predisposition to individualism' along with 'an overly simple view of the dynamic of personal freedom'.

3 Saints Margaret Clitherow, Jean Vianney and Thomas More being well known examples.

4 The general thrust of Häring's work is indicated by the titles of two of his best known works: *The Law of Christ* and *Free and Faithful in Christ*.

5 Ward notes that he has oversimplified the Catholic and Protestant positions he has described, and accepts that 'they are no doubt unrepresentative of the best in Catholic and Protestant thought.

6 There is the culture of one's family, one's school, one's society, one's trade or profession, one's sport, one's religion, etc.

7 It is, of course, possible that, in a case such as the one now provoking feelings of guilt, the original authority figures concerned would have made an exception to the rule that they taught. Because small children are unlikely to understand subtleties and abstractions, parents and other people who exercise authority over them tend to speak of moral rules in terms that appear not to admit of exceptions – for instance, 'Don't *ever* do that again.'

8 *Summa Theologiae* I, q. 79, a. 12. Aquinas picked up the term from Saint Jerome's *Commentary on Ezechiel*. There has been a good deal of debate about whether or not the term *synderesis* resulted from a mistake by Jerome or by a later copyist. Regardless of this, however, the fact remains that numerous authors have found it to be useful.

9 For further reflection on this point see Hoose 2006.

10 Makkot, 1.10.

11 For an introduction to the subject of virtues see Keenan 1998, pp. 84–94.

12 Rigali 2004. The argument runs throughout the chapter.

Bibliography

Martin Buber, 1966, *The Way of Man According to the Teaching of the Hasidim*, New York: Citadel Press.

Charles E. Curran, 1997, *The Origins of Moral Theology in the United States: Three Different Approaches*, Washington, DC: Georgetown University Press.

Richard Gula, 1989, *Reason Informed by Faith: Foundations of Catholic Morality*, New York: Paulist Press.

Richard Gula, 2004, 'Morality and Spirituality', in James Keating (ed.), *Moral Theology: New Directions and Fundamental Issues*, New York: Paulist Press.

James P. Hanigan, 2004, 'Conscience and the Holy Spirit', in Charles E. Curran (ed.), *Readings in Moral Theology*, no. 14: *Conscience*. New York: Paulist Press.

Bernard Hoose, 1999, 'Natural Law, Acts and Persons', in Todd Salzman (ed.), *Method and Catholic Moral Theology: The Ongoing Reconstruction*. Omaha: Creighton University Press, pp. 44–67.

Bernard Hoose, 2006, 'Intuition and Moral Theology', *Theological Studies* 67, pp. 602–24.

James F. Keenan, 1998, 'Virtue Ethics', in B. Hoose (ed.), *Christian Ethics: An Introduction*, London: Continuum.

John Mahoney, 1987, *The Making of Moral Theology: A Study of the Roman Catholic Tradition*, Oxford: Clarendon Press.

David Novak, 2004, 'Can Capital Punishment Ever Be Justified in the Jewish Tradition?', in E. C. Owens, J. D. Carlson and E. P. Eshtain (eds), *Religion and the Death Penalty: A Call for Reckoning*, Grand Rapids: Wm. B. Eerdmans.

Timothy E. O'Connell, 1978, *Principles for a Catholic Morality*, New York: Seabury Press.

Mark O'Keefe, 1999, 'Purity of Heart and the Christian Moral Life', in Todd Salzman (ed.), *Method and Catholic Moral Theology: The Ongoing Reconstruction*, Omaha: Creighton University Press.

Sean O'Riordan, 1998, 'The Problem of Pastoral Theology', in Raphael Gallagher and Sean Cannon (eds), *Sean O'Riordan, A Theologian of Development: Selected Essays*, Dublin: Columba Press.

Norbert Rigali, 2004, 'On Theology of the Christian Life', in James Keating (ed.), *Moral Theology: New Directions and Fundamental Issues*, New York: Paulist Press.

William C. Spohn, 2004, 'Jesus and Moral Theology', in James Keating (ed.), *Moral Theology: New Directions and Fundamental Issues*, New York: Paulist Press.

Vatican II, 1975, *Gaudium et spes*, the Pastoral Constitution on the Church in the Modern World, in Austin Flannery (ed.), *Vatican Council II: The Conciliar and Post Conciliar Documents*, Northport, NY: Costello.

Keith Ward, 1976, *The Divine Image: The Foundations of Christian Morality*, London: SPCK.

14

Theology, Law and Christian Life

BRENDAN KILLEEN

I received an email from the administrative staff at Heythrop for an update of my personal records. On the form that was attached I had to include the academic code for my discipline. I checked the appropriate website and found a list of such codes, ranging from A100 for pre-clinical medicine to X990 for education. As a canon lawyer I am convinced that canon law is intimately connected to theological disciplines. I thus put down the code for Christian studies. When I read the instructions more closely, I discovered that I was allowed to include two codes. It was at this point that I weakened and inserted a second code, this time relating to law. In short, is canon law a theological discipline or a legal one? Despite my weakness, I believe that it is a practical and pastoral application of theology. In order for me to explain the present role of canon law it is helpful to have a look at its history.

Brief History

The great canonist, Gratian, taught at Bologna in the twelfth century. Like others of his time, he was overwhelmed by the large collections of opinions from theologians, church fathers, popes, bishops and saints. To make matters worse, on any single issue there could be a variety of opinions. Thus, in about 1140 Gratian compiled his mammoth *Concordia Discordantium Canonum* ('Concordance of Discordant Canons'). This work is often referred to simply as the '*Decretum*'. As the full name suggests, Gratian would take a particular issue concerning church life and collect together the various relevant sources. He would then synthesize the opinions that he found in these sources in order to give one clear position.

It must be said that a modern critical examination of Gratian's sources might raise concerns. Sources not included by Gratian for consideration would now be regarded as just as important as those that were included. Also, expressions such as 'Saint Augustine said . . .' would now be rewritten, 'If he had considered the matter, there is the possibility that Saint Augustine might have said . . .'. Moreover, once Gratian had collected the various opinions, many of his syntheses promoted his own ideas. However, despite these problems, it must be said that the *Decretum* is a most scholarly work and provides excellent sources for the canonist. Although the *Decretum* was never the official law of the Catholic Church, it soon influenced popes and thus the entire Church. Also, for a very long time after Gratian, the study of canon law meant the study of the *Decretum*. Indeed, a canonist was nobody until he had written a commentary on it.

Despite the comprehensive nature of the *Decretum*, it soon needed updating. This is because popes and councils continued to issue opinions, decrees and laws. Over the next few centuries additional collections of laws were produced. By the beginning of the twentieth century it became apparent that it was becoming increasingly complicated to follow a theme from one collection to another. Thus, in 1904 Pope Pius X began the process of drafting a new book that would systematically set out the laws governing the Church. A special commission of cardinals was established, with Pius X as chairman and Cardinal Pietro Gasparri as secretary.

In 1917 Pope Benedict XV promulgated the Code of Canon Law, which assumed the force of law the following year. An analysis of the text shows that it does not have the variation in terminology that is often found in documents produced by committees. Also, its ecclesiology is homogeneous. The reason for these phenomena is that Cardinal Gasparri was personally involved in the drafting and editing processes. Within the 1917 Code there are 2,414 rules, each of which is called a 'canon'. Once the Code had been promulgated, Gasparri produced detailed lists of sources for each canon. As with Gratian, the study of a canon from the 1917 Code must involve a critical examination of Gasparri's use of sources.

The 1983 Code of Canon Law

On 25 January 1959 Pope John XXIII announced that he was going to convene a council. In the same breath he also stated that the 1917 Code was to be revised. It was not until March 1963 that he formed the first commission to start the process. It held its first plenary session in the

November. At that session the committee came to a decision, which initially seems to have made the meeting an anticlimax. The decision was to suspend the commission's activity until the Second Vatican Council had concluded its work. However, this decision was most important and proved to be fundamental with regard to emphasizing the true role of canon law. The members of the commission realized that the Council would enrich the Church's theology, moral theology and ecclesiology. Thus, the revised code would have to help apply these developments. That is, canon law would need to be at the service of the Council. In November 1965, only a month before the end of the Council, the commission held its second plenary session. It was then that Paul VI officially began the work of the commission.

On 25 January 1983 Pope John Paul II promulgated the new Code of Canon Law with the apostolic constitution *Sacrae disciplinae leges*. A few days later, on 3 February, the official text of the Code (*Codex Iuris Canonici*) was issued.[1] The new Code came into force on 27 November 1983, which was the first Sunday of Advent and so marked the start of a new year in the Church. The ten-month delay between the promulgation of the Code and it becoming law allowed various members of the Church to become acquainted with it and to prepare for its implementation.

The Code of the Second Vatican Council

It is quite clear from John Paul II's constitution *Sacrae disciplinae leges* that the 1983 Code is meant to implement the teaching of the Second Vatican Council. As the drafting commission had noted previously, the Code is to be at the service of the Council and directed by it. John Paul II stated:

> Indeed it is possible to assert that from this derives that characteristic whereby the Code is regarded as a complement to the authentic teaching proposed by the Second Vatican Council and particularly to its dogmatic and pastoral constitutions.
>
> From this it follows that the fundamental basis of the 'newness' which, while never straying from the Church's legislative tradition, is found in the Second Vatican Council and especially in its ecclesiological teaching, generates also the mark of 'newness' in the new Code. (Caparros et al. 1993, p. 53)

It must be acknowledged that, in practice, it is not always remembered that canon law is at the service of the other sacred disciplines. This is because a new mindset takes time to be achieved. However, change has and is taking place. Thus, from this new perspective, attitudes in the past might seem rather antiquated and even amusing. For example, a schema on marriage was needed for discussion at the Second Vatican Council. Accordingly, the Sacred Congregation for the Discipline of the Sacraments produced one. However, an examination of it soon reveals that the members of the Sacred Congregation had simply used the marriage canons of the 1917 Code (Mackin 1982, p. 248). This schema was not adopted by the Council. It would be unfair to judge the Sacred Congregation by post-conciliar standards. However, this is a good example of the understanding of the role of canon law before the Council and the 1983 Code.

The fact that the 1983 Code is meant to implement the teaching of the Council gives it an incarnational quality. The Council produced 16 documents on various issues central to the life and mission of the Church. These documents can be found on bookshelves in countless libraries and studies. An inspection of the spines of these publications might reveal that they have been opened and read. However, they remain words. The canon lawyer will look at these words and say, 'So what?' This question is not asked in a dismissive tone. On the contrary, it is asked in a positive and enthusiastic tone. That is, the canon lawyer is asking how the words of the Council may be put into action. Like other theological disciplines, it is a task of canon law to give these words flesh – to enable the ideas and vision of the Council to be put into concrete action. In this way canon law is practical – it is about doing. It has been said that talking is somewhere between thinking and doing; and that it is often a substitute for both. One of the roles of canon law is to help members of the Church avoid falling into the trap of talking about the vision of the Council while not actually living it.

Catholic Law

All churches and ecclesial groups require a certain number of regulations in order to function smoothly. The Catholic Church's present-day canon law is unique because of its direct connection with the Second Vatican Council. Catholic canon law also tends to have a greater international quality than that of other churches. For example, the 21 Eastern Catholic Churches have their own code of laws, which was promulgated in October 1990 and which took effect the following October. These Eastern Catholic Churches are in full communion with the Latin Catholic Church and so their canon law is very similar. However, there are variations based upon differences in culture, history and spirituality. For example, the Eastern Code allows married men to be ordained priests. Many people on either side of the debate about whether there should be married priests within the Catholic Church forget that priests in the Eastern Catholic Churches are permitted to marry.

Although the Catholic Church and the Church of England have a common heritage, their systems of law have developed differently since the Reformation. For example, the role of the Church of England parish church within villages is special. It is often a focal point for everyone, irrespective of religious persuasion. This special role is protected by laws concerning baptisms, weddings, funerals and church closures. Also, the law of the Church of England has a more intimate link with the law of the land. For example, it will be more particular with regard to financial contracts. Catholic canon law, on the other hand, will speak in more general terms because it is intended to be more international. With regard to matters such as financial contracts it will usually leave these to the law of the country in question.

Between the various churches there can be found differences in ecclesiology. This will manifest itself in the laws of each church. For example, the participation of lay people in governance will vary. Some churches have lay elders who appoint their ministers. If one compares parochial church councils in the Church of England with parish councils within the Catholic Church, lay people in the former have greater statutory power than those in the latter. The same can be said if one compares lay participation in Church of England synods with that in Catholic synods.

Underlying canon law is a very practical and good pastoral principle – namely, that the legislator could not have thought of every conceivable eventuality when drafting the law. Therefore, it is acknowledged that the law might be inappropriate in a particular circumstance. Although this is not applicable to those laws that are regarded as being of divine origin or based on 'nature', this acknowledgement still provides great flexibility. This goes against the character of civil law, which does not like exceptions to the rule of law. Catholic canon law, therefore, allows for the exercise of *epikeia* in the interpretation and application of the law. That is, when an individual realizes that following the letter of the law in a particular situation actually goes against its spirit and causes harm, then he or she can be flexible in his or her application of the law.

Canon law is to be interpreted and applied in terms of the intention of the legislator. *Epikeia* involves interpreting the mind of the legislator: 'If he (the legislator) had known about this situation he would not expect the law to apply.' For example, in the days of the strict Friday abstinence from meat, Catholics often found themselves visiting non-Catholics who, despite being poor, had bought meat and had enthusiastically prepared a meal for them. The Catholics sometimes exercised *epikeia* by eating a little meat so as not to hurt their hosts' feelings, thus exercising charity towards their hosts.

Canon law goes one step further than *epikeia* and actually allows the law to be relaxed in a particular instance. This is called a dispensation and is often described as a *vulnus legis* ('a wounding of the law'). Somebody in authority, such as a diocesan bishop, is allowed to relax a certain rule for a specific occasion if there is sufficient cause. This is a great strength of canon law and provides solutions to many difficult pastoral problems. For example, the first paragraph of canon 1086 does not allow Catholics to marry unbaptized persons. This is because the difference in faith could cause tensions, especially with regard to the religious upbringing of any children. However, such a general rule cannot be appropriate in every occasion. Thus, if a Catholic approaches a priest with the intention of marrying an unbaptized person, the priest can easily obtain a dispensation from this law if it is apparent that the difference in religion is not a problem. This system of granting dispensations recognizes the uniqueness of individual members of the Church. That is, one set of rigid laws cannot fit everyone.

The Orthodox Churches go further still in the interpretation and application of their law. They practise what is technically called *oikonomia*. This is a sacramental solution to pastoral problems and not merely a legal one. An example will help explain. An Orthodox man marries but his marriage fails. After receiving a divorce he goes through a civil wedding with another woman and stops practising his faith. Many years later he wishes to be reconciled with the Church. However, the Church does not recognize his second wife because he is divorced. He cannot leave her because they have a family that is dependent upon him. A rigorous approach to the law does not help the man on his faith journey. If he stays with this second woman he is living with somebody who is not his wife. However, if he leaves her then the family suffers. *Oikonomia* can be applied. It involves calling upon God to heal the situation. God is not bound by the law. Thus, a bishop, acting as a channel for God's grace, can allow the man to marry the second woman in a church wedding. In this example, God has worked through the bishop so that the man can progress on his journey of faith by being fully involved in the Church with his wife and family. Such a solution is not present within the Catholic Church. As somebody who often deals with marriage cases, I find it heartbreaking to see so many people who entered marriage at relatively young ages now living in second marriages that cannot be recognized by the Catholic Church. Attempts at declaring their first marriages invalid might have failed and they cannot participate fully in the sacramental life of the Church. However, although *oikonomia* might initially seem a helpful pastoral solution it may be argued that it would undermine the Catholic Church's teaching on the indissolubility of marriage.

Legal Texts

Practitioners in every branch of theology have to work with texts. It will be helpful to explain how canonists use their texts within the pastoral life of the Church. In Roman law, the 'Digest' quotes the jurist Modestinus as saying that the purpose of the law is to command, prohibit, permit and punish.[2] These four functions of the law found their way into the *Books of Etymologies* by Saint Isidore of Seville at the beginning of the seventh century.[3] Later, Thomas Aquinas refers to them in his *Summa Theologica*.[4] A reading of the 1917 Code shows that its canons tend to be limited to these four acts or functions of law.

The language of the 1983 Code, however, is much more varied and performs other functions. Yes, there are canons that command; others that prohibit, permit or punish. However, there are also many other linguistic acts. For example, there are canons that define. A good illustration of this is canon 369, which defines what a diocese is. This definition is taken verbatim from article 11 of the Second Vatican Council's 'Decree on the Pastoral Office of Bishops in the Church' (*Christus Dominus*). There are also canons that are meant to state facts. For example, canon 208 states that there is a genuine equality of dignity among all the baptized members of the Church. This canon uses almost the very same words as article 32 of the Council's 'Dogmatic Constitution on the Church' (*Lumen gentium*). One can also find canons that make recommendations. For example, canon 918 recommends that it is within Mass that Holy Communion should be received; although it can be received outside Mass for a good reason. Also, among the various linguistic acts or functions found in the 1983 Code, there are canons that make requests. For instance, the second paragraph of canon 401 repeats article 21 of the 'Decree on the Pastoral Office of Bishops in the Church' and earnestly requests diocesan bishops to offer their resignation should they become too ill to fulfil their duties.

It can thus be seen that the language of the 1983 Code is much richer than that of the 1917 Code, while the Code itself echoes the dogmatic and pastoral theology of the Council, even to the extent of direct quotation. This is so that the teaching of the Vatican Council can be implemented through the Code. This new Code is intended to enable every member of the Church to live out his or her role within the Church so that the Church as a whole can carry out her mission. It is for this reason that the language of 'must' and 'must not' is insufficient in practice.

The majority of the Church's law is found within the 1983 Code (or in the 1990 Code for the Eastern Catholic Churches). However, there are many other official ecclesiastical documents that must be taken into account and other ways in the Catholic Church by which law comes into being. For example, the Pope can sign a document prepared by a Vatican department and make its contents law. One instance of this is a decree by the Congregation for the Clergy called *Mos iugiter*, which regulates donations received by priests for celebrating Mass. It was explicitly signed by Pope John Paul II to make it law. Two other examples of law found outside the 1983 Code are rules for religious orders and laws promulgated by bishops for their dioceses. In both cases the laws are binding provided they do not contradict any law promulgated by a higher legislator, such as the Pope.

The 1983 Code gives rules for interpreting all these legal texts. These rules are intended to protect individuals within the Church. Thus, canon 10 explains that a law is to be considered invalidating only if it expressly says it is. An example will help explain this canon. When a couple wish to marry there are a number of legal formalities that need to be followed concerning paperwork and the ceremony itself. It is possible that the parish priest could make a mistake and not follow all these legal requirements. If the mistake is not too serious then the couple are still regarded by the church authorities as married. However, a serious failure can result in their marriage not being recognized. In legal terms such a marriage is said to be 'invalid'. Canon 10 restricts those occasions when things can be called invalid. That is, a law can declare something to be invalid only if it expressly says so. The pastoral advantage of this is, clearly, that it settles arguments, doubts or scruples about the validity of a particular marriage. Here, too, the law is at the service of the Church and its members and acts as an instrument of good pastoral care.

Important aspects of such pastoral care are to offer guidance in the right implementation of canon law and protection against abuse, mis-interpretation or misapplication of the law. Help on these matters is incorporated into the 1983 Code. Hence, canon 17 explains that eccle-siastical laws are to be understood according to the proper meaning of the words considered in their text and context. If the meaning remains unclear then an examination of parallel laws can be made. Also, the purpose and the circumstance of the law can be considered, as well as the intention of the legislator. With regard to the latter, such things as sermons and addresses given by the Pope can manifest his intention. For example, canons 1680 and 1574 require ecclesiastical judges to seek the advice of experts when needed (such as psychologists in certain marriage cases). However, are the judges bound to follow the advice given? In 1987 Pope John Paul II gave his annual address to the senior ecclesiastical judges of the Catholic Church. In it he explained that judges are not bound to follow the advice of such experts (Woestman 1994, pp. 191–6). Thus, the Pope's address shows what his intention was when he promulgated canons 1680 and 1574 and so how they are to be understood.

It has been seen that the language of the 1983 Code is varied. There-fore, many canons are not black and white. For example, the expression 'a good and reasonable cause' is often used. Canon 906 illustrates this. That is, a priest should not celebrate Mass without at least one mem-ber of the faithful being present unless there is 'a good and reasonable cause'. In practice, this expression might give rise to debate. One priest might think that there is a good and reasonable cause; whereas others might disagree. There is thus the real danger of arbitrariness with regard to applying the law. The example just given concerning priests celebrat-ing Mass on their own is not too serious, but what about those canons that prescribe penalties or restrict the free exercise of rights? It is these laws that can inflict real damage if applied too harshly.

Canon 18 explains which laws must be interpreted strictly. Among those listed are those laws that prescribe penalties or restrict the exer-cise of rights. These must be given a narrow interpretation so that they cannot be applied liberally. For example, a law that prescribes a penalty must be understood and applied in such a way that it avoids being applied across a wide range of circumstances. The same must be done with laws that can restrict the free exercise of rights. Canon 18 is based upon two ancient principles of law. The first states: 'In penal matters, the more benign interpretation is to be made' (*In poenis benignior est interpretatio facienda*). The second says: 'It is fitting that hateful things be restricted and that favours be extended' (*Odia restringi, et favores convenit ampliari*). These legal principles are numbers 49 and 15 respectively of 88 'rules of law' (*regulae iuris*) compiled by Boniface VIII, who was Pope from 1294 to 1303 (Gauthier 1996, pp. 107–17).

The purpose of canon 18 is to ensure that members of the Church can freely exercise their baptismal rights without fear of penalties or restrictions. All the baptized are involved in the mission of the Church and share in the threefold office of priest, prophet and king, and a right and proper use of canon law enables them to do this.

Law and *Communio*

The exercise of rights within the Code is balanced by the call to remember one's obligations to the wider ecclesial community. This is why the Code often speaks in terms of 'obligations and rights'. The order of words is meant to remind members of the Church of their obligations towards each other. For example, the section consisting of canons 208 to 223 is called 'The obligations and rights of all Christ's faithful' (*De omnium Christifidelium obligationibus et iuribus*).

Once again, the Code is trying to be practical and to enable the members of the Church to live out their baptismal calling. School teachers often say in jest that they have their classes all carefully planned and that everything runs smoothly until the children turn up to them. Similarly, the Council emphasized the equality of all the baptized. That is, we are all called to holiness and are all involved in the mission of the Church in the world. In theory this might not cause problems but as soon as real people step into the picture then there are the inevitable tensions.

These tensions often stem from an imbalance in power or authority. For example, there are tensions between bishops and priests, between priests and deacons, between priests and parishioners, between catechists and parents. The list could go on! The canons are an attempt to get the different parts of the Church to relate well to each other and to the Church as a whole. Person A relates to person B in that person A has certain obligations towards him or her. Also, person A can expect certain things from person B. At the same time, person B has certain obligations towards person A and can expect certain things from him or her. Although the complex relationship that exists in reality between two persons can never be reduced to just obligations and rights, such a reduction does allow the law to give basic principles concerning how these two people are to interact. Within canon law every person in the Church relates to others in terms of obligations and rights. It is the intention of those responsible for the law that this legal framework will allow mutual respect and tolerance; that it will allow everyone to exercise his or her charisms for the good of the Church and the world irrespective of his or her own shortcomings.

Christian life involves relating to others; be they members of the Church or not. These relationships should transform those concerned. That is, they are dynamic. It is as if we are being invited to dance with each other. However, dancing can be frightening because it involves risk. A lot can go wrong. Canon law provides a framework in which it is safe to trip, stumble and fall. One of the important tasks of the canonist is to help pick people up, correct mistakes and solve problems so that they may continue on their Christian journey. For example, diocesan tribunals spend a fair proportion of their time trying to help those whose marriages have failed. Also, in recent years, canon lawyers have become more involved in the process of making the Church safer for children and vulnerable adults.

Conclusion

For the reasons given, I believe that canon law is a theological discipline. Moreover, I see it as both practical and pastoral. The role of the canonist cannot be reduced to thumping the table and saying that something is against canon number . . . , as if the law is the ultimate yardstick. On the contrary, the canonist must use the documents, vision and theology of the Second Vatican Council and examine and apply the law in the light of them. Thus, if there is a yardstick, it is the Council. However, the canonist must also be more radical than that. There is the constant need to study theology and its various related disciplines in order to ensure that the law of the Church is assisting all the members of the Church on their pilgrim way, helping them respond to the universal call to holiness, truly recognizing their baptismal charisms, enabling them to participate in the Church's mission in the world and protecting their rights while preserving the unity of the Church. When that happens, canon law makes a necessary and notable contribution to the pastoral ministry of the Church.

Notes

1 A special supplement to *Acta Apostolicae Sedis* 75 (1983) was issued. In it the following can be found: '*Sacrae disciplinae leges*', pp. vii–xiv; '*Praefatio*', pp. xvii–xxx; '*Codex Iuris Canonici*', pp. 1–301; '*Index*', pp. 305–17; '*Corrigenda*', pp. 321–4.

2 D 1.3.7.

3 *Libri Etymologiarum*, book 5, chapter 19.

4 *Prima Secundae Partis*, Q. 92, Art. 2.

Bibliography

Official church documents in chronological order

Benedict XV, 1917, *Codex Iuris Canonici Pii X Pontificis Maximi Iussu Digestus, Benedicti Papae XV Auctoritate Promulgatus, Praefatione Emi Petri Card. Gasparri et Indice Analytico-Alphabetico Auctus*, Rome: Typis Polyglottis Vaticanis.

P. Gasparri (ed.), 1917, *Codex Iuris Canonici Pii X Pontificis Maximi Iussu Digestus, Benedicti Papae XV Auctoritate Promulgatus, Praefatione, Fontium Annotatione et Indice Analytico-Alphabetico*, Rome: Typis Polyglottis Vaticanis.

P. Gasparri and I. Seredi (eds), 1923–39, *Codex Iuris Canonici Fontes*, 9 vols, Rome: Typis Polyglottis Vaticanis.

Vatican II, 1960–1, *Acta et Documenta Concilio Oecumenico Vaticano II Apparando. Series I (Antepraeparatoria)*, vol. III: *Proposita et Monita Sacrarum Congregationum Curiae Romanae*, Rome: Typis Polyglottis Vaticanis, pp. 93–102.

Vatican II, 1965, 'Lumen gentium', *Acta Apostolicae Sedis* 57, pp. 5–71.

Vatican II, 1966, 'Christus Dominus', *Acta Apostolicae Sedis* 58, pp. 673–701.

John Paul II, 1983, 'Apostolic Constitution "Sacrae disciplinae leges"', *Acta Apostolicae Sedis* 75–supplement, pp. vii–xiv.

John Paul II, 1983, *Codex Iuris Canonici Auctoritate Ioannis Pauli PP. II Promulgatus*, Vatican City: Libreria Editrice Vaticana.

Also: 1983, *Acta Apostolicae Sedis* 75 – supplement, pp. 1–301.

John Paul II, 1987, 'Address to the Sacred Roman Rota', *Acta Apostolicae Sedis* 79, pp. 1453–9.

John Paul II, 1990, 'Codex canonum Ecclesiarum Orientalium, auctoritate Ioannis Pauli PP. II promulgatus', *Acta Apostolicae Sedis* 82, pp. 1032–1363, 1702.

Congregation for the Clergy, 1991, 'Decree "Mos iugiter"', *Acta Apostolicae Sedis* 83, pp. 443–6.

Other works

J. Alesandro, 1990, 'The Revision of the *Code of Canon Law*: A Background Study', *Studia Canonica* 24, pp. 91–146.

Thomas Aquinas, 1894, *Summa Theologica (Editio Altera Romana)*, 6 vols, Rome: Forzani and Co., vol. II: *Prima Secundae Partis*.

E. Caparros, M. Theriault and J. Thorn (eds), 1993, *Code of Canon Law Annotated*, Montreal: Wilson & Lafleur.

E. Corecco, 1992, *The Theology of Canon Law: A Methodological Question*, Pittsburgh: Duquesne University Press.

J. Coriden, 1997, *The Parish in the Catholic Tradition: History, Theology and Canon Law*, New Jersey: Paulist Press.

J. Coriden, 2000, *Canon Law as Ministry: Freedom and Good Order for the Church*, New Jersey: Paulist Press.

R. Cunningham, 1970, 'The Principles Guiding the Revision of the Code of Canon Law', *The Jurist* 30, pp. 447–55.

N. Doe, 1998, *Canon Law in the Anglican Communion: A Worldwide Perspective*, Oxford: Clarendon Press.

A. Gauthier, 1996, *Roman Law and Its Contribution to the Development of Canon Law*, 2nd edn, Ottawa: Saint Paul University Press.

T. Green, 1986, 'The Revised *Code of Canon Law*: Some Theological Issues', *Theological Studies* 47, pp. 617–52.

M. Hill, 2001, *Ecclesiastical Law*, 2nd edn, Oxford: Oxford University Press.

J. Hite and D. Ward, 1990, *Readings, Cases, Materials in Canon Law: A Textbook for Ministerial Students*, rev. edn, Collegeville, MN: Liturgical Press.

Isidore of Seville, 1878–90, *Libri Etymologiarum*, book 5, chapter 19; Latin text in J.-P. Migne (ed.), *Patrologiae Cursus Completus: Series Latina*, Paris: Garnier Fratres, vol. 82, cols 73–728.

S. Kuttner, 1994, 'The Unfinished Reform of the Second Vatican Council', *The Jurist* 54, pp. 216–27.

R. Latourelle (ed.), 1988–9, *Vatican II: Assessment and Perspectives. Twenty-Five Years After (1962–1987)*, 3 vols, New York: Paulist Press.

T. Mackin, 1982, *Marriage in the Catholic Church: What is Marriage?*, New York: Paulist Press.

F. Morrisey, 1978–9, 'The Spirit of Canon Law: Teachings of Pope Paul VI', *Origins* 8, pp. 33, 35–40.

H. Muller, 1992, 'How the Local Church Lives and Affirms its Catholicity', *The Jurist* 52, pp. 340–64.

L. Orsy, 1992, *Theology and Canon Law: New Horizons for Legislation and Interpretation*, Collegeville, MN: The Liturgical Press.

L. Orsy, 1992–3, 'How to Relate Theology and Canon Law', *Origins* 22, pp. 549–52.

E. Pfnausch (ed.), 1992, *Code, Community, Ministry: Selected Studies for the Parish Minister Introducing the Code of Canon Law*, 2nd edn, Washington, DC: Canon Law Society of America.

M. Place, 1985, 'A Theologian Looks at the Revised Code of Canon Law', *The Jurist* 45, pp. 259–74.

A. Richter and A. Friedberg (eds), 1922, *Corpus Iuris Canonici*, 2nd edn, 2 vols, Leipzig: Bernhard Tauchnitz, vol. I: *Pars Prior: Decretum Magistri Gratiani*.

A. Watson (ed.), 1985, *The Digest of Justinian*, 4 vols, Philadelphia: University of Pennsylvania Press.

W. Woestman (ed.), 1994, *Papal Allocutions to the Roman Rota 1939–1994*, Ottawa: Saint Paul University.

15

Keeping Faith in Practice: An African
Woman's Dream

LILIAN DUBE

This chapter introduces a practical theology from a feminist perspective and, from the global South, a black Catholic theology in sub-Saharan Africa and its significance in the very specific context of 22 million people infected by HIV, 1.9 million new infections in 2007 and 1.5 million HIV/AIDS-related deaths in the same year (UNAIDS 2008).[1] It discusses the Catholic pastoral theology that is relevant to communities who are at the crossroads of life and death in Africa, and searches for godly responses to the wailing songs of agony that rise from traumatized communities amidst last rites and burial ceremonies. The discussion re-examines theological guidelines that define the gender and sex taboos that are to be found both within the Catholic Church and in African communities, and their implications for African Catholics in the context of HIV and AIDS. This comparative study explores liberating sexualities and searches for messages of hope in a context where it is argued by some people that the teaching of the Catholic Church indirectly contributes to serious harm in this twenty-first HIV and AIDS century. Those same people also claim that the Catholic Church bequeaths an anti-sexuality faith to African Catholicism. The study offers the Church instead the urgent challenge to search for a liberating sexuality. Could this be another Catholic feminist dream?

African Theology

African Theology can be loosely described as 'Christian Theology done historically by African men for men and women'. It is a theology that is constantly challenged by socio-cultural and political scandals that make keeping faith in practice a struggle. African Theology continues to be transformed by events. Jean Marc Ela is convinced that the urgent problems of Africa must become the new locus of theological revolution (Stinton 2004, p. 113), arguing that 'the liberation of the oppressed must be the primary condition for any authentic inculturation of the Christian message' (Ela et al. 1988, p. iv). The challenge is for African Theology to go beyond cultural and political humiliations and extend the discourse to HIV and AIDS, poverty, hunger and violence, and to the different ways these affect women as Nyamiti posits (Nyamiti 1994, p. 66). Teresia Hinga places feminist theology between colonialism and inculturation and refutes a redundant 'monolithic feminist theology'. She proposes that African women distance themselves from ideals of 'generic woman' with 'generic experiences' and a 'generic feminist theology' (see Fiorenza and Copeland 1996, p. 26). Political and cultural liberation theologies have limited appeal to contemporary African feminist theologians struggling with gender justice in the postcolonial African Church and society.

Feminist theology in Africa is concerned with the search for African women's dignity, space and voice. It interrogates the kind of inculturation that was embraced in pastoral/practical theological discourse without gender critique following Vatican II. Thus while acknowledging the great African theological strides in creating African Christianity and dismantling the shackles of colonialism in church and society, African feminist theologians employ the cultural hermeneutical approach in gender analysis as they find themselves at the crossroads with the Catholic Church's social ethics on gender, sex and HIV/AIDS. Thus, these Catholic feminist theologians fiercely distance themselves from the Church's inculturation drive of the 1960s (Stinton 2004, p. 111), critiquing disturbing parallels between African and Catholic traditions on gender vis-à-vis AIDS prevention.

Despite the huge success in recreating African liturgy with the drum and the dance, revision of the sacraments in sync with the African rites of passage, and the shift in ecclesiastical power from male white clergy to African male clergy reflected numerically in the appointment of African bishops, the Catholic Church has sidelined culture-motivated gender injustice; hence the discontent among some of the feminist theologians from Africa. This chapter discusses the perspectives of such theologians in dialogue with Concerned African Women Theologians from diverse religious, ethnic, and class lines through the Circle.[2] They tackle cultures of violence against women embedded in African traditional practices and claim that they are perpetuated by the Catholic Church's teaching on marriage and sexuality. They employ the cultural hermeneutical approach to expose injustice masquerading as African cultural heritage, with the result of its uncritical acceptance, receiving no open chastisement from the Catholic pastoral teaching crafted to support the Church's unequivocal commitment to inculturation after Vatican II. Through these feminist lenses, this chapter re-examines Catholic moral ethics on abstinence and condom use against the backdrop of African ethical traditions of initiation rituals and matrimony.

The challenge for African women to speak and define new boundaries governing gender-biased sexual taboos is emphasized in this discussion. It accords the greater responsibility for judging and modifying African cultures and religious guidelines for femininity to women practitioners of the rituals. Oduyoye concludes that men and Western strangers should stop writing exclusively about Africa and representing African women (Oduyoye and Kanyoro 1992, pp. 9–10). The challenge of doing feminist theology through African women's eyes is constantly to draw from their experiences of celebration and tribulation even though the temptation to do feminist theology 'as men' is huge. As Oduyoye points out, women doing theology that differs in no way, neither in substance nor in style, from that done by men are allowed to remain as one of the 'boys'; they enjoy male privileges and are not singled out for condemnation (see Gibellini 1994, p. 166). This discussion, therefore, strives consciously to articulate African women's lived realities and perceptions shaped by their unstable experiences of the struggle for fullness of life as they do theology practically and academically. It brings the Catholic Church tradition into dialogue with traditional wisdom, problems and aspirations and is both practical and analytical.

Inculturation, Liberation and Beyond

African Cultural Theology emerged during the 1950s and 1960s when the struggle against colonialism brought political independence and cultural revolutions across Africa. The radical reaffirmation of African identity and integrity was a reaction of African nationalists to the colonial disdain for African religions, cultures, dress, music and dance forms, even African names (Stinton 2004, p. 110). The theology of the Second Vatican Council, which marked a radical reappraisal of Christian doctrine and practice, challenged the Church to be tolerant with other living faiths and encouraged the cultural revival of an African Renaissance typified by *négritude* in Francophone Africa. When Pope Paul VI challenged African bishops gathered in Accra, Ghana, in 1969 to have an 'African Christianity', the fire of cultural theology was fanned (see Stinton 2004, p. 111). African theologians who had formulated an apologetic for maintaining a Christianity that was split between the nationalist cause and missionary domination of the Church celebrated the advent of cultural theological liberation in Africa.

The Church became proactive in revitalizing indigenous cultures that Catholic practical theology energetically expressed through art, music and dance. The Hebrew Bible was translated into African languages. Shorter argues that inculturation liberates the Church and African theology when the interaction between culture and Christianity is mutually beneficial and transforming (Shorter 1988, p. 14). Sadly, however, inculturation did not adequately address the socio-economic and political pains of oppression such as those created by apartheid in South Africa, racial marginality and class infringement. This prompted further research on liberation. While African theology continues to reclaim African cultures and religious heritage and integrate it with the Catholic faith in order to ensure the integrity of African Christian heritage (Bediako 1992, p. 1), a lot remains to be desired around gender justice in church and society.

Black theology in South Africa confronted apartheid and its evil laws that created social oppression and injustice though racial and class divides. It spoke directly to the horrors of apartheid in the context of South Africa and witnessed the Church taking action to bring down an evil giant. The Kairos Document became a manifesto for the prophetic theologians who prescribed new ways of keeping faith in practice by defining the Kairos moment of the era as a rare moment in God's time for the liberation of black Africans (Kairos Theologians 1986). On the political front, Nelson Mandela was released from prison, marking a new era in society; it also marked a theological void and a yearning to keep faith in practice shared by post-independent African theologians who write from experiences of disillusionment with the flag-flying independence amidst mass rape and killings in war-torn Africa, and starvation, mass migration and HIV/AIDS destabilizing African community life. How, then, should Catholic pastoral theology engage the dimensions of life in contemporary Africa?

'An Irruption Within an Irruption'

Theology from the vantage point of African women's practical and academic experiences as they participate in Africa's postcolonial socio-economic and religious history is described by Oduyoye as 'an irruption within an irruption, trumpeting the existence of some other hurts, spotlighting women's marginalization from the theological enterprise and indeed from decision making in the churches' (see King 1994, p. 25). This is a reaction of African women still trapped in abject poverty. Their theology addresses sexism and the political sidelining of women in church and society. It is concerned with African women's experiences as another locus for liberation. African feminist theologians take a critical distance from any theology that does not recognize African women's experiences of poverty and cultures of gender violence that disgrace women and violate their dignity through rites of passage and rape in war-torn Africa. They seek to communicate their own understanding of God from painful dislocations. Thus, their African contexts dictate the themes that guide their theologies and the urgency of their will to arise and survive. Catholic theologians join the chorus of voices from the margins as active members of the Circle of Concerned Women Theologians (Circle).

African women's written theological contributions start in the 1970s though their participation goes well beyond that. The bulk of this work comes from the Ecumenical Association of Third World Theologians (EATWOT) Women's Commission and later from Circle. Teresia Hinga, a Catholic founder member of the Circle herself, describes the 1989 African women's meeting in Accra, which gave birth to this most powerful feminist theological body in Africa to date, as a turning-point in the emergence of a more formal and systematic feminist theology in Africa (see Fiorenza and Copeland 1996, p. 26). Thus guided by the goals of the Circle, feminist theology in Africa critiques religion and cultures of Africa and struggles for political empowerment and economic justice. The process requires African feminist theologians consciously to resist privileging experiences of elite women as normative for theology. It seeks to create opportunities for genuine dialogue with all women where they speak for themselves regardless of their social status or religious background, and it extends this dialogue to the global community. The well-being of the community as a whole takes precedence over individual visions and dreams. It is therefore this communal focus and justice-centred approach that can reliably inform pastoral theology in Africa and provide guidance for keeping faith in practice.

While it invites dialogue and strives to appeal to global feminist theological quests, African women's theology also gives prominence to the local by drawing from the immediate and diverse experiences of African women. It accords the oral and written theological forms equal importance. Thus, African women's stories become credible sources of feminist theology in Africa that can also reliably inform pastoral theology in mostly semi-literate African women's communities. These life stories, not classical philosophical theories, form the basis of feminist theologizing that Catholic pastoral theology in Africa needs in order to keep faith in practice at the grassroots level.

Oduyoye argues:

> The stories we tell of our hurts and joys are sacred. Telling them makes us vulnerable, but without this sharing we cannot build community and solidarity. Our stories are precious paths on which we have walked with God, and struggled for a passage to our full humanity. They are events through which we have received blessings of life from the hands of God. The stories we tell are sacred, for they are indications of how we struggled with God. (2001, p. 21)

It can be argued, therefore, that the African women's story-centred narrative theology brings back the personal into academic studies through the stories of socially oppressed women who suffer injustice and depend on God for liberation. As Boesak posits, the ethics of liberation which goes beyond survival to be grounded in transforming praxis is the rationale for liberation theology discourse. African women's theology as a liberation theology, therefore, derives from the Christian story of Jesus Christ, who becomes Saviour by representing both suffering and liberation. While a high level of analysis and critique is maintained in African women's theologies, it is driven by extreme passion for the will of God for humanity. Thus African women's theology stems from compassionate hearts and justice-seeking minds.

African women theologians passionately search for alternative interpretations of what God says to African women journeying through life steeped in traditional cultures that still define their spaces. They search the Hebrew Bible for stories of a God who participates in history and cultures, for crucial themes of liberation that speak to their social contexts as African women carving out their spaces in the history of God's people. Thus, reading for liberation becomes a mandatory approach to their Bible study and reinterpretation of the gospel for African women's liberation – a 'reclamation of the Christian heritage' (Boesak in Parratt 2004, p. 135).

Nevertheless, there is no consensus on what constitutes the African feminist agenda, given women's diverse identities as farmers, housewives, mothers and scholars. Yet the cultural hermeneutical approach to socio-cultural issues is a popular theological method. Thus Oduyoye calls for cultural exegesis to identify cultures that keep women in bondage and to avoid internalizing suffering as an integral part of African feminine identity (Oduyoye 1995, p. 81). The distinguishing mark of African feminist theologians comes from the critical voices arising from a culturally framed experience that is different from that of both Euro-American feminist and male African inculturation and liberation. Here, it is crucial to note that African women still view themselves as custodians of life, sustainers of the community and transmitters and upholders of culture (Oduyoye 2001, p. 24). Thus, they face huge challenges to carry on 'mothering'; and this is a version of how they see themselves in spite of the double and triple loads of burdens on their backs. This is the spirit of survival, for themselves and for their communities, which characterizes their vision as women in church and society. This is the theoretical framework that informs Catholic pastoral theology as it relates to African communities.

Within this general frame of reference, we can now examine the church response to two critical issues – HIV/AIDS and the practice of female genital modification – that trouble African women and communities. The argument here is that to tackle such issues it is necessary to deploy a theology that is practical and pastoral rather than simply theoretical and idealistic; there are deeply rooted cultural dimensions here that arise from African social, communal and familial practice, and this needs to be critiqued rather than lazily legitimized by Christian idealism.

Sexism, Poverty and HIV/AIDS

Medical, moral and feminist research underscores the social contexts of gender inequality, poverty and religion as breeding grounds for HIV and AIDS.[3] Teresa Okure, another Catholic founder member of the Circle and a biblical scholar from Nigeria, describes sexism and global poverty as 'two viruses more dangerous than HIV', which also fuel the rapid spread of HIV and AIDS among society's most vulnerable people, married women and children (see Kelly 2005, p. 325). Okure is joined by many African women theologians who argue that any analysis of HIV and AIDS in Africa that does not take religion, poverty and gender into account cannot produce holistic pastoral solutions. Their analysis links HIV/AIDS to socio-cultural norms that deprive women of the power even to negotiate safer sex; and 60 per cent of those living with HIV are women. While the role of Catholic-funded hospitals and clinics in facilitating healthcare in a postcolonial Africa characterized by crumbling health sectors and grinding poverty must not be underplayed, there are some sexuality traditions that are a challenge to pastoral theology.

The rural location of most church health institutions enables the Church to reach out to the forgotten poorest of the poor through subsidized health infrastructure. The Catholic Church's pastoral work in Zimbabwe's most vulnerable communities affected by hunger, starvation and HIV/AIDS illustrates the point. It should be noted that the Catholic Relief Services (CRS) work closely with the Zimbabwe Association of Church Related Hospitals (ZACH) in this endeavour. Despite many divisions, Christians in Zimbabwe have achieved at least a measure of practical co-operation in the field of healthcare, education and social services.[4] ZACH provides 45 per cent of all hospital beds in Zimbabwe and 68 per cent of all rural hospital beds (UN Humanitarian Support Team 2004). This life-saving ecumenical partnership dictates the pace for ecumenism in pastoral theology. The Catholic Church is pragmatic in its approach to poor communities with no resources for healthcare and severe food crises threatening millions with starvation. Through the Catholic Relief Services (CRS), it provides food assistance in Zimbabwe's rural hospitals targeting approximately 150,000 people (Catholic Relief Services in Zimbabwe, October 2002). In so doing, CRS strengthens and improves the lives of the disadvantaged in southern Africa. The Catholic Church's mandate to serve the brothers and sisters in need forms the basis of Catholic pastoral theological discourse that keeps faith in practice through prayer and distribution of food and AIDS relief services to the poor, who are mostly women. This raises the need for a more holistic approach to HIV/AIDS, relating it more directly to poverty and gender disparities; but this constitutes a challenge for a church that shies away from sexuality and proposes abstinence as the key factor in AIDS control.

'Abstinence not Condoms'

The Catholic theological tradition is not always in conflict with African traditional wisdom on gender issues. A relevant theology for the HIV/AIDS era requires rethinking not only African cultures that expose women and children to HIV/AIDS, but those Catholic Church traditions about gender and sexuality taboos that can also render women vulnerable. Such rethinking requires an exploration of recent debates in this area that inform pastoral guidance and may help answer widespread condemnations of the Church's position.

The Congolese Catholic theologian and founder member of the Circle, Bernadette Mbuy Beya argues that Roman Catholic teaching on sexuality has created inordinate burdens of guilt around sexuality for the faithful in Africa (see Oduyoye and Kanyoro 1992, p. 172). Teachings that place a high value on celibacy and promote abstinence can create sex taboos that have become death-traps for African girls and women. The teachings that prohibit contraceptives and uphold the indissolubility of marriage represent a double challenge for girls and women in African communities dominated by HIV/AIDS, whose traditional cultures demand the same self-sacrifice. This has increasingly become a bone of contention, critique and analytical focus for Catholic feminists in Africa who question the Church's teaching in this area in the wake of HIV/AIDS. Their argument is a critique of the advocacy of Catholic bishops' conferences for the traditional moral teachings of the Church on sexual behaviour and marital relationships when dealing with the AIDS crisis.[5] These theological voices rising from African feminist theologians responding to the AIDS epidemic claim that a Kairos moment has been reached which should not be missed by Catholic pastoral theologians concerned with social justice.

On his first pilgrimage as pontiff to Africa on 17 March 2009, Pope Benedict XVI addressed the issue. His predecessor, Pope John Paul II, argued that sexual abstinence not condoms was the best way to prevent the spread of the disease. This set the tone for the controversial position of the Catholic Church in contemporary Africa. Speaking about the HIV/AIDS impasse during his trip to Yaoundé, Cameroon, in 2009, Pope Benedict declared, 'You can't resolve it with the distribution of condoms. On the contrary, it increases the problem.' He urged African communities to adopt responsible and moral attitudes toward sex in the fight against AIDS. His message was a clear rejection of condoms, as part of the Church's overall teaching against artificial contraception.

The Catholic Church has strongly promoted the traditional ecclesial message of fidelity in marriage and abstinence from premarital sex as key weapons in the fight against AIDS in sub-Saharan Africa. This has had a troubling effect on many of the faithful.[6]

The task to keep faith in practice beyond the AIDS impasse is monumental. It could be argued that it requires rethinking the Catholic Church's pro-life commitment to *include* condom use in the context of HIV/AIDS. The challenge facing Catholic pastoral theology is to frame the saving message of the gospel and to be able to proclaim it loud and clear so that the light of Christ can shine into the darkness of people's lives; and this, some might suggest, is a challenge to rethink condom use in HIV/AIDS Africa. How can the light of Christ shine on thousands of Catholic women victims of gang rape in war-torn Africa when their husbands reject them for fear of being infected without protection? What will save women from infections when their husbands return from mines and war fronts after prolonged periods? What gospel message would bring a smile to the virgin bride infected on her wedding night or be the message of hope for a million poor, unskilled, displaced women struggling to survive? These faith questions form the feminist Catholic pastoral debate in contemporary Africa, the fastest-growing region for the Catholic Church.

The official Catholic position is that the best form of protection from illness and HIV/AIDS for individuals and society comes from education in a sexuality based on an integrated understanding of human personhood, and from changes in behaviour. The underlying belief is that sexual abstinence outside and fidelity within marriage are the only morally correct and medically sure ways to prevent the spread of HIV/AIDS. It is further believed that the use of prophylactics is technically unreliable and effectively constitutes promotion of behaviour that is morally unacceptable. Nevertheless, bishops' conferences in France and the United States and some individual bishops have implied in their public statements that accurate public information about condom use is acceptable and even that the use of condoms may be condoned where sexual activity is an established pattern of behaviour and grave risk is involved.[7] The 'Message of Hope' of the Catholic bishops of southern Africa, however, condemned condom use in the battle against HIV/AIDS on the grounds that it goes against human dignity, changes the act of love into a selfish search for pleasure while rejecting personal responsibility, does not guarantee protection and may be one of the main reasons for the spread of the disease. This statement, with the Catholic position in general, has provoked widespread outrage and condemnation within the scientific community worldwide and has often been met with little understanding, even within church circles.

A further complication derives from the Church's failure to provide pragmatic support for its idealistic teachings on abstinence. What are the implications for the Church's 'no condoms but abstinence' stance when, worldwide, HIV is still largely driven by heterosexual transmission and Africa registers the majority of all new infections? How does Catholic pastoral theology empower African women who form 60 per cent of adults living with HIV in sub-Saharan Africa (UNAIDS 2008)? The challenge for pastoral theology to reconcile 'no condoms, but abstinence' with these statistics might witness a mass exodus of African Catholics in search of pro-life spiritualities. Arguments against condom use in such cases hinge on the perceived devaluing of the rich meaning of marital sex and the frustration of the Creator's design in an act open to procreation. It is posited that if the Church were to approve the use of condoms in such cases, it would collude with an unacceptable lifestyle promoted by a hedonistic culture and undermine church teaching on birth control, whereas if marriage partners truly love one another and assume their mutual responsibility they will forgo sex in order to protect the non-infected partner and safeguard the well-being of their children.

Some voices from within the Catholic pastoral theology tradition, however, maintain that condom use in this case is 'pro-life', since it aims at protection against a deadly disease, and the contraceptive effect of prophylactic use is not intended for its own sake (a type of 'double-effect' reasoning). While the Catholic ideal is of marital sex that preserves the unitive and procreative dimensions of intercourse, there is also, they say, an obligation to act responsibly when high ideals cannot be enacted, since the higher good of preservation of life outweighs rules governing birth control and the preservation of procreative capacity. Above all, teaching against condom use in marriage may endanger the lives of women who do not have the power to negotiate sex with their HIV-positive male partners. Given the potential harm to individuals and to society as a whole, the common good requires the prevention of disease above the proclamation of lofty but unattainable ideals.

A failure to recognize power and gender inequalities, say these theologians, leads to a neglect of strands of church teaching that have long included the acceptance of secondary effects (the contraceptive effects of condoms used for prophylactic purposes) and the concept of the lesser of two evils (condom use as opposed to death). After all, the Catholic moral tradition has applied the principle of double effect where there is a proportionately grave reason for permitting the indirect bad effect (artificial contraception) in order to try to bring about the good (the preservation of life). According to this principle a woman could be allowed to use a certain kind of medication to regularize her periods or to deal with some aspect of endometriosis, even if the same medication has a contraceptive side-effect. It must be noted, however, that the principle of double effect requires that only the good effect may be intended. The bad effect is foreseen, but unintended. Intention here refers to the reason for acting.

Female Genital Modifications

The unwavering traditional stance of the Catholic Church on sexuality causes some serious problems for African feminist theologians struggling to eradicate practices linked to sex taboos in African cultures. In recent years, these theologians have worked with the UN and other engaged human rights groups, including the Catholic Church, to eradicate and/or modify the practice of female genital modification (FGM) now listed as a violation of human rights. In this context, however, the Church's insistence on abstinence strikes a chord with, and may become too easily allied with, many traditional sex prohibitions around the rites of passage of African girls into womanhood. FGM rituals have been utilized to curb women's sexual desire, in among the aesthetic and religious reasons that are advanced for its perpetuation. Thus, while Catholic pastoral theology negotiates on the tradition with ordinary believers, the faithful may be heading back to the traditional female genital cutters for coerced abstinence and infibulations.

Female circumcision ranges from excision of specific parts of the female sexual organs to the excision of part or all of the external genitalia and stitching and narrowing the vaginal opening, called infibulations (Abusharaf 2006, p. 60). It has been celebrated by more than three-quarters of Kenya's ethnocultural groups. In the far west district of Kisii, 97 per cent of women over 15 were circumcised, and 87 per cent of adult Masaai women fall into this category according to Mohamud, Radeny and Ringheim (in Abusharaf 2006, p. 78). The ritual celebrates and affirms unity between the community and the individual, who takes pride in being accepted into an important age set of gendered adults through rigorous cultural schooling concerning acceptable femininity.

Female genital cuttings can be traced back to the times of the ancient civilizations of Egypt and Sudan, and scholars have argued that it was widely practised by Egyptians, Phoenicians, Hittites and Ethiopians around 500 BC (Assad 1980; Sanderson 1981; Rushwan et al. 1983 – all quoted in Gruenbaum 2001, p. 43), and in the second century BC by tribes on the western coast of the Red Sea, Egypt. The practice is linked to a history steeped in mythical beliefs in the bisexuality of the gods mirrored in all mortals. Thus, the feminine soul of the man and the male soul of the woman are believed to be located in their sexual organs. In order for boys to become men and girls women and for both to realize healthy gender development, the excision of the female soul from the man and the male soul from the woman has to be initiated (Meinardus 1967, pp. 388–9). A fifteenth- and sixteenth-century report associates female genital cuttings with Sudanese sex slaves sold in Egypt and Arabia, who fetched higher prices if sewn up; hence the close association between Islamic conversions and slave routes is a leading clue to female genital modifications in Islamic regions, as slaves had to be sewn up for value (Mackie 1996, quoted in Boyle 2002, p. 28). The Islamic basis of female circumcision is contestable since the practice predates Islam, it does not occur in most Middle Eastern countries, and is not explicitly required by the Koran, and non-Muslim African groups have the same practice (Boyle 2002, p. 31).

When women pin down little girls and young women for the purposes of genital modification they never intend for those girls to experience eternal celibacy. When they celebrate female circumcision and give presents to the girls who have symbolically come of age they encourage the continued celebration of this initiation rite of passage as feminine ways of being in communion with men. A phenomenological reflection on circumcision portrays celebrated masculinities where de-infibulating men are treated as heroes for carrying out the honourable act of marrying a sealed virgin. The morning after their wedding night, the man who displays a blood-stained blanket or white sheet is often met with ululation and victory dances. The show of the blood of honour is for the bride, her family and the whole community that participated in preserving her dignity through forced enclosures to guarantee abstinence – although this may also be her fateful night of infection.

The argument espoused by some pastoral theologians is that African female initiation rites achieve the same objective of abstinence as is espoused by the Catholic tradition, and it is urgent to re-examine any theological guidelines that reinforce sexuality taboos that increase women's vulnerability to oppression as well as to HIV/AIDS. The taboos that sustain FGM and are also associated with theological norms paint a grim picture of matrimony and sexuality in poverty-stricken Africa as it faces the crisis of HIV/AIDS. Questioning the theological foundation of the ritual, Nawal Saadawi, an Egyptian physician and writer who was herself excised, critiques the practice thus:

If religion comes from God, how can it order man to cut off an organ created by Him as long as that organ is not diseased or deformed? God does not create the organs of the body haphazardly without a plan. It is not possible that He should have created the clitoris in a woman's body only in order that it be cut off at an early stage in life. (El Saadawi Nawal 1980, p. 42)

This would agree with Catholic teaching on mutilation, which clearly forbids the removal of the clitoris in such cases. Surgery is, of course, permitted in case of disease, but, even then, only if no less damaging alternative is available. While it is clearly difficult to follow rulings in a context where women have little or no freedom over their own bodies, and many commentators have a low understanding of the value of abstinence, it needs to be made clear that the abstinence preached by the Church involves personal attitude and conviction on the part of women and men. The right attitude and conviction could never be achieved by any amount of surgery.

On the other hand, some theologians might argue that statements concerning such cases – as, for example that of St Maria Goretti – can convey the impression that what is important is the woman's efforts to preserve her physical virginity. This could give the impression that women being raped or coerced sexually are wrong if they do not fight to the death to prevent penetration. Church leaders and theologians need to work hard to correct this impression, or any impression that women's lives are expendable in support of a principle.

Here is an instance of practical theology functioning in properly critical mode. As it analyses actual concrete practice it opens up a further critical dialogue with established norms and theological understandings, not to overturn them in some simplistic fashion but to understand them in greater depth, reinterpret them as necessary and apply them more accurately.

Conclusion

During the patristic period, much of a pessimistic nature was written about sex. Intending to procreate, it seemed, was the only thing that could justify indulging in it. This pessimism had a lasting effect on Catholic teaching and thinking about sexuality in general. However, changes gradually came about, resulting eventually in considerably more positive statements in the second half of the twentieth century. Vatican II's Pastoral Constitution on the Church in the Modern World, *Gaudium et spes*, 49, describes acts of marital intimacy as noble and honourable. In *Humanae vitae*, moreover, Paul VI taught that all sexual activity should be unitive, as well as open to the possibility of procreation. This demand for the unitive dimension rules out rape or any form of coercion in marriage. These teachings, and indeed those forbidding the mutilation that is female circumcision, need to be much better known. Otherwise, the impression can easily be given that church teaching supports what it clearly does not support. Additionally, however, some theologians would argue that it is time to consider the possibility of seeing condom use in some cases as the lesser evil, and perhaps to consider the possibility of applying a kind of double-effect thinking where appropriate. A life-affirming view of gender and sexuality is indeed the African feminist's dream.

Notes

1 Joint United Nations Programme on HIV/AIDS publishes a new 'Report on the global AIDS epidemic' every two years compiled from the best available data from countries and provides an overview and commentary on the epidemic and the international response.

2 The Circle of Concerned African Women Theologians is a theological body founded by Mercy Amba Oduyoye and inaugurated in Legon, Ghana, in September 1989 with the vision of empowering African women to contribute their critical thinking and analysis to advance current knowledge of theology, religion and culture.

3 In late 2006 UNAIDS reported that 39.5 million adults and children were living with AIDS, with 15–24-year-old married women in Sub-Saharan Africa at greatest risk for HIV infection – women who practise abstinence and fidelity but whose husbands do not.

4 Acknowledged by the Zimbabwe Catholic Bishops' Conference, 10 May 2004.

5 Catherine Machyo, http://www.fiuc.org/iaup/esap/publications/cuea/eajourn1aidsch.php

6 See http://www.aegis.com/news/ap/2009/AP090320.html

7 Statements of the US Bishops' Conference, 11 December 1987 and the French Bishops' Conference, 12 February 1996.

Bibliography

Rogaia Mustafa Abusharaf (ed.), 2006, *Female Circumcision: Multicultural Perspectives*, Philadelphia: University of Pennsylvania Press.
Marrie Bassili Assad, 1980, 'Female Circumcision in Egypt: Social Implications, Current Research, and Prospects for Change', *Studies in Family Planning* 11.1, pp. 3–16.

Antony Battaglia, 2000, 'The Hellenistic Understanding of the Body and its Legacy for the Christian Social Ethics', in Sylvia Marcos (ed.), *Gender/Bodies/Religions*, Cuernavaca, Mexico: ALER, pp. 137–53.

Kwame Bediako, 1992, *Theology and Identity: The Impact of Culture upon Christian Thought in the Second Century and Modern Africa*, Oxford: Regnum.

Elizabeth Heger Boyle, 2002, *Female Genital Cutting: Cultural Conflict in the Global Community*, Baltimore: Johns Hopkins University Press.

Catholic Relief Services in Africa: www.catholicrelief.org/where_we_work/africa/zimbabwe/index.cfm

Catholic Relief Services in Zimbabwe, October 2002: www.salt.claretianpubs.org/sjnews/2002/11/sjno211c.html

Jean Marc Ela, John Brown and Susan Perry (eds), 1988, *My Faith as an African*, Maryknoll, NY: Orbis Books.

Elizabeth S. Fiorenza and Shawn Copeland (eds), 1996, *Feminist Theology in Different Contexts*, Maryknoll, NY: Orbis Books.

Rosin Gibellini (ed.), 1994, *Paths of African Theology*, Maryknoll, NY: Orbis Books.

Ellen Gruenbaum, 2001, *The Female Circumcision Controversy: An Anthropological Perspective*, Philadelphia: University of Pennsylvania Press.

Kairos Theologians, 1986, *The Kairos Document: Challenge to the Church: A Theological Comment on the Political Crisis in South Africa*, 2nd edn, Johannesburg: Skotaville.

Kevin Kelly, 2005, 'Conclusion: A Moral Theologian Faces the New Millennium in a time of AIDS', in James F. Keenan, Jon Fuller, Lisa Sowle Cahill and Kevin T. Kelly (eds), *Catholic Ethicists on HIV/AIDS Prevention*, New York: Continuum, pp. 324–32.

Ursula King (ed.), 1994, *Feminist Theology from the Third World: A Reader*, Maryknoll, NY: Orbis Books.

Sylvia Marcos, 2000, 'Embodied Religious Thought: Gender Categories in Mesoamerica', in Sylvia Marcos (ed.), *Gender/Bodies/Religions*, Cuernavaca, Mexico: ALER, pp. 93–135.

Catherine Machyo, 'The Catholic Church and the HIV/AIDS Pandemic in Kenya: An Exploration of Issues', *Eastern African Journal of Humanity and Social Sciences (e-journal)* http://www.fiuc.org/iaup/esap/publications/cuea/eajourn1aidsch.php.

Otto Meinardus, 1967, 'Mythological, Historical and Sociological Aspects of the Practice of Female Circumcision Among Egyptians', *Acta Ethnographica Academiae Scientiarum Hungaricae* 17, pp. 387–97.

El Saadawi Nawal, 1980, *The Hidden Face of Eve: Women in the Arab World*, London: Zed Books.

Charles Nyamiti, 1994, 'Contemporary African Christologies: Assessment and Practical Suggestions', in Rosin Gibellini (ed.), *Paths of African Theology*, Maryknoll, NY: Orbis Books, pp. 62–77.

Mercy Amba Oduyoye, 1990, *Talitha Qumi: The Proceedings of the Convocation of African Women Theologians*, Ibadan: Daystar.

Mercy Amba Oduyoye, 1994, 'Reflections from a Third World Woman's Perspective: Women's Experience and Liberation Theologies', in Ursula King (ed.), *Feminist Theology from the Third World: A Reader*, Maryknoll, NY: Orbis Books, pp. 23–34.

Mercy Amba Oduyoye, 1995, *Daughters of Anowa: African Women and Patriarchy*, Maryknoll, NY: Orbis Books.

Mercy Amba Oduyoye, 2001, *Introductions in Feminist Theology: Introducing African Women's Theology*, Sheffield: Sheffield Academic Press.

Mercy Amba Oduyoye and R. A. Kanyoro (eds), 1992, *The Will to Arise: Women, Tradition and the Church in Africa*, Maryknoll, NY: Orbis Books.

John Parratt (ed.), 2004, *An Introduction to Third World Theologies*, Cambridge: Cambridge University Press.

Aylward Shorter, 1988, *Towards a Theology of Inculturation*, Maryknoll, NY: Orbis Books.

Diane Stinton, 2004, 'Africa East and West', in John Parratt (ed.), *An Introduction to Third World Theologies*, Cambridge: Cambridge University Press, pp. 105–36.

UN Humanitarian Support Team, 2004, Consolidated Appeal Zimbabwe Food Security, Urban Assessment Executive Summary': www.zimrelief.info/index.php.

UNAIDS, 2008, *Report on the Global AIDS Epidemic*, Joint United Nations Programme on HIV/AIDS.

16

'Poetry Changes Nothing'? Literature, Imagination and Pastoral Theology

DAVID LONSDALE

My interest and questions in this chapter have to do with relationships between the arts, and more specifically literature, on the one hand, and Christian faith, theology and practice on the other. In general terms, I am interested in questions such as the following. Are there ways of reading and reflecting theologically about literature – poetry, drama, the novel – such that this reading and reflection can contribute to pastoral theology, Christian faith and life and the Church's engagement with contemporary culture and society? What is the place of literature in relation to pastoral theology and Christian life? What is involved in a Christian engagement with literature of readers who are also people of faith? Is there any sense in which literature of both past and present can inform theology, spirituality and pastoral life? What is the value of the contributions of theologians who have addressed or are addressing these issues?

These are big questions and my aim in this chapter, which is intended to explore possibilities rather than to evaluate critically, is more modest. In the first part of the chapter I give an account of aspects of the thought on these issues of a major Catholic theologian of the twentieth century, Karl Rahner. The second part moves on to Seamus Heaney's idea of 'the redress of poetry' in relation to pastoral theological reflection. Finally I draw some tentative conclusions from this material. I should also perhaps add that art and literature that have explicit religious content are not my main concern here, since their relation to Christian faith, theology and practice is comparatively simple. The more interesting and complex questions have to do with the religious and theological value of works of art and literature that are not explicitly or thematically religious.

This area, sometimes called 'theological aesthetics', is relatively new as a subject of study and a focus of scholars' attention – an 'emerging discipline'.[1] And although I have been a reader of different forms of literature for several decades and have taught religion and literature at different levels, only recently have I begun to develop serious research interests around the points where literature, theology and spirituality meet. This is proving to be a very interesting path and this chapter represents work in progress.

The questions that I have just raised also seem to me to be important in the present religious climate, and there may be several reasons for this. Interest in these issues among Christians in general and Christian scholars in particular may be a response to a postmodern tendency to see the cultivation of the aesthetic and the ironic, and sometimes very superficial or trivial versions of them, as the primary or even the only value. The reflective, engaged Christian humanism that Rahner and others represented is under threat, on the one hand from the fundamentalist tendency and on the other from postmodern aesthetics. But there are also other trends in the churches, some of which are reflected in Christian postgraduate students in theology and spirituality. It is not unusual for theological students to be uncritically dismissive of so-called 'secular' culture, which is taken to be whatever is outside the explicit sphere of Christianity, as wholly decadent. This is grist to a teacher's mill in a seminar, of course, but worrying when it comes from young clergy preparing for parish work. In a recent article, Philip Sheldrake drew attention to some theological assumptions that often go unexamined but which may underpin such attitudes. He places these assumptions by reference to polarities that express a hierarchy of value, as for example, inwardness versus outer existence, personal experience versus social action, an elevated 'spiritual' realm as against the every-day and mundane, an idealized future (or past) against the present. At the root of these polarizations, he argues, lies a more fundamental contrast between the 'sacred' and the 'secular' (Sheldrake 2007, p. 93). Sheldrake traces some conventional interpretations of the sacred to the influence of Mircea Eliade and Rudolf Otto, for whom the sacred was '"wholly other" than the mundane and separated from everyday life and experience'. Furthermore, Eliade identified the 'secular' with the 'profane', which is everything that is outside what is explicitly dedi-cated to the sacred. 'The difficulty with this approach, which is still very influential, is that [Eliade] once again collapses "the profane" and "the secular", thus underwriting a radical contrast between, on the one hand, a sacred realm, and, on the other, the everyday or mundane.'

The result of this polarization is a tendency to value one pole over another, even to the extent of excluding the other, rather than trying to integrate the two; to value, it may be, the 'inner' life against outer life, personal experience against social action (and hence a separation of spirituality from ethics), an elevated 'spiritual' realm against the every-day and ordinary, an idealized future (or past) against the present.

Hence, in more practical terms, people may retreat to a safe 'sacred' place and refuse to engage with the secular, a move that is well captured in the image of 'campfire Christianity': Christians sitting in a circle, lit and warmed by the fire, reading the Bible and singing songs while 'pro-fane' darkness presses in threateningly all around. Others seem to want to rebuild the fortress Church, though they are too young to remember what life was really like in there. Others look for 'spirituality', but in the form of an exalted but warm, contemplative, interior space in which peace reigns. Sheldrake also notes the priority given in graduate studies in the United States to contemplative, monastic, mystical texts, in the apophatic tradition. What Sheldrake misses in all this is 'full-blooded attention to the kataphatic dimension, by which I mean . . . the way "the sacred" is encountered in and materialized by cultural or social practices and everyday human existence' (Sheldrake 2007, pp. 93–4).

Of course, the questions with which I began this paper are not new. From the start Christianity has always engaged, positively or negatively or with considerable ambiguity, both with and without much reflec-tion, with the arts and literature of the cultures among which it pitched its tent. The New Testament writers entered into dialogue both with the Jewish scriptures and with Greek philosophy. Augustine will per-haps serve as a representative of the kinds of questions that were being addressed and the kinds of answers given, not only in his times but also later. Augustine's relationship with classical and contemporary litera-ture was complex and seems to have changed over time. In the *City of God* he certainly engages with the literature of the earthly city, but largely in the form of a fierce polemic against much of it. In his work on teaching Christianity, he states it as a kind of principle that 'every good and true Christian should understand that wherever truth may be found it belongs to his Master'.[2] His advice to Christian teachers is to adopt a carefully discriminating approach to non-Christian literature and learning:

Accordingly, I think that it is well to warn studious and able young men, who fear God and are seeking for happiness of life, not to ven-ture heedlessly upon the pursuit of the branches of learning that are in vogue beyond the pale of the Church of Christ, as if these could secure for them the happiness they seek; but soberly and carefully to discriminate among them.[3]

Non-Christian literature and learning are also the 'spoils of Egypt'. According to Augustine's reading of Exodus, the Israelites, not on their own initiative, but with the authority of God, stole the property of the Egyptians, which the Egyptians were misusing, and which was designed for a better use. All branches of heathen learning contain 'false and superstitious fancies' which Christians, 'when going out under the leadership of Christ from the fellowship of the heathen', should abhor and avoid. But heathen learning also contains 'liberal instruction which is better adapted to the use of the truth and some most excellent precepts of morality' as well as 'some truths in regard even to the worship of the one God'. These are the spoils of Egypt which 'the Christian, when he separates himself in spirit from the miserable fellowship of these men, ought to take away from them and devote to their proper use in preaching the gospel'.[4]

Karl Rahner

Several reasons have prompted me to choose Rahner as a topic for discussion. First, his personal and theological writings suggest a man who was able to integrate faithful membership of the Catholic Church, an outstanding critical intellect, a profound spirituality and a reflective engagement with the arts and literature to an extent that is not often found in earthen vessels. Second, he was among the first major Christian theologians of the twentieth century to address issues of the arts in relation to Christian living. Third, this is an aspect of his work that has not so far received much attention from scholars.[5] And finally, Rahner's contribution in this area seems to me distinctive and worth further discussion.

Rahner's discussion of the arts in relation to Christian faith, theology and life comes in the form of a few relatively short essays and talks. Internal evidence suggests that at least some were written for a specific audience or readership, but it is not always possible to recapture the original settings. These pieces also come from different times of his life: those from the 1960s and early 1970s, for example, seem to have the abolition of the *Index of Prohibited Books* in the mid-1960s in the background, and it is obvious that he sometimes recycled earlier material more or less verbatim in later publications. In these writings his method is to extend some of the fundamentals of his philosophical and theological thought into a discussion of questions surrounding the arts in relation to Christian theology and Christian life, while in one essay he develops a rather distinctive theology of the word.

Art and Religious Experience

Rahner saw an intrinsic link between theology and both the 'non-verbal' arts (painting, sculpture and, with qualifications, architecture) and the 'verbal' arts (literature). Among the latter, he wrote more about poetry and the writer in general than about the novel or drama. Both theology and the arts speak about human matters, and in that sense theology is and has to be 'subjective', 'insofar as it has to speak of faith, hope and love and about our personal relationship with God'. Likewise, both theology and the arts are 'meant to be expressions, human self-expressions which embody, in one way or another, the process of human self-discovery' (Rahner 1982, pp. 17–19, 24). The major difference between them is that 'theology is man's self-reflexive self-expression about himself in the light of divine revelation' (1982, p. 24).

The 'verbal arts', however, share with theology the medium of the human word. From a theological point of view, one advantage, for Rahner, of the arts over a 'reflexive, purely conceptual and rational theology', is their capacity to 'put a person in touch with the depths of human experience in which religious experience takes place' (1982, p. 25). And that is so, even when a work of art has no explicit religious content. For Rahner, the term 'religious experience' has a particular meaning that is quite different from what it means in the work of William James, for example. Religious experience, in Rahner's eyes, 'takes place in the depths of existence' and 'a genuine and radical religious response is involved' (1982, p. 27). 'Religious', too, is to be understood in a special sense: a religious experience is one in which the whole question of existence, its meaning or meaninglessness, is awakened in a person (1982, p. 27). The question of existence and its meaning is a religious question, for Rahner, because it confronts a person with the question of God, of humanity's relation to God and an individual's existential (and not merely theoretical) response to this question. 'Religious', therefore, also means in some sense mediating divine mystery.

Both verbal and non-verbal arts, even when their subject matter is not overtly religious in a conventional sense, have the capacity to evoke a religious experience. '[I]t could be that a painting of Rembrandt, even if it is not religious in its thematic, objective content, nevertheless confronts a person in his total self in such a way as to awaken in him the whole question of existence' (1982, p. 27). And, 'I can understand Dürer's "The Hare" as a *concretissimum*, as an utterly concrete and definite given in an innocuous human experience. But if I really look at it with the eyes of the artist, there looks out at me, if I can put it this way, the very infinity and incomprehensibility of God' (1982, p. 29).

Literature and a Theology of Grace

Further explanation of how and why a work of art or literature that has no explicit religious content can evoke religious experience and the mystery of God is to be found in Rahner's theology of grace. The foundation of this theology is the principle that all human life and activity take place within a context or economy of grace that is all-pervasive. Rahner's thesis, therefore, in a piece called 'The Task of the Writer in relation to Christian Living', published in 1971, is that 'the author as such stands under the summons of Christ in grace and his Christianity must be conditioned by this fact' (Rahner 1971). In this article Rahner uses the term 'Anonymous Christians' and related ideas.[6] As this term does not seem particularly helpful, I will try to give an account of Rahner's position without using the phrase.

As is well-known, Rahner developed the notion of grace as God's self-gift, self-communication in love to humanity. Strikingly, 'It is the gift which is God himself and it is the gift of accepting the gift which bestows itself.' Grace is a hidden reality that permeates human existence and operates secretly in the depths of that existence. Rahner insists that grace so understood is not one of the conditions of human life that come and go with changing circumstances. On the contrary, grace is one of the transcendent 'existentials' of all human existence, that is to say, one of its permanent features or conditions. Whether we know it or not, whether we like it or not, we live in a world of grace and we cannot escape:

> Human existence is inevitably and inescapably subject to certain transcendent conditions such that, while they may indeed be denied, they do not thereby cease to be so, and constantly remain in force whether we recognize them consciously or not, whether we accept them or protest against them. (Rahner 1971, p. 113)

That is because each and every person is 'loved by God with the absolute and unreserved self-offering of the innermost depths of God's own true life'; because 'God has willed the incarnation of the eternal logos to take effect in his existence' and because 'the grace of God is applied to [each] permanently and enduringly'. The purpose of God's self-gift in love is 'to support the life of humanity from within'. Rahner understands grace in human life as an active force that 'appeals to all, empowers all and invites all'; 'it wells up from the depths of a person's heart in a thousand different ways'; it makes human beings restless, and it is through grace that human existence in all its aspects is constantly open to the infinite (Rahner 1971, pp. 113–14).

If all human existence is conditioned by grace so understood, then so is the life of the writer. And if we consider the human act or process of writing, then it has to be seen as a free act, an act that a person chooses to do. As such, the act of writing, as the act of speaking, 'has a moral relevance prior to and independent of the content of what is being said', at least if it is considered in its formal aspect (1971, p. 116). In the light of these premises, Rahner argues that any act or process of writing 'constitutes a response, either affirmative or negative, to Christianity [that is grace] as such', whether a writer is aware of this conditioning of human life or not, whether she accepts it or protests against it (1971, p. 115). And this is true even though writers may not grasp the full significance of what they are saying, or may be saying more than they intended. Consequently, it would be wrong of Christians to dismiss the books of writers who are not explicitly Christian or who oppose Christianity. An author's expression of an 'anguished atheism' may in fact be in reality 'a sharing in the desolation of the Cross' (1971, p. 118). And even when a writer implicitly or explicitly denies Christianity, such writing may in fact be the 'false or inadequate explanation and interpretation of a quest for the fullness of life which is, nevertheless, under God's blessing, which is Christian' (1971, p. 118).

When a writer writes about human life as it really is, the result is necessarily ambiguous. 'It is no accident, but rather inherent in the nature of the case, that the great creative writings of mankind are obscure and for the most part leave us with the unanswered question of whether it is the mystery of grace or that of perdition' that they describe. It could not be otherwise. Writers and artists deal with the concrete, the particular rather than trying to make general and universal principles dance like marionettes (1971, p. 120), and the concrete and particular constitute 'a mystery which will only be unveiled by that unique judgement which belongs to God alone' (1971, p. 120). Nonetheless, there is a difference between 'genuine creative writing' and 'that which conveys a message of sheer unbelief and immorality under the pretence of being creative writing' and Christians must learn to distinguish them (1971, p. 121).

Genuine creative writing, then, in Rahner's view, is a gift and work of grace and implicitly a fruit of redemption by Christ. The moral or religious ambivalence and ambiguity of great poetry, novels or drama are virtues because they reflect the reality of human existence, draw readers in to the dark and obscure depths where fundamental questions about human existence arise and have the potential to mediate an encounter with the mystery of God. In the case in which a literary work appears largely evil and destructive in its intent, content and likely effect, it is important for Christians to recognize that they are Christians and not Manichees and that 'evil as such is nothing'. Great sin is terrible, but it is great partly because it shares in the greatness of humanity. 'The only possible way in which sin can come to be so great is that in it much of the greatness of humanity itself is realised and revealed' (Rahner 1971, p. 120).

A Theology of the Word

'Christianity, as the religion of the word proclaimed, of faith which hears and of a sacred scripture, has a special intrinsic relationship to the *word* and hence cannot be without such a special relationship to the *poetic* word' (Rahner 1966). These remarks appear in an essay, 'Poetry and the Christian', which was published in 1966. In Rahner's theology God is a God who takes initiatives, in creation, revelation, grace (as God's self-communication) and incarnation. Rahner understands creation (and evolution within the world) as God's preparation to enable God to give himself in love and forgiveness to that which is other than God (Doud 1983, p. 448). One aspect of that preparation in humans is the development of the capacity to hear a 'poetic' word as a precondition for hearing the word of the gospel, the word of God's self-revelation and of human salvation. In the essay Rahner sets out four prerequisites that must be present if a person is to hear the word of the gospel without misunderstanding it.

The first condition is that human ears be 'open for *the word* through which the silent mystery is present' (1966, p. 358). In this word humanity is approached by 'what is incomprehensible, the nameless silent power that rules all but is itself unruled' (1966, p. 358). It is therefore through temporal and finite words that the eternal and infinite comes to humanity, and anyone who wants to hear the message of Christianity must be able to hear the human word in which 'the silent mystery' makes itself heard (1966, p. 359).

The second requisite is a capacity 'to hear words which reach *the heart*, the centre of man' (1966, p. 360). The heart is Rahner's term for the hidden centre of a human person from which knowledge, love and human action spring, 'the primordial faculty of the inmost spirit of man' (1966, p. 360). Among the words that reach the heart, and hence affect the whole person, are 'primary' words, and they 'strike the inmost depths . . . killing and bringing to life, transforming, judging and graciously favouring' (1966, p. 360). Both poetry and Christianity use such words.

A third requisite is a capacity to hear the word that unites. Typically, human words distinguish, define, separate, especially in technical or purely functional contexts. But there are also words that unite, reconcile and liberate. Poetic metaphors bring together into a unity different and sometimes apparently incompatible layers of meaning. Words of truth, love and forgiveness reconcile, unite and set free. A capacity to hear the uniting words of poetry prepares human beings to hear the reconciling, liberating words of Christianity. 'Only when one can hear the secret sound of unifying love in sundering words has one the ears to perceive truly the message of Christianity' (1966, p. 361).

The fourth condition for hearing aright the gospel is the capacity to recognize the inexpressible mystery of God expressed in the Word made flesh (1966, p. 361). The consequence for human language of the Word becoming flesh is striking: 'In every word, the gracious incarnation of God's own abiding Word and so of God himself can take place.' Hence, the human word can become 'the word of eternal love by the very fact that it expresses man and his world' (1966, p. 362).

The human word capable of performing all these functions is the word of poetry. If humanity lost the capacity to hear the poetic word, then human beings 'could no longer hear the word of God in the word of man' (1966, p. 363).

Rahner then outlines some of the implications of this discussion. First of all poetry is a necessity. 'We Christians must love and fight for the poetic word because we must defend what is human, since God himself has assumed it into his eternal reality' (1966, p. 364). Second, there is an 'inner kinship' between 'great Christianity' and 'great poetry', though they are not the same thing. Rahner believed that great poetry exists only when human beings radically face what they truly are (1966,

p. 365). Those who venture into this as poets or as readers are more likely to meet God there than 'those who skirt cautiously the chasms of existence' (1966, p. 365). Third, Rahner points to the need to exercise discernment of spirits in reading literature, because, as we have already seen, great literature usually leaves unanswered or ambiguous 'as to whether it was the mystery of grace or perdition' that was played out in it.

On this basis one might also argue for seeing an 'inner kinship' between 'great poetry' in Rahner's sense, and pastoral theology on the grounds that both deal with what human beings radically are, fundamental questions of the meaning of human existence and the practical living out of that meaning at all levels. Like great literature, its subject is 'humanity, humanity redeemed or in need of redemption and capable of redemption' (1966, p. 365).

Delight and Redress

I now want to move away from Rahner towards Seamus Heaney and in particular one of the lectures that he gave in Oxford as Professor of Poetry in 1989. The lectures were published as a book called *The Redress of Poetry*, which is also the title of the first lecture. An aspect of pastoral theology that gets a good deal of attention these days is its power to bring about change in personal lives and in communities. There are those who claim that such transformation is the primary task of pastoral or practical theology (see, for example, Graham 2000, pp. 104–17). And certainly the personal and communal lives of a whole generation were profoundly transformed by the pastoral theology of the Second Vatican Council. This topic also brings me closer to the question mark that I set against Auden's statement, 'Poetry changes nothing' in the title of my chapter. Intriguingly, Seamus Heaney seems to think that poetry can and does change things, make things happen, and that it has a unique way of doing it.

Change comes about through the capacity of poetry (and implicitly other forms of creative literature, though Heaney discusses only poetry in this lecture) to offer imagined alternatives to present reality, 'poetic fictions', 'the dream of alternative worlds' (Heaney 1995, p. 1). These imaginings hold out the hope of redress of what is oppressive, bigoted, unjust, destructive in the here and now, and new possibilities for human living. Thus poetry, according to Heaney, has a 'counterweighting function' (1995, p. 8). Poets 'conjure with their own and their readers' sense of what is possible, desirable or, indeed imaginable' to offer redress.

Heaney came under criticism throughout 'the Troubles' in Northern Ireland for not taking sides, not writing overtly political poetry in support of a cause. In his lecture he points out how dissatisfied the political activist, whether on the side of those in power or the revolutionaries, is going to be with mere poetic fictions.

> Engaged parties are not going to be grateful for a mere image – no matter how inventive or original – of the field of force of which they are a part. They will always want the redress of poetry to be an exercise of leverage on behalf of *their* point of view. (1995, p. 2)

Pastoral activists are likely to react in a similar way. The redress of poetry or fiction does not come in the form of a pastoral programme, and a fiction's power precisely as fiction with a capacity to offer redress is often in inverse proportion to its programmatic character. To read *Measure for Measure* as no more than the implementation of the Duke's pastoral strategy for Vienna is to lose more than the plot. It is, however, interesting to wonder what some of our pastoral plans would look like if they were allowed to be more informed, even if at several removes, by vividly imagined poetic fictions that offer redress. And like political activists, workers at the pastoral coal face are not necessarily going to be impressed by being offered no more than a dream of an alternative. My main point here, however, is that the 'redress of poetry' has an essential role as a resource for pastoral theology and pastoral action.

But it is crucial to remember how the redress of poetry works. What I know of Rahner suggests to me that he had a view of literature as exalted, even sublime, a matter of high seriousness, a view that was perhaps not untinged by German Romanticism. As we have seen, he is worried about us when we are 'narrow-minded and bourgeois' and avoid doubt – and God – by being superficial and trivial. And he celebrates literature's power to confront us with the serious, fundamental questions of human existence upon which matters of life or death depend. Seamus Heaney, too, stresses the seriousness of literature, but he also reminds us that poetry – and the redress of poetry – work by pleasure, delight, a particular kind of enjoyment. He quotes Borges, 'what is essential is . . . the thrill, the almost physical emotion that comes with each reading' and comments: 'Borges is talking about the fluid, exhilarating moment which lies at the heart of any memorable reading, the undisappointed joy of finding that everything holds up and answers the desire that it awakens' (Heaney 1995, pp. 8–9). This moment of delight stems from the beauty of the poem, its being something 'fully realized' (1995, p. 8) in its play and patterns of sounds, its images, words, rhythms, what in the same lecture Heaney calls 'proportion and pace and measure', 'winding forms and woven metaphors' (1995, p. 16). The redress of poetry (and of other forms of literature) 'works' through this kind of experience, through delight, by way of 'those unforeseen images and stanzas that send our reader's mind sweeping and veering away in delighted reflex' (1995, p. 16). In both writing and reading, 'the movement is from delight to wisdom, and not vice versa' (1995, p. 5).

Delight itself is the source of poetry's power to redress. What Heaney says in this lecture about culture and politics is perhaps not irrelevant to pastoral theology and practice:

> [I]n considering poetry's possible service to programmes of cultural and political realignment . . . I don't want to give the impression that its force must always be exercised in earnest, morally premeditated ways. On the contrary, I want to profess the surprise of poetry . . . I want to celebrate its given, unforeseeable thereness, the way it enters our field of vision and animates our physical and intelligent being. (1995, p. 16)

And as a metaphor of the way in which poetry offers redress, he draws on the phenomenon in which real birds have been known to change direction suddenly when they catch sight of images of birds stencilled on the transparent surfaces of glass. (1995, p. 15)

Conclusion: Literature and Pastoral Theology

In a recent book, the American theologian Mark McIntosh suggests a connection between spirituality and theology that needs to be maintained if both are to be healthy.

> Perhaps one might think initially in terms of encounter with God as the common ground of spirituality and theology: spirituality being the impression that this encounter makes in the transforming life of people, and theology being the expression that this encounter calls forth as people attempt to understand and speak of the encounter. (McIntosh 1998, p. 6)

Rahner's thinking on literature, the arts and Christian life and theology leads to the conclusion, as we have seen, that works of literature that have no explicit religious or Christian content nonetheless have the capacity to effect just such an encounter with God that McIntosh is talking about. Seeds of the divine word are hidden in the words of novelist, dramatist and poet. Moreover, Seamus Heaney's discussion of the experience of poetry suggests that what he calls 'delight' is integral to this encounter. Pastoral theology, as many of the chapters in this book affirm, has to do with the place where tradition, experience and present-day contexts meet and the conversation that ensues. The way in which McIntosh links encounter and theology suggests that, if literature is the place and moment of such an encounter, then pastoral theology is one of the forms of theology 'that this encounter calls forth as people attempt to understand and speak of the encounter'. Pastoral theology may be thought of as involving reflection in two directions. In one direction there is reflection on the founding events of the life, death and resurrection of Jesus, as mediated and interpreted by the community down the ages (that is to say in Scripture and tradition) in the light of a particular present-day context. In the other direction, pastoral theology reads particular contemporary experience and context through or in the light of those events as mediated by tradition. And this reflection is done with a view to transforming praxis.

All of this, moreover, raises questions for further investigation. Rahner's argument about non-religious, non-Christian literature's capacity to draw readers into the mystery of God does not mean, obviously, that reading literature is *ipso facto* 'sacramental', as it were, in and of itself a moment of grace. Rahner recognizes very clearly that what literature offers us is morally and spiritually ambivalent. Reading can be both healthy and dangerous; it can both lead towards fullness of life in the love of God on the one hand or corrupt and undermine our human well-being on the other. Literature can be both creative and destructive for the reader; it mediates evil as well as grace. In other words, the moments of delight that Seamus Heaney describes so eloquently are not unambiguously moments of grace, movements towards a deeper faith, hope and love of God and neighbour. They may also corrupt the reader, draw the reader in the direction of sin – injustice, oppression, narcissism, destructive attitudes and patterns of behaviour. They may bring us face to face with the mystery of evil as well as the mystery of grace. Though it may be true, as Heaney says, that the movement is from delight to wisdom, there can equally be a movement from delight to unwisdom and evil.

If literature is a resource for pastoral theology, there is a further need to understand and explore ways of reading that include what the Christian spiritual tradition calls 'discernment of spirits', methods of reading and reflection that allow us to distinguish between those moments, whether of delight or its opposite, that mediate grace and those that lead to evil. For moments of profound appreciation of a poem, a novel, a story, a play, we need ways of reading and reflection that distinguish between the movement of the Spirit of God and that which works in us as readers and as human beings to oppose and undermine the Spirit.[7] These are questions for another occasion.

Notes

1 There are currently two readers in English: Robert Detweiler and David Jasper (eds), 2000, *Religion and Literature: A Reader*, Louisville: Westminster John Knox; Gesa Elsbeth Thiessen (ed.), 2004, *Theological Aesthetics: A Reader*, London: SCM Press.

2 Augustine, *De Doctrina Christiana*, Bk II, Chapter 18.

3 *De Doctrina Christiana*, Bk II, Chapter 39.

4 *De Doctrina Christiana*, Bk II, Chapter 40.

5 There have been a few articles in journals and handbooks, for example, Robert E. Dould, 'Poetry and Sensibility in the Vision of Karl Rahner', *Thought* 58, no. 231; Gesa Elsbeth Thiessen, 'Karl Rahner: Toward a Theological Aesthetics', in Declan Marmion and Mary E. Hines (eds), 2005, *The Cambridge Companion to Karl Rahner*, Cambridge: Cambridge University Press, pp. 225–34. The first book-length study that has come to my attention is Antonio Spadaro, 2006, *La Grazia della Parola: Karl Rahner e la Poesia*, Milan: Jaca.

6 For an explanation of 'Anonymous Christians', see Karl Rahner, *Theological Investigations*, vol. VI, pp. 390–8.

7 I have discussed these issues in a recent conference address, '*Tolle, lege*: Reading, Discernment and Personal Transformation', which will be published in due course.

Bibliography

Robert Detweiler and David Jasper (eds), 2000, *Religion and Literature: A Reader*, Louisville: Westminster John Knox Press.

Robert E. Doud, 1983, 'Poetry and Sensibility in the Vision of Karl Rahner', *Thought*, vol. 58, no. 231 (December 1983).

Elaine Graham, 2000, 'Practical Theology as Transforming Practice', in James Woodward and Stephen Pattison (eds), *The Blackwell Reader in Pastoral and Practical Theology*, Oxford: Blackwell, pp. 104–17.

Seamus Heaney, 1995, *The Redress of Poetry: Oxford Lectures*, London: Faber & Faber.

Mark A. McIntosh, 1998, *Mystical Theology: The Integrity of Spirituality and Theology*, Oxford: Blackwell.

Karl Rahner, 1966, 'Poetry and the Christian', in *Theological Investigations*, vol. IV, London: Darton, Longman & Todd.

Karl Rahner, 1971, 'The Task of the Writer in relation to Christian Living', in *Theological Investigations*, vol. VIII, London: Darton, Longman & Todd.

Karl Rahner, 1982, 'Theology and the Arts', *Thought* 57, pp. 17–29.

Philip Sheldrake, 2007, 'Spirituality and the Integrity of Theology', *Spiritus* 7.

Antonio Spadaro, 2006, *La Grazia della Parola: Karl Rahner e la Poesia*, Milan: Jaca.

Gesa Elsbeth Thiessen (ed.), 2004, *Theological Aesthetics: A Reader*, London: SCM Press.

Gesa Elsbeth Thiessen, 2005, 'Karl Rahner: Toward a Theological Aesthetics', in Declan Marmion and Mary E. Hines (eds), *The Cambridge Companion to Karl Rahner*, Cambridge: Cambridge University Press.

17

Practical Theological Research:
A Case Study

JAMES SWEENEY CP (with D. BHATTI,
H. CAMERON, C. DUCE AND C. WATKINS,
THE ARCS RESEARCH TEAM)

Introduction

One of the practices of interest to practical theology is the practice
of theology itself, and of theological research – the fundamental practice of the academic world. But theology, and even more theological
research, is not well appreciated as a practice among practices in the life
of the Church. It tends to be confined, and may confine itself, to academic circles, withdrawn from scrutiny as a practice in which faith and
ecclesial living are involved. Such a separation of theology from faith
practice not only limits its contribution to Christian life but withdraws
it from evaluation on a faith basis.

This chapter discusses research in pastoral/practical theology and
how it can be sustained as a properly theological exercise. It draws
on the work of the ARCS project at Heythrop College, University
of London.[1] This project sees its purpose explicitly as an exercise in
responsible theological intervention in support of practices of evangelization, renewal and church social action.[2] It views these as not only
faith practices but embodied theologies, and the intention is to bring
the theological resources of the Christian tradition to bear on this
embodied theology, while at the same time re-examining the tradition
in the light of embodied practice. This is a practical kind of theology in
virtue of the direct reference to practice; and a practical result is envisaged – enhanced, theologically mature practice. Most importantly, the
emerging forms of mission in the Church today are taken at face value
as faith enterprises, inspired and motivated by religious and theological

ideas, and not to be reductively theorized in terms of other forms of discourse.

Roman Catholic and Anglican groups are involved in the project, primarily from the London area. In its first research period (2006–8) ARCS was engaged with seven groups, and an additional three took part in the previous, set-up phase (2004–6). Six groups continued into the second period (2008 onwards), two of which had been involved from 2004, and some new groups began to come on stream.[3] They represent a wide spectrum of church mission – from evangelism to social action, large-scale agencies to local groups, younger to older, church sector to national charity, and an ecumenical mix. This has generated a rich and expanding database.

Renewal and Mission – a Diocesan Pastoral Plan

As an illustration of this work, we can take the example of the RC Diocese of Portsmouth and its diocesan plan and stewardship process.[4]

The Diocese, building on a previous programme 'Growing Together in Christ' under the leadership of Bishop Crispian Hollis, produced its Pastoral Plan, *Go Out and Bear Fruit*, in 2005.[5] The plan is based on the centrality of the Eucharist and it has required the creation of pastoral areas larger than the individual parish, therefore touching on the central practice of the celebration of Sunday Mass. It was launched at a diocesan conference in summer 2005 and then cascaded through the diocese with a series of launch evenings in parishes. A major strand was to support the development of stewardship in parishes and pastoral areas:

> We are stewards of the gift of creation and all that life brings: our time, our treasure our talents and one another. Therefore we have a duty to ensure that we make the best use of all we have, and that we do this in a way which respects the dignity of every person and promotes the common good. (Roman Catholic Diocese of Portsmouth, 2005, p. 28)

The diocese adopted its Stewardship approach from one developed in the United States. Diocesan personnel took part in conferences and training events in the USA, although back in the diocese they tailored the materials to local conditions. A few parishes piloted Stewardship in 2005–6 and others built on their experience. People throughout the diocese, in parishes and schools, are encouraged to grow in an under-standing of stewardship as a way of life, a 'disciple's response' of conversion to Jesus Christ. This implies both structural adaptation and spiritual renewal. The process is supported by a Trustees' Committee, a Schools' Stewardship Group, a part-time Advisor to the Clergy on Stewardship, and a full-time Advisor for Stewardship and Collabora-tive Ministry in the Department for Pastoral Formation.

ARCS became involved in 2005 and undertook interviews with key diocesan personnel, a review of their literature and a visit to one of the parish groups. The data was analysed according to grounded theory procedures. Diocesan personnel took part in research symposium in May 2006. A formal agreement to proceed into an action research phase was reached, and a co-researcher from within the diocese was appointed to carry out interviews and focus groups.[6] Subsequent data was again analysed using grounded theory to identify emerging themes; a theological response paper was prepared by the theologian on the ARCS team examining the key questions that arose. Theological ques-tions and issues were around the various dimensions of eucharistic practice, leadership in the ecclesial community and the theology of orders, and Christology and the 'visibility' of the person of Jesus in the emerging spirituality.

These materials were considered at three meetings between the ARCS team and different diocesan groups, at two of which the bishop partici-pated. The need was identified to generate a more sustained process of theological reflection internally within the diocesan process, and a 24-hour workshop to build up capacity for this was facilitated by ARCS personnel.

This Portsmouth example shows how ARCS works; the theological issues that emerged will be covered later. The other groups, of course, are all quite different and each requires its own approach; a diocese-wide programme has to take a broad sweep, whereas movements such as CaFE or Youth 2000 have a more precise focus. Space does not allow coverage of all the details, although the theological issues will emerge.

A Theologal Field[7]

In this pastoral-theological research, ARCS frames the 'reality' it is handling on a basic assumption: that for 'faith groups' faith perceptions are constitutive of their self-awareness; that, therefore, whenever they speak about their identity or purposes faith and some form of theology is being articulated; that even if they do not use explicitly theological or religious terminology they are giving expression to a practical kind of theology; and that this embedded 'theologal' dimension to their life and action is of primary significance for theological reflection on, and a starting-point for theological understanding of, practice, and ultimately for the development of theology itself.

In faith practices 'process' is an integral and prominent feature. A diocesan plan, for example, or the social action projects of an agency such as Housing Justice, are much more than whatever the glossy booklets may lay out as their theological principles and aims and objectives and stages. The project is an emerging and unfolding feature of the life of the diocesan community or organization. The pastoral plan (and any such pastoral project) is a representation of what may be termed the 'theologal force field'. It portrays a dynamic field of energy and action. The actors are all those involved – in the case of a diocese, bishop and parishioner, staff in the diocesan offices and parish priests, mothers and fathers and children, members of movements and of parish groups, teachers and pastoral workers, and many more. As process – in its set-up, its negotiation, its implementation – a pastoral project is *performative*, involving a multitude of actors; and it is in the performance rather than some quantifiable 'results' that its purpose is achieved (Schechner 1988). A Shakespeare production is not rated artistically by the number of theatre tickets sold but by its inherent quality – and ticket sales will follow. Pastoral practices are not to be assessed theologically by easily observable 'results' – nor even, since they stand under the sign of the Cross, simply by eventual 'ticket sales'[8] – but by the good that is internal to them.[9]

Four Theological Voices

The heuristic framework ARCS uses to explore this theologal reality views it as the confluence of four theological streams. At the level of 'lived theology', there is (a) the *espoused* theology that groups formally adhere to and (b) an *operant* theology that is evident from their actual life and activities, with the two streams in greater or lesser correspondence.[10] These streams at the lived level are dynamically related (in varied ways) to theological streams and influences at the institutional level. Lived theology is not autonomously constructed but is determined and patterned, to a greater or lesser degree, by (c) *formal* theology as developed by professional theologians and (d) the *normative* theology of the Christian churches (Scripture, creeds, magisterial teaching).

Practical Theological Research

Within the process of pastoral life, theological research itself becomes part of the process; it is always to some degree a performative act. The same would be true of non-theological intervention, an organizational or a sociological study for instance, which cannot escape becoming part of the narrative of the group under investigation; but theological engagement has the added implication of being an 'insider' to the group's values and beliefs and their normative force. Theological research of this kind – the art of practical theology – may be thought of as a particular kind of performance – engaging in a conversation about the interconnections between the four streams of espoused, operant, formal and normative theology, with the purpose of strengthening the theologal force field of the group's life and mission by building up the capacity for ongoing theological reflection.

Theology is often – even mainly – carried out 'factually', or in operant mode (Astley 2002; Watkins 2006). The community of faith is a community of living faith practice, and so of embedded theology, where human experience has its proper place as a locus of revelation. Attention to this fact is all the more important in our times as aspects of culture and context increasingly emphasize the significance and authority of personal experience, with a characteristic 'turn to the subject'. Our data shows that talk is mostly about 'my faith'– a perspective encouraged by the various practices of faith-sharing and small community nurture – but 'my faith' is not the same as 'the faith' ('what the Church teaches' or Christian tradition). Today's cultural diversity, pluralism and consumerism, and the consequent individualism and relativism of opinion, heightens the significance of the lived, operant stream of theology. It becomes all the more important, then, to relate this to the formal and normative theologies at the institutional level, and open up an examination of how contemporary Christian practice stands in relation to the historic tradition of Christianity. This necessarily raises issues such as legitimation, validation and institutional control.[11]

The word 'theology', however, can be off-putting to some, and may be seen reductively as 'head' rather than 'heart', theory rather than practice. But at its simplest theology is a matter of finding words to give expression to lived faith; it's a matter of language. By exploring with the members of a faith group the theologal dimension of their life, and distinguishing between their espoused and operant theology, it is possible to spot differences between what they think they are doing (or thinking) and what they are actually doing (or thinking). More importantly, it also brings to light the ways that both theoretical (or notional) and factual (real) belief and commitment (assent) are in play. So, for example, the belief in the Eucharist as a sharing in the Body of Christ – both his Body that is the sacrament and his Body which is the Church – can be truly held as a 'notion', and it is held as 'real' when this dual characteristic is embedded in day-to-day practice (Lubac 2006). This is something that the Portsmouth programme, for example, centred on a eucharistic theology, seeks to establish, and on which the success of its reorganization of parish and diocesan structures depends.

Theological Reflection

Complex manoeuvres are involved across this theologal force field and a complex psychology, because in daily life we use other 'languages' as well – cultural, technological, scientific, literary – and articulating theological discourse in relation to such diverse areas is a challenge. If theological language is to work, it has to be appropriate or apt for context – apt for the work it has to do (in proclamation, catechesis, spirituality, social action, liturgy); apt for today's cultural sensitivities; and apt for giving expression to the transcendent realities of faith. Theology requires a rich vocabulary and careful modes of expression, and a capacity that goes beyond simple theological literacy to theological *fluency* – the ability to speak an appropriate theological language appropriately.[12]

Formal theological reflection, whether the practitioner's direct reflection on practice or that undertaken by the academic theologian, is *fides quaerens intellectum*, an intellectual work that is secondary to the direct apprehension of the religious act of faith and which, while it is in service of that faith, involves critical thinking.[13] This is structured in ARCS as mutually critical interchange between the four theological streams. These, of course, are asymmetrical – operant theology is not of a piece with normative; nor may a group's espoused theology be totally convergent with the best theology of the theologians. This leads to the probing of some fundamental notions, such as 'community', which routinely crop up in theology and pepper the discourse of groups. We need to ask how 'community' is being used in practice and with what connotations. Does it operantly mean simple togetherness or an awareness of our *communio in Christo*? The language of evangelization also needs unpacking. Words can mask reality, and an espoused theology of mission may be hiding a more inward-looking operant theology of renewal. Culturally acceptable words such as 'inclusiveness' are particularly slippery: code, perhaps, for openness to those with 'alternative lifestyles' but not to those with different ecclesial (still less political) sympathies. It is around such issues that serious practical-theological work needs to be done.

On the other hand, the embedded theologies of practice probe and question the positions of formal theology. Practices that don't fit with established notions – the return of traditional liturgy and devotional practices (for example, Youth 2000's emphasis on eucharistic adoration) – can be taken as a spur to develop fresh theology. In such reflection, taking us beyond our comfortable routines, theological language is remoulded, images are refreshed and concepts are honed to become more apt for expressing and stimulating practice.

Research Methodology

The research process in pastoral and practical theology clearly has to keep practical purposes in view. The methodology developed by ARCS deploys an action research programme within which a variety of methods is used (Bhatti et al. 2008, pp. 48–53). The steps are: (a) agreement on the research question and project with the partner group; (b) data gathering in the field; (c) coding and analysis of the data, using NVivo and a broad grounded theory approach; (d) reflection on the emerging themes within the ARCS team employing sociological and theological perspectives; (e) written feedback to the partner group; (f) theological reflection within the partner group on the data and the ARCS feedback; (g) reflection together by the ARCS team and the partner group, leading to discernment of action and the possibility of a further research phase. It is an iterative conversational process. Of course, this represents an ideal, and in practice resource constraints dictate how much can be done at each step along the way. In addition to its action research work, ARCS engages in a meta-level of analysis and theoretical reflection spanning the data from across the partner groups and using it to contribute to missiology and pastoral-practical theology, and feeding this back to the groups as well.[14]

It is important to stress the conversational aspect. The data gathered from the partner groups comes in the form of interview transcripts, participant observation notes, focus group reports, etc. Having undergone a first analysis and coding, the interpretation *in conversation with* the partner group and not in isolation from them is essential, not only to serve the purposes of change in action research but, more fundamentally, as a matter of hermeneutics; it is an acknowledgement that research intervention in faith practices participates in the practice, and stands within not outside the 'performance'.

The Problem of Bias

But this then raises the intractable problem of objectivity. Nicholas Healy, in his chapter in this volume, says that empirical accounts are required for practical ecclesiology (and by extension practical theology), and have to be generated by appropriate social-scientific methods without reliance on theological presuppositions or doctrines; but that nevertheless doctrine, in addition to ensuring the overall theological nature of the project, does somehow guide the empirical investigation, for example towards privileging a group's own language in its self-description (see also Healy 2000). There is a tension here between subjective participation and outsider perspective, insider and outsider (emic–etic) viewpoints, and a proper balance has to be struck (Arweck and Stringer 2002). Both perspectives have their presuppositions. The emic viewpoint, operating from within the experience, attributes an essential reality and validity to the practices of faith, while an etic view situates them comparatively within some wider class of practices – and may remain neutral about their validity, or take overtly or covertly a positive or negative view of them. The point is, as Healy shows, that empirical research can never be presupposition-less; and if not theological then some non-theological presuppositions will be in operation. However, objectivity (or, perhaps better, accuracy) must be guarded, especially in an overtly theological research project such as ARCS if it is to be trusted as *bona fide* empirical enquiry.

Here, there are three related issues: accuracy, data analysis and interpretation. Objectivity may be thought of as both an art and the fruit of technical method, and this applies at different points. For the phenomenology, objectivity is served by accurate observation; within analysis, it is served by detailed and systematic procedure; and at the level of interpretation, objectivity requires reflexivity and the development of an account that remains open to further elaboration, in reflective ongoing conversation.

Assuming the basic skills of accurate observation in fieldwork, it is the procedures for analysing and interpreting data that are crucial. The grounded theory approach to data analysis, or some variant of it, allows gathered data to suggest its own theory before formal theological resources are brought to bear. This is an emic technique in that it develops internally to the data, but also etic in that it imposes strict systems of coding and classification. At its fullest it involves detailed coding of data, sorting codes into a hierarchy of categories and concepts, returning to the field for theoretical sampling to check the accuracy of data, and eventually creating an exhaustive grounded theory (Charmaz 2006).[15] This is a corrective for subjective bias and ensures a measured and objective approach to data. A picture is built up of the life of the group and of its espoused and operant theologies, and generic and contrasting themes are identified as a basis for properly theological reflection.

Hermeneutics

Proceeding further, into the realm of hermeneutics, the emerging practice of partner groups is open to interrogation and questioning from a number of points of view. In ARCS, pedagogical and sociological critique has been brought to bear (Sweeney et al. 2006, pp. 15–16; Bhatti et al. 2008, pp. 23–4, 33–6). This, in the first instance, is in order to benefit from insights from the social science disciplines, but it also helps ensure proper rigour of analysis. Finally, the explicitly theological level of questioning can be broached, opening the conversation with formal-normative theologies. This presents its own challenges. There is, first, the blunt problem of maintaining the research as true theology, and that the theology does not simply become the icing on a cake already baked in the oven of social analysis. Moreover, it must be emphasized that theology does not make its appearance only at this late stage, as if previously the research effort had been simply social scientific or organizational; the theology runs right through the project as its main structuring principle and guide to the research questions. Then there is an issue about the provenance of the actual theology that is brought to bear on practice. The question here is whose theology is at work, and how particular resources, themes and interpretations come to the fore. The tendency to be eclectic or partial in deploying the religious tradition has to be kept in mind.

However, theological materials are notoriously diffuse and open to contestation, all the more so when research is undertaken across denominational boundaries, and there is a danger of merely opinionizing. In ARCS this has been tackled by setting out a formal interpretative framework of theological themes, four interlocking themes of the theology of Grace, Church and World, Christology, Sacraments and Sacramentality, in terms of which the theological conversation can proceed (Sweeney et al. 2006, pp. 19–26). The specification of these theological themes draws on the resources of the tradition and biblical and magisterial teaching where appropriate. At the same time, such a summary cannot, and should not, be isolated from the issues and questions that arise in contemporary practice – this is a *contemporary* summary of the tradition. And in any case, the themes function in a dual way: they lay out the perspective within which practice can be assessed, while they themselves (and the theological resources on which they draw) are open to reverse interrogation and critique from the standpoint and insights of practice (Bhatti et al., 2008, pp. 25–33, 41–2).

Theological Conversation

It is here, in fact, that a truly interesting theological interplay begins. Partner groups have expressed warm appreciation about being drawn into an explicitly theological enquiry about their practice and how this deepens their perceptions.[16] A striking diversity of theological interpretations sometimes emerges; for example, how the call to serve the needs of others and even leave aside worship to do so can be seen in dramatic terms as 'the temple "passing away" as the kingdom breaks in', but also, more soberly, as the need 'to revivify the traditional and powerful connection between Eucharist and the giving away of ourselves in service, the connectedness of liturgy and life' (Bhatti et al. 2008, p. 28). The enquiry exposes the many ways in which theological language usage is culturally positioned – inevitably so, given its performative quality and the requirement of fluency in order to be communicative – and therefore the need to be on guard against culture simply overpowering theology. Perhaps most fascinating is how this kind of research exercise puts theology in touch with contemporary ecclesial practice as 'tradition in (its) tentative, growing mode, whose authority, whilst real, is different from that of the already discerned (and continually re-discerned) tradition of Christian history' (Bhatti et al. 2008, p. 41). The Catholic sensitivity to tradition impacts on theological work in the close attention given to magisterial teaching as the expression of an always evolving and emerging tradition.[17] Added to that, the *locus theologicus* that is the contemporary experience of the People of God is another fount of evolving tradition. To research this experience is to engage in an exposition of the living *sensus fidelium*.

Some Final Theology . . .

The model of research outlined above emerged rather tentatively over the years 2004–8 as the fruits of the research team's practice of theology, and no doubt there are many developments and clarifications still to come. While we feel justified in claiming some methodological originality for our project (we are not aware of any other examples of this kind of theologically framed action research), researchers in pastoral-practical theology will recognize the issues we faced and the paths we trod. But there is more to methodology than can be laid out in writing, particularly in the case of an ecclesial pastoral theology. The build-up of experience in the team, sensitivity to the research parameters, appreciation of key insights, awareness of the concrete details that go to make up a group's practice and mission are all carried in the shared life of the research team. This is more than just a matter of acquired skills or consolidated expertise that may be lost when the team disperses; their theological *practice* is in play. Assessing this theological practice in theological terms – in the same way that ARCS assesses the practice of its partner groups – leads to the notion of 'theologal theology', which according to Jon Sobrino 'must be a mystagogy'.

The theological theme within which this dimension of pastoral-practical theology can be explicated is that of revelation; and specifically, revelation 'realized by words and deeds' as expounded in *Dei Verbum* (n. 2).[18] Pastoral theology as a practical discipline concerns itself with the ongoing deeds realized in the Christian community through which God's saving action in Christ continues – a fundamental theological interpretation of the significance of practice. Deeds and words, however, are not simple correlates. To speak is already to do, obviously so in the case of preaching and proclamation; for example, Jesus' Sermon on the Mount (Matt. 5—7) or Peter's post-resurrection sermon (Acts 2.14–36).[19] Pastoral theology, understood as an ecclesial practice, is itself a work of both 'words and deeds' in service of the Church and society at large. As Karl Rahner puts it:

[I]n being this kind of theory practical theology is not simply an 'essential' science but a quite unique one, a testing of the spirits with a view to the act of committal; it implies a prophetic element – which one may be permitted to call 'political' – since it must be aware of the impulses of the Church's Spirit, which is not simply identical with the perpetually valid truth in the Church, but translates the latter into the concrete challenge valid at the particular hour. (Rahner 1972, pp. 103–4)

Practical theological research, then, such as in ARCS, brings with it responsibilities to more than the academic world. In the first place, clearly, there is a responsibility to research partners and the enhancement of their practice; and to make responsible use of their experience when drawing wider lessons about mission and evangelization, and to engage them through feedback and discussion at that level as well. More broadly, practical theology by definition does not exist in an 'ivory tower', and so it cannot avoid the responsibility of commitment to the issues in its field of enquiry. The ARCS story began with a wish to serve and strengthen the emerging practices of evangelization in the Church, and part of the journey has been coming to a deeper awareness that the theology of practice is itself a theologically laden practice.

Notes

1 The ARCS project at Heythrop (Action Research: Church and Society) works together with OxCEPT (Oxford Centre for Ecclesiology and Practical Theology) at Ripon College, Cuddesdon. See, D. Bhatti, H. Cameron, C. Duce, J. Sweeney and C. Watkins, 2008, *Living Church in the Global City: Theology in Practice*, Heythrop College, University of London.

2 The first phase of research was carried out by the Von Hügel Institute and the Margaret Beaufort Institute in Cambridge. See J. Sweeney, C. Watkins, P. Knights and D. Bhatti, 2006, *Going Forth: An Enquiry into Evangelisation & Renewal in the Roman Catholic Church in England & Wales*, Cambridge: Von Hügel Institute & Margaret Beaufort Institute of Theology.

3 The ten partner groups that have been involved in ARCS are: St Margaret Mary Parish, Liverpool; St Patrick's School of Evangelisation; Sion Community; Catholic Faith Exploration (CaFE); Youth 2000; RC Diocese of Portsmouth Pastoral Plan and Stewardship Process; RC Archdiocese of Westminster Agency for Evangelisation; C of E Diocese of Southwark Social Responsibility Network; Alpha at St Mary's Church, Battersea; Housing Justice.

4 See Bhatti et al. 2008, pp.16–17.

5 Available at the diocesan website: www.portsmouthdiocese.org.uk.

6 The research plan is formulated in a 'remit document' agreed by the partner group and ARCS. Different models of participation are possible – the appointment of an internal co-researcher, a 'reflective practitioner' model with fieldwork undertaken by ARCS, or a consultancy model with ARCS advising on some initial, exploratory research.

7 'Theologal', meaning God-directed, derives from the more familiar but distinct term 'theological', which has a more theoretical meaning. It is used by, among others, Jon Sobrino: 'A theologal theology must be a mystagogy – an introduction into the reality of God as God is; transcendent mystery, utterly resistant to manipulation, and yet our Father, near at hand, good and saving.' Jon Sobrino, 1988, *Spirituality of Liberation: Toward Political Holiness*, Maryknoll, NY: Orbis, p. 72.

8 In the jargon, 'bums on pews'.

9 Alasdair MacIntyre defines practice in such terms: 'a coherent and complex form of socially established cooperative activity through which goods internal to that activity are realized' (1981, p. 187).

10 This is similar to Newman's differentiation between 'notional assent' given to abstract inferences and 'real assent' given to concrete realities. This is not the opposition of unreal to real. Notional assent is an inferential pattern of operation or a theological deduction, whereas in real assent the object of the operation is a truth of religion. 'A dogma is a proposition; it stands for a notion or for a thing; and to believe it is to give the assent of the mind to it, as it stands for the one or for the other. To give a real assent to it is an act of religion; to give a notional, is a theological act. It is discerned, rested in, appropriated as a reality, by the religious imagination; it is held as a truth, by the theological intellect' (Newman 1985, p. 69).

11 Issues of both individual agency and institutional structure.

12 Communication depends on fluency. Enzo Pace, building on the example of John Paul II, suggests that pastoral strategy in the churches now takes shape as communication, a new mode of religious power and a communicative presence to society (Pace 2007, pp. 37–49).

13 Theology that combines faith and critical thinking is not the only mode of operation of theology, and may not be suited to all situations.

14 See: http://www.heythrop.ac.uk/index.php/content/view/1007/470.

15 ARCS has followed the constructivist approach in grounded theory; although, since grounded theory analysis is very time-consuming, NVivo coding has often come to be used instead.

16 See especially the Housing Justice report in Bhatti et al. 2008, pp. 13–15.

17 Catholic theology, of course, has its rules of critical interpretation of magisterial teaching. Ecumenical partners are often intrigued by, for example, the dominance of the documents of the Second Vatican Council in the theology of their Catholic partners.

18 See discussion of this in the chapter in this volume by James Sweeney, 'Catholic Theology and Practice Today'.

19 To do is also to speak – captured in the advice attributed to St Francis: 'Preach the Gospel, and if you must, use words.'

Bibliography

E. Arweck and M. Stringer (eds), 2002, *Theorizing Faith: The Insider/Outsider Problem in the Study of Ritual*, Birmingham: University of Birmingham Press.

J. Astley, 2002, *Ordinary Theology: Looking, Listening and Learning in Theology*, Aldershot: Ashgate.

D. Bhatti, H. Cameron, C. Duce, J. Sweeney and C. Watkins, 2008, *Living Church in the Global City: Theology in Practice*, Heythrop College, University of London.

K. Charmaz, 2006, *Constructing Grounded Theory: A Practical Guide through Qualitative Research*, London: Sage.

N. M. Healy, 2000, *Church, World and the Christian Life: Practical-Prophetic Ecclesiology*, Cambridge: Cambridge University Press.

H. de Lubac, 2006, *Corpus Mysticum: The Eucharist and the Church in the Middle Ages*, trans. G. Simmonds CJ with R. Price, London: SCM Press.

A. MacIntyre, 1981, *After Virtue: A Study in Moral Theory*, London: Duckworth.

J. H. Newman, 1985 (1870), *An Essay in Aid of a Grammar of Assent*, edited with introduction and notes by I. T. Ker, Oxford: Clarendon.

E. Pace, 2007 'Religion as Communication: The Changing Shape of Catholicism in Europe', in N. Ammerman (ed.), *Everyday Religion*, Oxford: Oxford University Press.

K. Rahner, 1972, 'Practical Theology within the Totality of Theological Disciplines' in *Theological Investigations*, vol. IX, trans. G. Harrison, London: Darton, Longman & Todd.

Roman Catholic Diocese of Portsmouth, 2005, *Go Out and Bear Fruit*, at www.portsmouthdiocese.org.uk

R. Schechner, 1988, *Performance Theory*, London and New York: Routledge.

J. Sobrino, 1988, *Spirituality of Liberation: Toward Political Holiness*, Maryknoll, NY: Orbis.

J. Sweeney, C. Watkins, P. Knights and D. Bhatti, 2006, *Going Forth: An Enquiry into Evangelisation and Renewal in the Roman Catholic Church in England and Wales*, Cambridge: Von Hügel Institute and Margaret Beaufort Institute of Theology.

C. Watkins, 2006, *Living Baptism: Called Out of the Ordinary*, London: Darton, Longman & Todd.

Conclusion

JAMES SWEENEY CP
WITH GEMMA SIMMONDS CJ AND
DAVID LONSDALE

The essays in this volume reflect the main issues in Catholic pastoral theology today, and while there is some international input they essentially come out of one particular location – the Catholic theological scene of Britain and Ireland. This is both their usefulness and their (inevitably) limited scope. There are many other perspectives and fields that could be added; they have been touched on only briefly here: biblical pastoral theology, ministry, ecology, catechesis and religious education, and so on.

It is hoped that the volume will be helpful to students and teachers and researchers in the different schools and traditions of pastoral and practical theology. As well as aiding understanding of the Catholic approach, the aim is to engage with the arguments over the nature and direction of this kind of theology. There is a lively discussion among Catholic pastoral theologians about the nature of their trade, and an equally lively discussion among those in other Christian traditions and between them and Catholics. To conclude, therefore, we make some suggestions about key issues and what might usefully be explored further in an ecumenical pastoral/practical conversation.

Two Traditions

Protestant and Catholic practical theologies have different genealogies, with their far origins in Schleiermacher and Tübingen respectively. This is not to say that there has been no interaction between them. Their recent development has been driven by different, but not entirely dissimilar, processes: on the one hand, by the crisis of metaphysical neo-scholastic theology in Catholicism, engineering a shift to the practical; and on the other hand, by a turn within theology in the Reformed traditions towards the social sciences in an effort to overcome theology's dissociation from practical matters. Catholic pastoral theology in these countries has emerged in piecemeal fashion, its intellectual and spiritual impetus coming largely from abroad, and its local development driven by immediate pressing pastoral needs. The Protestant tradition of practical theology, on the other hand, has been more university-led, but reacting to a merely academic theology which is perceived to be disconnected from the needs of either the Church or society. There is now a new opportunity to learn from each other. Indeed, the steady advance of ecumenical understanding at church congregational level (not the same as formal ecumenical schemes) would indicate that practice can only be realistically addressed in an inter-church (and, more and more, an inter-faith) way.

In Service of Mission

This leads to the practical intent of this theological enterprise. The classic definition of *fides quaerens intellectum* might need a bit of tweaking to fit it to pastoral and practical theology. Its goal goes beyond understanding – *intellectum* – and includes enhanced practice or action. This does not mean, in relation to the strictly theological exercise, the direct action of the social practitioner or the religious disciple; the theological trade is not a directly activist one. Rather, it is a matter of analysing what is involved in practices and then discerning and designing new ways. By this means, action – of individuals and, even more, of communities – is transformed; it becomes a transformative praxis which aims – always co-dependently on the action of God – to advance the transformation of humanity and the social cultural order within the Reign of God. If the specific focus of this theology is the theology of practices, then steadily deepening the notion and application of praxis is a necessity.

Defining the Venture

The definitional problem still troubles. Can pastoral/practical theology claim true disciplinary status? On the Catholic side, pastoral theology has a rather amorphous feel and it spreads out over diverse areas. Its primary areas such as ministry, moral theology and spirituality and fields such as liturgy and catechesis rely on classical systematic and sacramental theology and the human sciences, although in each case these will be in a somewhat different mix. Moral theology is reliant on systematic and biblical theology and philosophical ethics; ministry on systematic and sacramental theology and church history; liturgy on sacramental theology and studies of ritual; catechesis on biblical and systematic theology and pedagogy.

In each of these fields of study, the empirical dimension requires an appropriate methodology to analyse lived practice. All of them are instances of practical theology in that respect. So too, liberation theology, political theology, feminist theology, social theology are all practical theologies. Even a classic topic of systematic theology such as ecclesiology requires historical and empirical referents.

Is there, then, a substantive 'practical theology' over and above these branches? Might it be better understood as a theological methodology, or as one of the dimensions of theology as such, a characteristic of some theological projects? A useful comparison might be with education. This is a well established discipline in its own right, but it is depen-dent on other substantive subject areas (humanities, science, languages, religion) for its grounding. Practical theology might be understood in a similar fashion as the study of what is involved, across a variety of fields and from a specifically theological perspective, in sustaining the practical dimensions of religious faith – of 'keeping faith in practice'.

Practical theology, then, might be seen as both a theological method-ology with wide applicability in a variety of pastoral studies disciplines, and a particular and restricted substantive area of theological enquiry in its own right. Some issues and topics would seem to fall directly under its aegis. One area is the study of basic concepts and procedures, such as: the meaning of *locus theologicus*; the notions of practice and praxis; the definition of a properly *theological* practical methodology (avoiding its reduction to a religious form of social science). The topic of reading the signs of the times is fairly and squarely practical theo-logy; and this leads directly to the set of issues that falls under the headings of the Christian and society, Christ and culture, the Church in the world, and the historically bound nature of ecclesial institutions and practices. These are some of the conceptual issues that merit co-operation between the different traditions.

The Theological Truth Claim

The criticism of pastoral theology has been that it is 'only' practical and without theoretical interest. Leaving aside whether this is fair, it poses a challenge. The kind of pastoral and practical theology outlined in this volume takes us beyond the notion of 'applied theology', where the move is simply from theory to practice, and envisages instead a dialectical relationship of theory and practice. What this seeks is not only the transformation of practice but new theoretical insight. And this insight is, or should be, new *theological* insight, and not simply some generic insights into the theory of practice.

But this presents the greatest challenge of all. The epistemological question – deepening what is meant by truth, and the authority that pastoral theology can claim for the empirically grounded insights it deals in – needs to be explored more fully. Truth is much more than a quality of conceptual knowledge; it is to be grasped in the spiritual move in which it is accomplished. Here, the different traditions could come together to give grounding to the practical theological enterprise. Practical theologians need to articulate the contribution they have to make to systematic theology. And in co-operation with systematic theologians they have to work to specify the new understandings of Christian faith in action that are possible and the new expressions that are needed to grasp and live the faith that has been handed down. This, in the end, is likely to be the measure of the success of the practical theological venture.

Index

Lightning Source UK Ltd.
Milton Keynes UK
16 March 2010

151492UK00001B/17/P